Ecology
of the
Northern Lowland Bogs
and Conifer Forests

Academic Press Rapid Manuscript Reproduction

Ecology of the Northern Lowland Bogs and Conifer Forests

James A. Larsen

University–Industry Research Program
University of Wisconsin
Madison, Wisconsin

1982

ACADEMIC PRESS
A Subsidiary of Harcourt Brace Jovanovich, Publishers

New York   London
Paris   San Diego   San Francisco   São Paulo   Sydney   Tokyo   Toronto

ACADEMIC PRESS, INC.
111 Fifth Avenue, New York, New York 10003

United Kingdom Edition published by
ACADEMIC PRESS, INC. (LONDON) LTD.
24/28 Oval Road, London NW1   7DX

Library of Congress Cataloging in Publication Data

Larsen, James Arthur.
    Ecology of the northern lowland bogs and conifer
forests.

    Includes bibliographical references and index.
    1. Bog ecology--United States. 2. Bog ecology--Canada.
3. Forest ecology--United States. 4. Forest ecology--
Canada. 5. Conifers--United States--Ecology. 6. Conifers
--Canada--Ecology. I. Title.
QH104.L34 1982   581.5'26325   82-11368
ISBN 0-12-436860-3

PRINTED IN THE UNITED STATES OF AMERICA

82 83 84 85   9 8 7 6 5 4 3 2 1

Contents

Preface

It is a warm afternoon and the bright sun is setting in a cloudless sky. The few resident ducks sit quietly on a pond just visible in the distance. A marsh hawk has drifted past over sedges emergent in a shallow slough, the water rippling in the gentle breezes. The peace is so absolute it is almost unimaginable.

One is inclined to feel, against better judgment, that this placid scene will be perpetuated forever. It will, however, be broken in a day or a week by harsher winds and flights of migrant ducks. Wedges of geese will sweep in from the north. The idyllic Elysium will turn boisterous, the tamaracks will shade into brilliant gold. The spruces will be a black onyx set into the backdrop of higher hills beyond the bog. Both bog and adjacent marsh will be covered with a drifting of fallen leaves over dried sedges.

This is a book on the ecology of bogs and conifer swamps and, to some extent, the marshlands. An appreciation of bog and marshland ecology is as much an esthetic experience as is the perception of bog sights and sounds during the seasons of the year. To a scientist, there is an esthetics of science, just as to a composer there is a science of musicology. Often, sensuous appreciation of nature precedes intellectual maturing and fascination with the sciences.

The chapters that follow are, for the most part, a review of what is known about the northern bogs and lowland forests, written in the terminology of science in the hope, as well as the expectation, that such knowledge will be of value to those who appreciate the beauty of bogs and marshlands, to ecologists and other biological scientists, naturalists, wildlife conservationists, hunters, trappers, construction engineers, as well as to others whose vocations or avocations take them afield.

The discussion is devoted, at least primarily, to the ecology of one kind of wetland — the lowland bogs and conifer forests — and treats only in passing the marshlands and other kinds of vegetational communities that are also classified as wetlands. In general, the former can be distinguished from the latter by the presence in lowland bogs and conifer forests of the *Sphagnum* mosses and by accumulations of peat. The bogs and conifer forests are, therefore, known also as peatlands, but the distinction between the two kinds of communities — peatlands and marshes — is not always clear to the unpracticed eye.

A quick view of the northern landscape will, moreover, usually reveal that marshes, lowland bogs, and conifer forests are intermingled, and that these communities all grade into one another so that it is difficult to decide where one begins and another ends. We are concerned, however, with the lowland peat bogs and forests, particularly those that have developed to a point where their identity is indisputable for the simple reason that no other review of accumulated knowledge on these vegetational communities is presently available. Many books, articles, and research papers have been written on the marshlands, much fewer on the lowland bogs and conifer forests. This is perhaps because the marshlands are of value to hunters and trappers and all who are interested in wildlife. The marshes, too, are in most cases more accessible—a person can travel to them or through them easily by boat. The bogs and conifer swamps, on the other hand, are hard to get to, and even more difficult to get through—one must walk, and the walking is not easy, since feet sink into wet moss and peat at every step and the sense that one is mired is unsettling to say the least. Hence, the bogs and conifer forests have not been studied very much. By now, however, the importance of bogs and conifer swamps, in regions where they are found, is becoming more deeply appreciated, and research has expanded greatly and has begun to catch up with work on marshes in recent years.

Wetlands were once valued only as wildlife habitats or as areas of potential value for agriculture, highways, or buildings. The high intrinsic value of natural, undisturbed wetlands for ground water replenishment, flood control, as well as wildlife habitat has led both federal and state conservation agencies to enact protective legislation and to acquire wetlands for wildlife sanctuaries and for storage basins that insure continued supplies of water for lakes, rivers, and wells. The result has often pitted private gain against public good, but growing official concern and public awareness has given wetland conservation an impetus lacking in early days.

Even so, the Great Lakes Basin Commission estimated that 20,000 acres of Great Lakes Basin wetlands are drained or filled each year. No exact figures are available on the proportion of original native wetlands that now have been converted for other purposes, but nationally the figure is thought to range between 30 and 40 percent. In Wisconsin, figures exist to show that only about 25 percent of the original wetlands now remain in what might be considered an undisturbed condition, although some disturbance has, of course, occurred in all of them during the past century.

The lowland bogs and conifer swamps, which together form the peatlands, are usually adjacent to, or at least near, marshes and sloughs that provide food, shelter, and breeding ground for waterfowl, mink, and muskrats, as well as for other mammals such as raccoons and white-tailed deer. The peatlands store water that maintains adequate levels in the spawning grounds of walleye and northern pike, muskellunge, trout, perch, and other fish species. The lowland bogs are probably the only native plant community that is cropped extensively, and this for cranberries, of which Wisconsin and Michigan are the nation's top producers. This use does not seriously conflict with some of the other useful functions of bogs, such as water storage and control of sediment carried by runoff from surrounding uplands. Much commercially valuable timber is also found in the lowland forests—tree species such as northern white cedar and black spruce.

Regional economists have said that it is difficult to put an accurate price tag on any of the values that wetlands possess, but it is now clear that the preservation of the remaining wetlands may well prove vital to the environmental and economic well-being of the Great Lakes region as well as to areas where the lowland bogs and conifer forests may be found, among which are the Pacific Northwest, British Columbia, Alaska, central Canada, New England, and the Maritime Provinces.

It is my hope that the environmental and economic value of the northern lowland bogs and conifer forests, as well as an appreciation of the esthetic and scientific values of the research conducted there, will be communicated to those who read this book.

James A. Larsen

1 Lowland Bog and Conifer Forest Ecology: Historical Perspective

Looking back over the history of ecology in the United States--not in any systematic way but as revealed in a casual reading of a few issues of old botanical journals--the surprising thing is not that the material seems so old, but that it seems so new.

There have been no great revolutions in ecological thought. There have been refinements, more detailed observations, and now, recently, mathematical treatment of data and principles, but on the whole the basic foundations of ecology laid down as long as a century ago still stand.

It is significant that this should be the case. The same is true of all fundamental sciences--chemistry and physics, for example--in which underlying foundations established in the eighteenth and nineteenth centuries remain largely intact. This is only applicable, of course, to events at the level scientists were capable of studying at the time: events that can be made to occur in flasks and test tubes or that can be observed in nature, not the subatomic phenomena more recently studied with the use of an array of powerful instruments available to modern scientists.

The same cannot be said about the so-called soft sciences. The views held today about the nature of reality in psychology, sociology, behavior--if these can be called sciences in the true sense--are in many ways modified substantially from what they were at the turn of the century.

The point is that ecology does, indeed, seem more closely allied to basic sciences than to social sciences at least in these respects, although much ecological research employs statistical methods used in social sciences, such as factor analysis and principal component analysis, which rarely find use in basic sciences.

All of this is prelude to what, to me, are some surprisingly modern statements made in the early botanical papers dealing with the forests of the Upper Midwest--the western Great Lakes region--found in journals dating to the late years of the nineteenth and the early years of the twentieth century.

1

Ecology now encompasses an astonishing breadth of subject matter, with as many narrowly specialized subfields as any other science and so the discussion here must necessarily be narrow and specialized. Since we are dealing with the vegetation of an area in the Upper Midwest, it will concern one field--the ecology of plant life. It will concern one aspect of the plant life of this region--the native vegetation of parts of Michigan, Wisconsin, Minnesota, and Ontario within the Lake Superior watershed or, in some instances, the upper Mississippi River, and specifically the vegetation of the lowland bogs and conifer forests.

Ecology is concerned with relationships between living things and their environment. For a hint of what this definition means in terms of vegetation, we can take an example from an early ecologist who studied the forests of the Great Lakes region. In an essay on the forests of northern Michigan, Whitford (1901) wrote that the purpose of his study was to answer some of the questions involved in the development of forests:

In other words, the question is, why are there forests on certain physiographic formations and none on those which lies close by? Also within the forest itself there predominates now one and now another tree type. In some places the coniferous forest is prominent, in others the maple-beech-hemlock type is the chief feature. Indeed, if enough regions are studied an indefinite number of combinations may be observed. Thus not only must the presence or absence of trees be explained, but also where trees are present a reason must be given for the dominance of any particular kind of forest. If these questions can be answered satisfactorily, some light will be thrown on the origin and development of forests. In the answer three sets of factors are involved, climatic, ecological, and historical.*

FOREST INFLUENCES

Whitford described in more detail than we need be concerned with here the influence of the various environmental factors upon the vegetation that covered the landscape, using familiar phrases that can be found without major modification in meaning in recent publications on plant ecology:

By atmospheric factors are meant those which influence the aerial parts of plants. They include radiant energy in the form of heat and light, and also the influence of wind...

* Reprinted by permisssion of The University of Chicago Press.

Once a dense forest is established, all forms of low vegetation, except those species that have special shade adaptations, are driven out...

Again, the struggle may be between plant societies, as the forest and heath, or forest and prairie. The line along which two societies meet has been called the tension line. If the other ecological factors remain the same, the tension line does not change...

Not only may the struggle be between the forest on the one hand and some other type of plant society on the other, but it may be between different kinds of forests...

The three great physical media--soil, air, and water-- are all influential in bringing about certain plant societies. These, together with the biotic factors, make that variety in the landscape of any region which is shown in the plant societies that are present...

Since trees present a greater transpiration surface than other forms of plants they must occupy those positions where there is sufficient water to maintain the transpiration current. This excludes them from regions where the water content of the soil approaches the minimum; a stagnant condition of soil water is likewise injurious to trees...

The physical properties of the soil play an important role, for upon them depends the capacity of the soil to hold water...

The greater part of the eastern half of the United States is a potential forest. Here the two great climatic factors, temperature and moisture, are favorable to the development of forest trees...

Within this vast forest formation there are prairie, beach, dune, heath, swamp, and other plant societies; also the forest itself may be divided into a number of different forest societies...*

As a demonstration of the fact that these same general topics are those that concern ecologists at the present time, here are a few of the topical divisions of a modern ecology textbook (these are subheads within one section of the volume): "Light as an environmental factor," "The distribution of moisture within vegetation," "Air movement above the ground and within vegetation," "The soil environment," "Nitrogen supply." One author of a recent volume on physiological plant ecology (Bannister, 1976) summarizes the contemporary view by stating that "physiological responses to specific environmental variables can provide at least partial explanations of ecological phenomena." He adds that the variables together "form a picture of the whole complex of plant-environment relationships which constitutes plant ecology."

* Reprinted by permission of The University of Chicago Press.

DISCOVERY OF THE PRINCIPLES

The birth of what we now accept as the fundamental principles of ecology somehow seems to lack the drama and intensity of
purpose that marks the great discoveries of chemistry and physics,
but the parturition in each instance must have been preceded by
an intuitive insight, and a feeling of profound rightness, on
the part of the participants, just as Newton must have had and
just as was evidently the case for Einstein with his concept of
relativity. This kind of inspired flush of comprehension has
been described by Keynes as the product of intuition, and he says
of Newton that "his pre-eminence is due to his muscles of intuition being the strongest and most enduring..." The same must be
true, in perhaps lesser degree, of the botanists who saw that
plants have not been placed over the face of the earth by some
working of divine will, but rather by the influence of the environment. This was not always the accepted view; and the history of birth, denunciation, and final acceptance lies deep in
the past, as the history of science goes, just as does the history of Newton's formulation of the principles that bear his name.

In describing these origins, a noted figure in the history
of American ecology, Cowles, wrote as follows in 1911:

The earliest account which I have discovered that clearly
deals with vegetative dynamics is in a short paper in the
Philosophical Transactions in 1685, in which William King
gives a good account of the origin of bog vegetation from
floating mats; many times since, this has been reported as
an original discovery. Perhaps the first to have a real
glimmer of the doctrine of succession, as understood today,
was the great French naturalist Buffon. Although better
known for his spendid descriptions of animals, Buffon in his
earlier life was much interested in forestry, and 1742 he
noted that poplars precede oaks and beeches in the natural
development of a forest...Biberg, a student of the great
Linnaeus, published his thesis in 1749, and in this he describes the gradual development of vegetation on bare rocks;
here he observes accurately the pioneer activity of the
lichens and mosses, and he notes as well the importance of
Sphagnum in the development of bogs.
The seeds planted by Buffon and Biberg fell on sterile
soil; in France it was observed that Buffon was trespassing
on theological grounds, and he was obliged to recant any
views which implied that the world was not made in the
beginning once for all; in Sweden the influence of Linnaeus
was wholly against anything dynamic; he never published
anything dynamic himself, and when a student like Biberg
set his face in that direction, the master frowned, and
said that the student was departing from the true mission

of the botanist. It is not strange, therefore, that there
followed a sterile period of three-quarters of a century.*

Although Buffon was obviously speaking of succession in
his publication on plant communities in 1742, it was not until 1806 that the term came into use to mean the sequential
development of a community through a series of prior stages.
In the latter year, a botanist named De Luc wrote:

> The bottom of every dale is a meadow on a subsoil of
> peat; this, by gradually advancing into, contracts the
> original extent of the lakes; and, it was well-known...that
> many large lakes have been converted into smaller ones, by
> the peat advancing from the original shores, and in many
> places now meadows, and only traversed by a stream, had
> still a lake in them, in the memory of old people...The
> succession of these different zones, from the border of
> water towards the original border of sand, represents the
> succession of changes that have taken place through time
> in each of the anterior zones...

It was Hult, however, who was evidently the first to fully
recognize the fundamental importance of successional development in plant communities. He studied the forested land of
Blekinge, Finland, and in 1885 traced the succession of each
stage, seeing that grassland became heath, that the heath developed into forest. The early stages of forest development
were dominated by birch, and on dry soil this is followed by
pine, on wet soils by spruce. A birch forest can also be replaced by oak forest, which then develops into a beechwood. In
swamps, the succession goes from mosses to sedges to a moor
vegetation to birch and finally to a spruce forest.

These faint beginnings, in the dim distance of a century,
still possess some surprisingly modern aspects. So, too, do
the works of Humboldt and those also of Warming, who in 1895
published his *"Oecology of Plants."* In 1898, Schimper published *"Plant Geography on a Physiological Basis,"* translated
from German into English in 1903. Cowles published his classic,
*"The Ecological Relations of the Vegetation on the Sand Dunes
of Lake Michigan"* in 1899, followed in 1901 by *"The Physiographic Ecology of Chicago and Vicinity."*

EARLY AMERICANS

Cowles has already been mentioned, and he stands today as
one of the great hulking figures in early American plant ecology, standing beside--but slightly apart from--Clements, of
whom we speak today in perhaps somewhat awed but not entirely
sympathetic terms. Of Cowles there is not much to be said,

*Reprinted by permission of The University of Chicago Press.

as is so often the case with quiet, thoughtful figures in the
history of science. They exist as mileposts or turning points,
or perhaps represent final destinations in the history of a
science, but of their personal characteristics we know little,
for often they seem stamped from the academic mold and with
little individuality beyond that given them by their ancient
role as teacher and mentor. After about 1911, Cowles wrote
little, but the few papers published early in his career have
become classics. Cowles and Clements are associated with the
University of Chicago and the University of Nebraska, respectively, and where Cowles resembles the cloistered scholar, Clements comes on strong with a hint of Chautauqua or perhaps even
the barker in some illicit form of academic sideshow, or evan-
gelism on a Mississippi stern-wheeler. As Egler (1951) writes,
long after Clements held sway over American ecology, Clements
was "a prolific writer of all-encompassing scope, a composer
of textbooks, a solver of problems, an establisher of complete
systems and disciplines."

The solemn fact that Clements's "system" threw American
ecology off the rails for a number of decades is one of the
more ludicrous, if we may use the term, episodes in the history
of American ecology--ludicrous, in a sense, because it had no
great tragic consequences, but merely created a mythical and
almost ecclesiastical hierarchy in the vegetational types found
on the surface of the earth, and so shrouded ecology and ecologists in mystical veils that it was many years before anyone
peeked out again at the real world. It was parallel to, and
just as ridiculous as, the development of certain European
schools of community classification for vegetation, without
the incongruous backdrop of theology that seems to have been
needed to lend some authority to the European system, far re-
moved from the real world as it was. There was a good reason
for the European failure: it followed the mold of long-estab-
lished traditional ways of looking at things, the prevailing
intellectual temper of the times. In the case of Clements,
however, one simply wonders what drove him to create such a
conceptual monster. One can perhaps envision the academic
community at Chicago, where Cowles worked, as one that valued
quiet thought and contemplation. The one at Nebraska must have
had for Clements some of the early western appreciation for
hearty verve and vociferous spirit, exhilarating on the monotonous prairies but not especially rich in enduring intellectual content.

Clements had not been trained to deal with academic logic
and scientific method, and he classified and split plant communities into so many categories that others would inevitably
see that the cubbyholes into which he stuffed his communities
were artificial. In fact, placed side by side in the proper

order, they formed a continuum. However, Clements was a good fellow and a fine field man--evidently he could set ailing rangeland on the road to recovery in short order, although there is not much to be done with ailing rangeland except to leave it alone to recover naturally, in short, to remove the cows, or at least some of them. As Egler summarized in 1951,

> he had never let the ritual and dogma of his pseudo-theological system interfere with his common sense in applying remedial measures to an eroding hillside or an overgrazed range. Now that he has gone, it remains to be seen whether his followers will grasp the meaning behind his words, and whether they will wrangle interminably over the forms of terminological baptism and the particular phrases associated with their communion with nature...

Finally, Clements had split the climax into so many fragments that it included everything existing in the vegetation of a region. Therefore, why call it climax? Why not just call it vegetation? As Egler writes, "And if we do wish to use the term climax, we are back again to that favorite American query, 'What is the climax?'" It is, evidently, whatever is growing naturally at any given time on any given uncultivated or un-bulldozed plot of ground. When Clements first wrote the germinal words on his concept of vegetation, "The Development and Structure of Vegetation," that appeared in 1904, in the *Botanical Survey of Nebraska, Vol. 7,* he surely did not envision that this was the logical end of his speculative endeavors. He was undoubtedly attempting to build a theoretical structure that was to endure for all time; it was not more than two decades until its demise. Even this would be too long--the concept was not a fruitful one in terms of encouraging the development of the science. Or perhaps it was--the flurry of activity that occurred during the middle decades of the century, much of it inspired by the express intent to disprove Clements' theoretical structure, might not have occurred without the existence of a straw scarecrow to tackle.

PLANTS AND ENVIRONMENT

There was, however, another major theme in the drama, a quiet leitmotif that was ultimately to become the triumphal coda. By the time a decade had passed, the concepts of geographical distribution of vegetation and plant communities as caused by environmental factors had gained a firm hold upon plant ecology. Perhaps Transeau, writing in 1909, could be said to have summarized it most aptly:

Perhaps the most interesting and important advance that has been made during the past decade in the study of the relation of plants to environment is in regard to the point of view. It is difficult to say just when the movement began, but it is assuredly true that it has only recently gained recognition. To a certain extent the movement has involved the substitution of the ecological for the floristic method in geographical problems involving climate...The movement has further brought our attention to the necessity for investigating vegetation by experimental methods comparable to those by which plant processes have long been studied.

Transeau then quoted the *Yearbook* of the U. S. Department of Agriculture for 1894 as revealing both that the vegetation of the United States was now known in its broader aspects, and that there was, at that time, a certain deceptive complacency in the conviction that knowledge of why things grew where they did was available:

It appears, therefore, that in its broader aspects the study of the geographic distribution of life in North America is completed. The primary regions and their principal sub-divisions have been mapped, the problems involved in the control of distribution have been solved, and the laws themselves have been formulated.

Perhaps nothing could have been farther from the truth. As a consequence of the knowledge being acquired, the concept of vegetation was becoming more complex than could have been envisioned as late as a decade earlier. Moreover, the complexity of the environment had yet to be appreciated; more than a single decade would pass before ecologists would become fully aware of the complexity not only of the vegetation but of the environment as well. However, there are hints of this in Transeau's writings. He continues:

The appearance of the classics of Warming and Schimper served to impress all with the inherent complexity of the problem. We are no longer deeply concerned with the discussion as to whether temperature or moisture is the most important geographic factor. Neither do we hope to erect a stable system of geographic divisions upon either of these bases. When we recall that for North America alone not less than sixty different proposals of geographic zones and regions have been published during the last century, the futility of the point of view which disregards all but one or two climatic factors and emphasizes boundary lines, must be apparent. But we shall be still more impressed with the inadequacy of these proposals if we attempt to relate the actual distribution of plants or plant formations to these "regions."

Recently there has been a rapid increase of local ecological studies in which the successional processes of vegetation have been emphasized. These studies have apprehended to a greater or less extent the dynamics of the habitat and the plant formation. The separation of the local vegetation into stages has assumed the dominance in each, of a distinct complex of environmental factors. The occurrence of distinct boundaries has neither been assumed nor insisted upon.

The question of the behavior of the individual plants of the various species--a topic that was to evolve into one of dominant proportions and explosive impact--was also on Transeau's mind:

But the most striking fact about the geographic distribution of individual species is their dominance in some region and their decline in importance and frequency as we depart thence in any direction. Plant formations in their distribution show the same phenomenon. Further, it appears that the optimum areas of scores and hundreds of species nearly coincide...Probably the most promising field for experimentation at the present time is the investigation of the processes of vegetation. There are so many vague notions and dogmatic statements regarding the processes of competition, migration, adjustment, etc., in relation to the climatic factors, that the rewards for pioneer work will be ample.

There had thus, in the short space of a few years or decades at most, come the realization that the vegetation of the world, and of areas of North America in which these botanists had worked, was the consequence of interactions of many intrinsic characteristics of living plants and of the forces of environment, many of them obscure and virtually invisible.

There finally arose such a mingling of voices in the attempt to describe the endless variety of groupings of trees and shrubs and herbaceous species that botanical discussions would end in a shrill wrangling over what everyone meant by the terms "formation," "association," "community," "climax," "subclimax," "postclimax," "consociation," and so on, ad infinitum.

The multitude of voices was so loud and overpowering that there were echoes resounding across the boards as late as 1951, when a Wisconsin botanist studying the northern forests, a botanist with the appropriate name of Forest Stearns (1951), would still feel obliged to define his terms. He explored the structure of northern conifer-hardwood stands that could be

found uncut, ungrazed, and in near pristine condition.   He
wrote as follows:

> To the writer, the expression "community" serves to de-
> limit any particular grouping of plants regardless of
> successional stage. The term "stand" is used to designate
> a particularly geographic unit of a community or associa-
> tion. The term "association" has in past usage had a tre-
> mendous range of meaning varying from a widespread climax
> type to almost any grouping of plants, large or small, clim-
> ax or seral in nature... It seems reasonable to follow
> Beard (1944) who defines a climax as "...any community which
> is apparently stable, mature, and integrated." A climax
> community will ordinarily consist of the most mesic species
> present in the region and those which show the greatest
> tolerance of shade and of each other.

Stearns's definitions establish the usage that will be employed in the later chapters of this book, in which the structure and composition of the bog communities, a specific and
well-defined segment of the northern forest, will be discussed.
First, there is an interesting history to explore. It is the
history of the development of Clements's ideas of the commun-
ity--the climax community of forested regions--as an organism
in its own right, i.e., one that is born, lives, and dies. It
is a concept that gripped ecology like an octopus for more years
than one cares to recount.

2 The Organismic Forest: Historical Perspective Continued

The idea that natural vegetation of a region is dynamic, that it is in a continual process of change, was firmly established as a valid concept by the turn of the century when ecological studies began to be carried on in the Great Lakes region. Among the first to look at nature in this new light, to attempt to discern how factors of the environment influenced daily existence and successional behavior of native plant and animal life, especially in the western Great Lakes region, was Charles C. Adams, who followed Schimper, Warming, and Cowles by only a few years. Adams directed an ecological survey of northern Michigan, and in 1906 wrote:

> In this study, attention was directed particularly to the forces and conditions composing the environment, in order that the dominant forces might be recognized. This involved a careful analysis of the conditions, as it is only by such means that the laws of change can be recognized, and the dynamics of the habitat be understood. In this way, the habitat can be studied from the standpoint of *process* rather than from that of the end result or effects of such forces, for it is very evident that if the habitats are to be understood it must be by a study of their laws of change.

The early plant ecologists who dealt with the northern conifer-hardwood forests of the Great Lakes region began to ask a number of good questions:

> What is the role of the species in succession?
> What are the characteristics of the various species that attain dominance?
> Is long-term stability ever attained by any aggregation of species?
> Is there such a thing as a vegetational climax in the Great Lakes region, and, if so, what are its attributes?
> Is the regional climax forest readily identified and described, or is it variable and conceptually elusive? a polyclimax? a monoclimax? a pattern? a continuum of xeric, mesic,

hydric communities grading into one another, all stable at
maturity, all of various ages and stages of development,
each with its own distinct history of disturbance by fire,
disease, insect infestation, windthrow, and composed of
species each with its individual physiological response to
surroundings?

These were all pertinent questions, relevant not only to
practical forestry but to theoretical resolution of the question "Is there a regional climax vegetational community?" Does
such a vegetation ever exist anywhere except in the minds of
theoreticians? What is the regional climatic climax for the
western Great Lakes region?

The ultimate resolution of these questions probably would
have occurred with much greater celerity had Clements not step-
ped at this point onto the stage of Midwestern ecological development. We saw in Chapter 1 that Clements had broad knowledge, intense interest, and imagination. His writings are
voluminous and convincing. He had the urge, typical of all
theoreticians, to get the loose ends neatly tied down. If
there were errant facts, they could be swamped in the general
flood of convincing analogy or conveniently ignored. Clements,
moreover, had the courage of his convictions--he was certain
he saw things in the correct light. How else can we explain
the lengthy works that came from his pen, replete with a new
technical vocabulary to delineate the organismic theory of the
plant community, to fill in the details, to explain away the
odd fact that did not fit the hierarchical scheme of things, to
clean up the messy points where forests and prairies seemed not
to behave quite as an idealistic theoretician might expect them
to?

There is likely just enough in the way of apt analogy in
the organismic idea to give it some credence still among an
isolated researcher or two. Plants do not live in total in-
dependence of one another, but are obviously adapted to exist
in close proximity. They are not, however, mutually inter-
dependent as are the parts of a plant or an animal. There is
no analog in the plant community for, say, the heart and the
liver of an animal, or the leaves and meristematic tissue of
a plant; in neither case can the parts live alone, and the
absence of an important component species from a community does
not doom the community in the same way that the absence of
leaves or meristem would doom a plant.

In a plant community, on the other hand, there has to be
some degree of interdependence, to be sure, in the sense that
shade-tolerant herbaceous species need the shade of maple or
basswood trees, for example, to exclude the shade-intolerant
species that would otherwise be present as competitors. The

degree of interdependence between shade-tolerant species, however, is probably minimal or nonexistent. It would seem that
competition for water, nutrients, and light far outweigh in
importance any interdependence that might have developed, excluding perhaps rare instances of obligate parasitism, commensal-
ism, or saprophytism that may have arisen during the course of
evolution.

Clements began his classic report of 1916 to the Carnegie
Institution of Washington, of which he was then a staff member, with these words:

> The developmental study of vegetation necessarily rests
> upon the assumption that the unit or climax formation is an
> organic entity. As an organism, the formation arises, grows,
> matures, and dies. Its response to the habitat is shown in
> processes or functions and structures which are the record
> as well as the result of these functions. Furthermore,
> each climax formation is able to reproduce itself, repeating
> with essential fidelity the stages of its development. The
> life-history of a formation is a complex but definite pro-
> cess, comparable in its chief features with the life-his-
> tory of an individual plant. Succession is the universal
> process of formation development. It has occurred again
> and again in the history of every climax formation, and
> must recur whenever proper conditions arise. No climax
> area lacks frequent evidence of succession, and the greater
> number present it in bewildering abundance.

Clements then went on to build an intricate conceptual
edifice, in which every facet of the landscape--dunes, strands,
lakes, flood plains, bad-lands, rock outcrops, hills, valleys,
ant-heaps, rabbit-burrows, plow-furrows--and every species of
plant, from the mosses and lichens of the forest floor to the
most majestic tree, had a place. Only by reading this synthesis
of knowledge and these fanciful flights of imagination can the
enormity of the effort expended in its creation be appreciated.

There was evidently little opposition to the organismic
concept initially, at least in America. Some opposition would
come from Europe, perhaps surprisingly--but the European voices
were faint at that distance, and American ecologists were eager
to begin making themselves heard on the stage of international
science. Why not with a theory?

In the United States, Gleason voiced dissent, but it was as
though he had criticized the artistry of the "Mona Lisa." He
learned quickly that there are two kinds of truth: scientific
and poetic, and that at times one passes for the other. It is
prudent to keep one's counsel when the wave of popular opinion,
even in science, is strongly against one.

Gleasons' paper of 1917 remained for almost a decade an
isolated adverse comment on the enormously satisfying organis-

mic theory. There was just enough coincidence in the characteristics of organisms and plant communities for ecologists to
carry on meaningful research, add to knowledge, describe community structure, and list the species in forests, prairies,
and steppes, without running into serious difficulty, without
revealing, or admitting to themselves, that plant communities
do not behave like organisms, that they only seem to do so
when looked at with a poet's eye.

The organismic concept was an inspired and lyrical metaphor,
and even today one must admit that it is curiously intriguing.
There is a kind of correlation between evolving, developing,
active, resilient organisms and the evolving, developing, dynamic vegetational community. The poetic qualities of the concept concealed for years the fact that it was incongruous,
maladroit, and devoid of validity. When finally it was recognized as nothing but meretricious humbug, the response on the
part of ecologists was to wonder how this mountebank of a
theory had escaped unmasking for so long. Only then did they
realize that it had been unmasked as early as 1917, a year
after publication of Clements's report, but indignation had des-
cended upon the unmasker in such a widespread and vitriolic
avalanche that he had withdrawn onto silence. He sought else-
where--the safe haven of taxonomy--for his measure of worldly
acclaim. The contemned unmasker was forced to wait for his
vindication.

Those in the Clementsian tradition were Aristotelian in
their views, saying that there are discrete things in this
world, that a thing is what it is--not half of one thing and
half of another. All things exist outside the mind, and the
mind comprehends only to some degree the real world. The logic
inherent in the universe is the creation of a greater mind, a
greater logic than we can know, but it is nevertheless a logic,
and the majestical thing is to see the thread that ties together
all things, each part of another. There are thus hierarchies
in things; there is nothing that is part one thing, part another, with gradations between.

What more perfectly logical inference could one make from
the warp and woof of the carpet of vegetation over the earth
than that it is itself an organism? The species are the organs, working in a tight-knit unity, like the organs of animals
and plants, to bring to the whole a perfect balance and har-
mony that is a marvel to behold. The concept, it can be seen,
was likely to grip the mind, emotions, esthetic sense; it was,
moreover, revolutionary, revelatory, infallible, explaining
the inexplicable. Those who were opening up the science that
deals with plant communities took to the theory with enthusiasm.

Even the critical Gleason began his commentary on the
Clementsian theory by saying, "Ecological literature has re-

cently been enriched by the publication of an exceedingly important book on the structure and development of vegetation..."
However, the introduction led to a profound but inoffensively
worded questioning of the very fundamentals of the organismic
theory. Finally, Clements and his adherents realized that the
gauntlet had been dropped, delicately and with polish, but
dropped nonetheless. Gleason, however, had reckoned wrongly
the appeal of the organismic concept; the theory was at birth
universally accepted. Why this should have happened is not
clear. It was contrary to all the precepts of scientific method and of critical review. Gleason concluded: "It is probable
that some of the more radical ideas of the author may be accepted reluctantly and that others may be rejected completely,"
but the theory evidently had an appeal that was almost reli-
gious in intensity.

As late as 1929, Clements was still propounding the organismic concept. He had even amplified it to include some obviously needed emendations to account for, or explain away,
conflicting evidence, for example, that the life-form of all
the dominant trees in a climax community must be uniformly the
same, that there is no place, in other words, for conifers in
a hardwood climax community. This was awkward, for there were
often conifers--spruce and fir and pine--in considerable abundance in the Great Lakes hardwood forest climax communities.
They did not belong there, Clements said. He created another
climax for the Great Lakes regions, the spruce-pine climax,
impossible to find anywhere on the landscape, but it existed
because the system declared it must be so.

Almost 60 years later, the idea is still alive--more prevalent in romantic fiction, perhaps, than in scientific dis-
course--but it has an esthetic appeal as forceful as that of
a beautiful metaphysical system. A writer of Western tales of
wide renown was to write in the 1970s: "A forest is a living
thing like a human body, each part dependent on all the other
parts...Listen, and you can hear the forest breathe." This is
as pretty and as exciting a notion as anyone could have in regard to the fundamental nature of a forest, but it is more ex-
pressive of a quixotic affection for green landscapes than of
an objective assessment of biological reality. The concept was
so appealing that even as it died as a part of science it was
revived to endure in literary discourse long after it was discredited as anything but a chimerical metaphor.

Much valuable time and effort, finally, was expended in
the public refutation of the organismic concept, by logical discourse and, with greater impact, by new masses of data, many
of them gathered from living forests by ecologists using methods advocated by Clements himself--the use of quadrats for

the purpose of "determining the composition and structure of plant communities..."

The idea of the community as organism died hard, in part because it was so imaginatively engaging, and in part because Clements was himself not disillusioned. In deference to Clements, no one came forth to butt heads over the matter. The sense of urgency perhaps had passed. The theory would, sooner or later, expire with its creator. The effort to accumulate the evidence that would bury it forever was making possible an accurate description of the vegetation of North America and the world. The concept of the individualistic nature of species and the plant community--what Gleason had propounded--was generally accepted by midcentury: no plant community, climax or successional, is organismic in nature, it is rather a mix of species behaving as independently as conceivable in association with other species, each individual plant acting on its own, without organic connection with individuals of its own or other species with which it is associated.

3 Comprehending the Northern Plant Communities

Ecologists have gone to great length, have they not, to comprehend a natural phenomenon that for the most part no longer exists? In the upper Midwest, there are but few remnants of the primeval northern conifer-hardwood forests that were ubiquitous along the southern shores of Lake Superior, on the uplands of northern Wisconsin, Minnesota, and Michigan. Likewise, the wetlands--the bogs and marshlands--are now also disappearing. Why be concerned?

There are good reasons. At one end of the scale of practicality is antiquarian interest--of little value other than satisfaction of curiosity over what the country was like before the arrival of European immigrants. At the other end of the scale, knowledge of the ecology of the natural forest vegetation is of immediate and practical value to foresters, land managers, wildlife conservationists, and many others, for this knowledge is a basic tool of all their trades, providing a guide to what will grow, where, and what transformations in vegetation take place as time passes. It is a guide to what can be done to slow or speed succession if either is desirable.

So much for the rationale of ecological research. The vegetational communities are what interest us here: trees, open glades, leatherleaf bogs, conifer swamps, sedge marshes, grassy meadows, and shorelines of streams and lakes. We shall consider several of these in our discussion of the ericaceous bogs, for they are related, however distantly, by the schemes of successional development proposed by the early ecologists. First we must consider the mature upland forest, believed by many workers to be the regional climatic climax; the northern conifer-hardwood forest, to use the term commonly employed to designate a loosely definable entity, greatly varied in composition from one place to another.

The question we shall attempt to answer is this. "How do bogs, mature upland forest, as well as the other communities, become established?" Ecologists who first undertook to answer this question make up a most interesting cadre of professionals in an arcane but nevertheless significant episode in the early

17

history of the Great Lakes region. We saw previously that much
of what they had to say seems new even today. This is due to
the fact that they were hitting the mark in their interpretations of the dynamics of vegetation of the Great Lakes region.
The messianic fervor of Clements, however, then made them ig-
nore what had been said and what they had seen. When Clementsian views were discredited finally, the evidence had already
been available for nearly half a century. Much ecological effort expended between roughly 1905 and, say, 1940, provides an
example of a wild goose chase carried on with enthusiasm in pur-
suit of a scientific quarry more illusory than real.

Perhaps we ascribe too great a proportion of the error to
Clements. In these early writings--those appearing around the
turn of the century--there are hints everywhere of extrapolation beyond the bounds of the evidence available in the northern forests. For example, several ecologists hinted at belief
in irrevocable successional processes that lead ultimately to
a hypothetical climax, a climax that, in theory, would eventually blanket the entire landscape. This idea, actually, is
an almost inevitable conclusion to be drawn from simple observation of the forested landscape and construction of an
imagined endpoint of succession. It requires only extrapolation
far enough into the future. The early-day workers were tempted
to jump to theoretical conclusions, just as we are today. The
fact that 10,000 years had elapsed since retreat of the glacier
did not deter them. They said this had not been time enough for
establishment of a continuous blanket of vegetation in the form
of climax forest over the entire region, or even significant
portions of it.

In their eagerness they set up a number of different theoretical climax forests--depending on who did the work and where
it was done--as a final developmental stage that then seemed
as real as the pioneering or intermediate stages, even though
no one had ever seen a climax such as they proposed; the forest
had simply not yet reached its organismic maturity, they said.
They believed this, despite the fact that no one had ever seen
such a forest, nor was any evidence available that such a forest had ever existed in continuous unbroken carpet over the
western Great Lakes region.

EARLY VIEWS

Looking back today over the long and often acrimonious disputes among plant ecologists on these really rather simple and
self-evident matters, the striking thing is that there has been
so much violent disagreement over such small points. Much of
the fire has been consequent largely upon willful disregard or

failure to understand what the other fellow was saying. The
series of disputes resembles sterile theological bickering
over the place of angels in heavenly hierarchies--it is surely
not a dispassionate discussion of the meaning of inconclusive
data.

There is, however, a somewhat faint continuity in the conceptual development of the principles governing the way plants
behave in natural communities. Modern ecologists are, in fact,
still employing concepts developed by early pre-Clementsian
botanists to describe, in ever great detail, what the pre-
Clementsian pioneers saw in broad outline.

When one reads, for example, the writing of Cowles, Whitford, Transeau, Adams, and their colleagues, the accumulated
knowledge of the intervening years is seen to have confirmed
their views, to have amplified them with greater detail and
broader experience. The interesting thing is that they were
right in so many respects, and that they were right on the
basis largely of intuition rather than accumulated data. Cowles,
for example, published in 1901 his view that the slow progression of geological events would lead ultimately to a flat monotonous plain where today there are lakes and hills. He wrote:

In a young topography, such as the recently glaciated
areas of Michigan, Wisconsin, and Minnesota, there is a great
variety of topographic conditions and of plant societies.
Among these are the many hydrophytic lakes and swamps and
many xerophytic hills. The hills are being denuded and the
swamps and lakes are being filled, so that the hydrophytic
and xerophytic areas are becoming more and more restricted,
while the mesophytic areas are becoming more and more en-
larged. In passing from youth to old age then, a region
gradually loses its hydrophytic areas and also its xerophytic areas, though in the latter case there is usually at
first an increase in the xerophytic areas which is due to
the working back of the young streams into the hills...From
what has been stated it will be seen that the ultimate stage
of a region is mesophytic. The various plant societies pass
in a series of successive types from their original condition to the mesophytic forest, which may be regarded as the
climax or culminating type. These changes may be slow or
rapid; some habitats may be mesophytic from the start; undrained lakes and swamps fill up and become mesophytic with
great rapidity, whereas granite hills might take many centuries or even geological epochs in being reduced to the
mesophytic level. Again the stages may be direct or tor-
tuous; we have already seen how the first consequences of
stream erosion may be to make mesophytic areas xerophytic...
progressive phases often take long periods of time for their
full development, especially in their later stages.*

* Reprinted by permission of The University of Chicago Press.

This, conceptually, is virtually as we would have it today; no major revisions would be required to fit Cowles's views neatly into the ecological framework that we take today as being most modern in its formation. Perhaps we would be inclined to ask, "Over such long periods of time, how are we to know what the forest vegetation will ultimately be like?" There is no mention of the mosaic of forest developmental stages that are the consequence of recurrent fires. But these are details. What else does Cowles say?

> The above phenomena postulate congenial climates and more or less static crustal conditions. It is obvious, however, that erosive processes in a desert region do not result in a mesophytic flora; the same is true of alpine and arctic climates. Again, the climate of all regions is doubtless changing, as it has changed in past ages. So, too, there are crustal movements up and down. In other words the condition of equilibrium is never reached, and when we say that there is an approach to the mesophytic forest, we speak only roughly and approximately. As a matter of fact we have a variable approaching a variable rather than a constant... Retrogressive phases, i.e., away from the mesophytic and toward the hydrophytic or xerophytic, must be included as well as progressive phases away from the hydrophytic or xerophytic and toward the mesophytic. In this way, all possible conditions are accounted for...the upward movement of hills ...if a climate grows colder or more arid...crustal changes ...it is usually difficult to decipher their tendencies.*

There are thus, in this great natural pageant, forces that work to block the natural progression toward a vast, flat, monotonous mesophytic plain. Even Cowles, however, would on occasion fall into the trap of believing that succession on all landforms must eventually progress to a mesophytic forest climax. Note his statement on the dunes vegetation of Lake Michigan: "Nothing need be said in the way of further summary except to remark that dunes, like all other topographic forms in our climate, may ultimately develop a mesophytic forest, though the stages are far slower than in most of the other series." Today we do not believe that this is necessarily so. We believe that dunes can remain as dunes for thousands of years, that they have indeed done so since retreat of the Pleistocene glaciers, and that they can, indeed, remain so until advance of the next massive shelf of continental ice erases all trace of dune and forest alike from the landscapes of the Upper Midwest. The same is true of the bogs and wetlands.

We can see in the writing of Whitford, too, hints at the concept of the all-encompassing mesophytic forest climax, but at the same time he qualifies his statement: just as would the

* Reprinted by permission of The University of Chicago Press.

modern ecologist to whom the pattern of the communities over the
land--forest, bog, swamp, meadow--is itself the climax, the pattern as climax, the mosaic as polyclimax, not the one forest
community as climax but the whole range of communities, a kind
of kaleidoscopic climax, a dynamic changing pattern that is all
the more stable, all the more fascinating for the biologist,
than a monotonous carpet, a monoclimax. Whitford (1901) say:
"The greater part of the eastern half of the United States is
a potential forest." Then he adds: "But if a bird's-eye view
of any portion of this formation be obtained, there will be
found within it groups of other plant types...Within this vast
forest formation there are prairie, beach, dune, heath, swamp,
and other plant societies; also the forest itself may be divided into a number of different forest societies..."*

To summarize many pages of argument presented by many different ecologists, this is a theory that defies efforts to
prove it represents events occurring on the time scale of geo-
logic epochs. Even without the major disruption of native vegetation that resulted from industry and agriculture, there is
little chance that the postulated monoclimax would ever have
been attained--surely not within the lifetime of a human witness; existing plant species and plant communities show no
tendency toward establishment of such a regional uniformity as
was postulated by Clements and others, and so the whole conceptual structure resembles a metaphysical system that is invul-
nerable to attempts either to prove or disprove it. In the
case of upland areas, natural destructive agencies, fire and
windthrow most importantly, reduce any mature forest to rubble
with sufficient frequency to preclude formation of any uniform
blanket of vegetation over a large enough region to consider it
a regional climatic climax. So also, in the case of the bog
and conifer swamp communities, succession beyond a certain point
seems rarely if ever to occur; there is instead a cyclic repetition of decadence, destruction, and regeneration, which appears to recur, with no trend discernible over the span of years
that it has been possible to observe--both within historical
time and into the past as far as inference can be carried on
the basis of pollen analysis and other palynological techniques.

* Reprinted by permission of The University of Chicago Press.

4 A Thoreauvian Digression: Bog Community Composition and Structure

Studies of the life of northern swamps and bogs in sufficient detail to result in knowledge of scientific significance have required the fanatical dedication of a Thoreau. As evidence for the kind of fervor aroused in the heart of the ineffable Henry by so simple a landscape feature as a swamp, I quote the following from "A Week on the Concord and Merrimack Rivers:"

I can fancy that it would be a luxury to stand up to one's chin in some retired swamp a whole summer day, scenting wild honeysuckle and bilberry blows, and lulled by the minstrelsy of gnats and mosquitos! A day passed in the society of those Greek sages, such as described in the banquet of Xenophon, would not be comparable with the dry wet of decayed cranberry vines, and the fresh Attic salt of the moss-beds. Say twelve hours of genial and familiar converse with the leopard frog; the sun to rise behind alder and dogwood, and climb buoyantly to his meridian of two hands' breadth, and finally sink to rest behind some bold western hummock. To hear the evening chant of the mosquito from a thousand green chapels, and the bittern begin to boom from some concealed fort like a sunset gun!--Surely one may as profitably be soaked in the juices of swamp for one day as pick his way dry-shod over sand. Cold and damp,--are they not as rich an experience as warmth and dryness?

Perhaps so. But much can be learned without going to such 12-hour extremes of wet watchfulness. For one reason or another it is not always easy to yield credibility to Thoreau on the count of actually having carried out his own earnest recommendations. Perhaps there is more truth to his belief that:

We need the tonic of wildness,--to wade sometimes in marshes where the bittern and the meadow-hen lurk, and hear the booming of the snipe; to smell the whispering sedge where only some wilder and more solitary fowl builds her nest, and the mink crawls with its belly close to the ground.

At the same time that we are earnest to explore and learn
all things, we require that all things be mysterious and
unexplorable, that land and sea be infinitely wild, unsur-
veyed and unfathomed by us because unfathomable. We can
never have enough of Nature. We must be refreshed by the
sight of inexhaustible vigor, vast and Titanic features,
the seacoast with its wrecks, the wilderness with its living
and decaying trees, the thunder cloud, and the rain which
lasts three weeks and produces freshets. We need to witness
our own limits transgressed, and some life pasturing freely
where we never wander.

It is perhaps a need for refreshing wildness that sent ecologists into the swamps and bogs from time to time, and it is
likely that they did so with a feeling that they had been prison-
pent and that somewhere in the marshes they would find succor
and release. It is an unfortunate truth of life, of academic
life at least, that most of one's hours and days must be spent
in an urban environment--for the simple reason that universities
are in cities. When the opportunity affords, the call from the
wilderness is unmistakable, particularly for those familiar with
the pleasures that wilderness affords; and for ecologists, wildlife biologists, limnologists, and botanists the call is ir-
resistable. It is like the siren song that lured Ulysses to
the Forbidden Islands. It is, however, somewhat revealing that
of all the botanical and ecological studies conducted on the
vegetation of the northern regions, the fewest have been carried
out on the bogs and swamps, the fens, marshlands, sedge meadows,
and conifer lowlands. The reasons are probably obvious.

BOG PLANT COMMUNITIES

In his classic "The Vegetation of Wisconsin," Curtis (1959)
asserts that the meaning of the word "bog" ultimately traces
back in origin to wet and soft conditions of terrain in which
it is possible to bog down or become mired. In ecological
studies, he adds, the meaning of the word has been retracted
to the extent that it refers to a plant community made up of
a rather specialized group of shrub and herbaceous species
growing on a wet, acidic, peat substrate: "The bog as thus defined is a common feature of the glaciated landscapes of the
entire Northern Hemisphere and has a remarkably uniform structure and composition throughout the circumboreal regions"
(Fig. 1.)

In the Great Lakes region, the open bog plant community is
very closely related in species composition to the wet conifer
swamp, Curtis adds, and is usually a long-lived stage in primary hydrosere succession leading to the conifer swamp. It is

Fig. 1. A central pool of open water surrounded by a
lowland conifer forest with open bog encroaching over the lake
is typical of the bogs and lowland conifer forests. The pioneering species Chamaedaphne calyculata is shown in the fore-
ground, with stems stretching into the open water of the lake.
The trees are primarily Picea mariana.

also similar in some respects to the northern sedge meadow and
the fen. Bogs, fens, marshes, and swamps are all difficult if
not impossible to walk through or even to gain access to by
other means. They are neither wet enough for boats nor dry
enough for even such ingenious devices as long and wide swamp
skis. The plant communities of the bogs, fens, marshes, and
swamps have, as a consequence, been among the least studied
features of the biological landscape in northern regions despite their abundance in such areas as the Northern Highlands
State Forest of Wisconsin as well as other parts of the western Great Lakes region (Fig. 2).

Fig. 2. Labrador tea, Ledum groenlandicum, dominates the understory vegetation in the lowland conifer forests of many areas, with an occasional stem of C. calyculata also visible here. Only on the occasional site where trees have been re-moved by windfall, disease, or cutting is there sufficient light on the forest floor to permit the taking of useful photo-graphs.

For the purposes of his "The Vegetation of Wisconsin," Curtis (1959) studied 17 bogs, 6 fens, and 35 northern and 44 southern sedge meadows. Other studies employed by Curtis in his synthesis of knowledge of these wetlands include those by A. B. Stout, D. F. Costello, M. L. Partch, A. J. Catenhusen, J. H. Zimmerman, and J. J. Clausen. The basic differentiating characteristics of fens, meadows, bogs, and marshes can be summarized as shown in Table I.

Table I.   Community Characteristics

Community	Characteristics
Bog	Wet, very acid peat
Fen	Alkaline, neutral, or slightly acid wet peat
Heath	Wet to moist sandy soil with a shallow layer of peat
Marsh	Wet or periodically wet but not peaty soils
Moor	Upland heath on dry or damp but not wet peat
Meadow	Wet or periodically wet, with sedge peat or muck
Conifer swamp	Wet, mossy understory with spruce or tamarack trees in the over-story

The typical plant species found in each of these wetland communities are given in Table II.

Table II.   Typical Community Plant Species

Community	Dominant species
Bog	Bog ericads, cotton grass (*Eriophorum*), grasses, some Compositae, *Caltha, Iris, Cypripedium, Salix*
Heath	Ericaceous shrubs (bog ericads)
Marsh	Cattails, reeds, rushes
Moor	Bog ericads (ericaceous shrubs)
Meadow	Sedges, some Compositae, grasses, rushes

A summary of the synthesis by Curtis (1959) of the data available on the fens, bogs, meadows, and marshes is presented in "The Vegetation of Wisconsin." It is of interest that all of these communities are circumpolar in extent, with many of the species retaining their identity, although often in the form of varieties or subspecies, across the entire expanse of the circumpolar regions. Thus, *Carex stricta*, for example, as well as a number of other sedges plus a sizable group of herbaceous and shrub species are found in comparable communities in Europe and Asia. As Curtis points out, between the sedge meadow communities of south Germany and Wisconsin there are 15 of 60 species and 33 of 44 genera in common. Typical plants found in both regions are *Caltha palustris, Eleocharis palustris, Mentha arvensis, Poa palustris,* and *Scutellaria galericulata*. Of the species in the sedge meadows of Alberta, New England, and the Atlantic states, some 25-50% are found in the Wisconsin sedge meadows.

As to the general nature of the lowland bogs and conifer forests, most are small, many have a small central pool of open water, they are wet and soft to walk through, and if observed closely are seen to possess a layer of *Sphagnum* mosses on the surface, upon which grow the ericaceous shrubs and sedges that so typically dominate the plant community. A typical bog in northern Wisconsin, for example, one studied by Kratz (1981), was about 6.5 acres in area, and had a 0.2 ha oblong central lake with nearly vertical sides and an almost uniform depth of 1.5 m. The pH was 4.7 in July. Plant species around the perimeter of the lake and over the surface of the bog included the dominants *Chamaedaphne calyculata, Sphagnum* mosses, and *Carex oligosperma*.

Such a site, however, is not the only one that can be occupied by bog plant communities. Rigg (1940a,b), in addition to providing a general description of the processes of bog formation in kettle-hole lakes, lists other sites in which bog species can gain a foothold and create small communities. These include (1) portions of the margins of larger lakes, often on or beside logs that have lain in the same position for a long time, (2) small patches of bog, often floating on larger lakes, (3) very small, shallow ponds, (4) areas of marshland on which *Sphagnum* can encroach, (5) the edges of slow-moving rivers and streams, and (6), at least in some western regions, *Sphagnum* bogs formed over dense shrub communities.

The bog plant species are adapted to the distinctive environmental conditions designated as *ombrotrophic*--a term used frequently in describing a particular kind of environment. The set of ecological conditions designated as ombrotrophic form the central topic of this book, along with the plant communities most often found in the ombrotrophic bogs.

An ombrotrophic bog is one possessing a very low content of nutrients available for plant growth; the soil water is highly acidic; the soil itself is primarily peat, often in a deep deposit; and perhaps most important of all, there is little or no drainage of water from either streams or surrounding uplands through at least much of the bog. It is this latter characteristic that gives the ombrotrophic bogs their most distinctive feature; as a consequence of this lack of nutrient inflow from stream or runoff, most or all of the available nutrients for plant growth come from elements carried to the bog in precipitation and from dust falling on the surface of the peat.

The bog waters can be said to be analogous to the water of oligotrophic lakes; they are similarly low in mineral content, contrasting sharply with conditions in minerotrophic marshes and eutrophic lakes, both of which are high in nutrient content and are neutral or alkaline in pH. Thus, there is a direct correspondence between ombrotrophic and oligotrophic, and between minerotrophic and eutrophic. The distinction is one that should be remembered, because it will be referred to frequently in discussions throughout the book.

SPECIES OF THE COMMUNITIES

Plant communities are characterized--as are all communities--by the kinds, or species, of organisms existing therein, an attribute usually characterized by the term *composition*, and by the abundance with which each is represented, a characteristic often referred to as the *structure* of the community. There are, however, regional differences in the composition of what might be considered recognizable communties--conifer forest, for example, or lowland bog--and so species composition and structure of the communities differ from east to west and north to south over the range in which the lowland bogs and conifer forests are found.

To obtain an overall view of composition and structure of the lowland bogs and conifer forests, it is reasonable to begin with a description of some south-central bogs and forests and then range east, west, and north to depict differences encountered along these geographical axes. As a starting point then, we take those lowland bogs and conifer forests in Wisconsin, mentioned above as having been discussed in some detail by Curtis (1959). The species in Table III were those found to be most prevalent in the 17 bogs in northern Wisconsin studied by Curtis and associates, listed in order of presence (the percentage of bogs in which they were found).

Table III.   Prevalent Species in Northern Wisconsin Bogs

Species[a]	Presence (%)
Andromeda glaucophylla*	94
Chamaedaphne calyculata*	88
Kalmia polifolia*	82
Ledum groenlandicum	77
Vaccinium macrocarpon*	77
Smilacina trifolia	77
Sarracenia purpurea*	77
Vaccinium oxycoccus*	65
Vaccinium angustifolium	59
Vaccinium myrtilloides	59
Carex trisperma	53
Drosera rotundifolia*	53
Cornus canadensis	53
Calla palustris*	47
Cypripedium acaule*	47
Dryopteris cristata	47
Gaultheria hispidula	47
Iris versicolor*	47
Potentilla palustris*	47
Menyanthes trifoliata*	41
Gaultheria procumbens	41
Eriophorum spissum	35

[a]Species marked with an asterisk were also modal, i.e.,
their presence values were higher in bogs than in any other
plant community.

Other species found in bogs, but with lower presence values, although all were modal, include those in Table IV.
The close relationships between the open bogs and lowland
conifer forests dominated by Picea mariana, Larix laricina,
Thuja occidentalis, and Abies balsamea are revealed by comparing these listings with comparable ones obtained from 71 northern lowland conifer forest stands in Wisconsin studied by Curtis (Table V).
Other species of lower presence are given in Table VI.
Modal species of lower presence were Carex pauciflora (19),
Cinna latifolia (18), Rhamnus alnifolia (17), Arceuthobium
pusillum (12), Carex interior (8), Lonicera villosa (7), Carex
canescens (6), Agrostis perennans (5), Equisetum scirpoides (4),
Eriophorum tenellum (4), Habenaria clavellata (4), and Carex
comosa (3).

Table IV. Other Common Species in Northern Wisconsin Bogs

Species[a]	Presence (%)
Betula glandulosa*	29
Eriophorum angustifolium*	29
Carex lasiocarpa*	29
Triadenum virginicum*	29
Carex oligosperma*	24
Drosera intermedia*	24
Rhynchospora alba*	24
Pogonia ophioglossoides*	18
Myrica gale*	18
Calopogon pulchellus*	18
Dulichium arundinaceum*	12
Rhus vernix*	12
Scirpus rubrotinctus*	12
Triglochin maritima*	12
Arethusa bulbosa*	6
Bidens tripartita*	6
Brasenia schreberi*	6
Dryopteris bootii*	6
Habenaria dilatata*	6
Salix candida*	6

[a]See footnote to Table III.

Black spruce, Picea mariana, is a tree species that is ubiquitous in bogs across the continent, found in scattered clumps in the open bogs, forming a densely canopied stand in the lowland conifer forests, often in association with Larix laricina, tamarack, in open bogs, and with Thuja occidentalis, northern white cedar, and Abies balsamea, balsam fir, in the forests particularly of the eastern part of the continent. Larix laricina is often a pioneer with P. mariana in the open bogs, but is intolerant of the deep shade in the closed-canopy forests.

Picea mariana occupies the lowland bogs and conifer forests along the southern margin of its range from eastern North America across the continent to Alaska. It does not, however, reach the Pacific Coast except in southwestern Alaska, and is replaced in the far western coastal bogs by species characteristic of the Pacific coastal forest. Larix laricina follows roughly a similar distribution, except its western limit is somewhat farther from the Pacific coast than that of P. mariana and it is somewhat more scattered than P. mariana in north-central Alaska, where it reaches nearly to the coast.

Table V. Prevalent Species in Northern Wisconsin Lowland
Conifer Forests

Species[a]	Presence (%)
Carex trisperma*	86
Ledum groenlandicum*	82
Smilacina trifolia*	77
Gaultheria hispidula*	76
Vaccinium myrtilloides*	73
Dryopteris austriaca	63
Cornus canadensis	61
Alnus rugosa	59
Chamaedaphne calyculata	58
Trientalis borealis	58
Kalmia polifolia	56
Vaccinium angustifolium	55
Maianthemum canadense	52
Osmunda cinnamomea	51
Andromeda glaucophylla	49
Viola pallens*	49

[a]See footnote to Table III.

Table VI. Other Common Species in Northern Wisconsin Lowland
Conifer Forests

Species[a]	Presence (%)
Coptis trifolia	47
Rubus pubescens	46
Cypripedium acaule	45
Gaultheria procumbens	45
Dryopteris cristata	42
Eriophorum spissum*	42
Nemopanthus mucronatus*	42
Parthenocissus vitacea	41
Linnaea borealis	38
Carex disperma	37
Eriophorum virginicum	36
Aralia nudicaulis	35
Sarracenia purpurea	31
Equisetum fluviatile	29
Vaccinium oxycoccus	28

[a]See footnote in Table III.

Species of the Pacific coastal region that are found in
bogs are also widespread on uplands, in contrast to the ecological amplitude of *P. mariana* and *L. laricina,* which are almost exclusively lowland species along the southern margin of
range across the continent. The most abundant coastal forest
trees inhabiting the western bogs are *Tsuga heterophylla* (western hemlock), *Thuja plicata* (western red cedar), *Chamaecyparis
nootkatensis* (Alaska yellow cedar or cypress), and *Pinus monticola* (western white pine, found mostly southward).

The tree species found in bogs along the Pacific Coast are
thus quite distinct from those occupying bogs in the rest of
the continent, but the herb and shrub species found in the long
stretch of coast from northern United Stated to southern Alaska are, with a few exceptions, familiar to botanists studying
the bogs elsewhere. Among the exceptions are such species
found in Pacific coastal bogs as *Ledum columbianum, Menziesia
ferruginea, Sorbus sitchensis, Gaultheria shallon, Rhododendron
californicum, Gentiana sceptrum, Trientalis arctica, Tofieldia
intermedia, Drosera anglica, Lysichitum americanum,* and (northward) *Loiseleuria procumbens, Salix reticulata, Vaccinium uliginosum, Rubus chamaemorus, Saxifraga hirculis,* and additional
species listed by Rigg (1940a,b), Griggs (1936), and other
authors who have written on the bogs of the Pacific Coast region from Oregon to Alaska.

Some of the species found in the Pacific coastal bogs,
particularly northward and into southern Alaska, are arctic
and alpine species that range southward along the mountains inland from the coast. These species include, in addition to *L.
procumbens,* such species with arctic affinities as *Ledum decumbens (Ledum palustre), Empetrum nigrum, Andromeda polifolia,
Vaccinium vitis-idaea,* and other species that are generally
thought of as being found more generally in arctic and alpine
regions than in the more southern bogs.

The presence of these species in the bogs, however, tends
to support the concept, discussed in detail in later chapters,
that at least many species in the bogs of North America have
adaptations fitting them to the environment of the bogs more or
less incidentally, and that they are primarily adapted to arctic and alpine habitats. The latter idea is supported also by
the fact that the southern edge of the range of many of the
species dominant in the bogs of the northern United States and
southern Canada is coincident with southern edge of the glaciated region, where kettle-hole lakes are available for the formation of bog communities. These species range far north into
boreal forest and arctic tundra of Canada.

The stands in a forested area of north-central Manitoba,
for example, had these species as dominants: *P. mariana, Ledum
groenlandicum, C. calyculata, Kalmia polifolia, Oxycoccus mi-*

crocarpus *(Vaccinium microcarpus)*, *Andromeda glaucophylla*, *Betula glandulosa*, *Myrica gale*, *Smilacina trifolia*, *Drosera rotundifolia*, and *Potentilla palustris* (Larsen 1980; Sims and Stewart 1981), all of which are represented, or represented by closely related species, in the lowland conifer forests of the northern United States.

For a comparison of species composition of more southern lowland bogs and forests, such as those of Wisconsin, with open bogs or muskegs of northern regions, Tables VII-X list species in communities of northern Manitoba and southern Mackenzie, Canada, which can be taken as representative. The listing of species is taken from unpublished data from the author's research in boreal forest and tundra of Canada (Larsen, 1980); the frequency data given refer to the frequencies of the species in transects of 20 1-m square quadrats.

Table VII. Frequency of Species in a String Bog in Manitoba[a]

Species	*Frequency (%)*
Andromeda polifolia	100
Carex limosa	100
Menyanthes trifoliata	100
Vaccinium oxycoccus (V. microcarpus)	95
Utricularia intermedia	60
Larix laricina (seedlings)	55
Equisetum fluviatile	40
Betula glandulosa	30
Kalmia polifolia	30
Chamaedaphne calyculata	30
Drosera rotundifolia	25
Smilacina trifolia	15
Carex rostrata	10
Drosera intermedia	5
Sarracenia purpurea	5

[a]*Northwestern Manitoba 57ºN, 101 W.*

Table VIII.   Species in an Open Muskeg in Manitoba

Species	Frequency (%)
Ledum groenlandicum	100
Rubus chamaemorus	100
Chamaedaphne calyculata	85
Vaccinium oxycoccus (V. micro-carpus)	65
Kalmia polifolia	60
Picea mariana (seedlings)	30
Vaccinium vitis-idaea	25
Eriophorum spissum	5

Also present in the string bog but in lower frequencies were A. glaucophylla, L. groenlandicum, Rubus chamaemorus, a number of species of Carex, as well as abundant mosses and lichen species. Dominant species in an open muskeg are given in Table VIII. In this community, Carex was also present in addition to abundant lichen and moss species. Species in an open muskeg in Southern Mackenzie are given in Table IX.

In this stand mosses and lichens were abundant and with high cover value.

A distinctive characteristic of the bog plant communities is the high relative abundance of two families, the Orchidaceae and the Ericaceae, the latter more important in terms of dominance since the total density and cover afforded by the ericads are much greater than that of the northern wild orchids. Using data on the northern bogs taken from Curtis (1959), the comparisons in Table X can be made among several wetland communities (the values given are percentages of prevalence of the family in the communities).

It is apparent that the ericaceous shrubs give the bog and lowland conifer communities an identity distinct from all others, and in Chapter 5 some attention is given to the members of this most fascinating plant family.

Table IX. Species in an Open Muskeg in Southern Mackenzie, Canada[a]

Species	Frequency (%)
Carex species	90
Ledum groenlandicum	85
Empetrum nigrum	80
Rubus chamaemorus	80
Vaccinium oxycoccus (*V. micro-carpus*)	80
Vaccinium vitis-idaea	75
Vaccinium uliginosum	75
Ledum decumbens	65
Equisetum species	55
Drosera rotundifolia	50
Picea mariana (seedlings)	30
Larix laricina (seedlings)	20
Epilobium angustifolium	15
Eriophorum spissum	10
Chamaedaphne calyculata	5
Petasites sagittatus	5
Pyrola secunda	5
Salix glauca	5

[a] *61°N, 118°W*

Table X.   Comparisons of Families in Wetland Communities[a]

Family	Open bog	Wet forest	Wet-mesic forest	Sedge meadow	Boreal forest	Mesic forest
Ericaceae	9.2	6.7	...	...	...	...
Cyperaceae	9.2	13.5	12.5	9.0	5.7	7.5
Compositae	6.7	6.7	8.8	15.8	9.8	5.7
Gramineae	5.9	5.7	7.4	9.0	4.7	...
Orchidaceae	5.0	...	...	...	...	...
Rosaceae	...	5.7	...	6.8	...	5.7
Ranunculaceae	...	...	6.7	...	5.7	4.8
Liliaceae	...	...	6.4	...	5.7	8.4
Labiatae	...	...	...	6.2	...	...

[a] *Dots indicate that values are much lower.*

5 Plant Species of the Bogs—I

The Ericads or ericaceous shrubs are members of the wide-ranging family Ericaceae, with many species representing the group in Africa, Asia, and Australia. Since many of the northern ericaceous shrubs are also known as heath plants, perhaps we can diverge from our central topic for a moment to discuss the origins of the term. The words heath and heather are found in Old English, and the word heathen is also derived from early times. It seems that in the days of the Roman Empire, the teachings of Christianity were accepted more rapidly in the cities than in the rural areas--hence the dwellers on the heaths were the last to hear of it, and were thus unbelievers, called heathens.

It has long been recognized that there are close relationships among genera that traditionally fall into the Ericaceae and other genera such as *Pyrola, Monotropa, Pterospora, Moneses,* and *Chimaphila,* although the latter have been considered by some taxonomists to belong in separate families, the Pyrolaceae and the Monotropaceae. Some taxonomists separate the Pyrolaceae and Monotropaceae, others put *Monotropa* and *Moneses* in the Pyrolaceae, and a few include the entire group, *Pyrola* and Monotropaceae and all the rest, in the Ericaceae. Whatever the preference, and there seems to be ample latitude to exercise one's subjective judgment here, the mutual relationships among all the genera included at one time or another in these families have long been recognized. Moreover, they are also related to the Empetraceae, of which the species *Empetrum nigrum* is a wide-ranging and well-known member; evidently, the same can be said for *Diapensia* of the Diapensaceae.

The above relationships are of course based on morphological characteristics, the structure of the flowers in particular. However, some other factors also tend to confirm that all the genera of the Ericaceae, Pyrolaceae, Monotropaceae, and other mutually related families are so close in evolutionary terms that they all might well be considered members of a single family. Perhaps the most significant evidence is ecological or physiological--a large proportion of the species

require fungal root associates known as mycorrhizae to grow
successfully. Members of the order Ericales, which includes
the Ericaceae, Pyrolaceae, and Monotropaceae, are more dependent upon mycorrhizae than most plant groups, and some, the
Monotropaceae, have become so dependent upon the fungal part-
ner that they have given up photosynthesis--have lost their
chlorophyll and hence ability to make their own food.

It is also known that many members of the heath family
possess compounds in their tissues that are toxic to animals.
In all of these, the toxic substance is the same, which further
indicates the close relationship among these species. As
Swingle (1946) pointed out, members of the family have little
forage value, but they have been responsible for poisoning
livestock throughout recorded history, largely at times when
other forage was not available for one reason or another.
Laurels and rhododendrons are most notorious for their toxic
qualities. In general they are unpalatable, but when feed is
scarce animals may be forced to eat them. The poisonous compound was first called andromedotoxin, since it was first isolated from a species of *Andromeda,* but it has been characterized chemically and has been now given the somewhat different
chemical name acetylandromedol. The effects of the substance
when ingested are discussed more fully under the descriptions
of the various species presented later in this volume.

The Ericaceae is essentially a shrubby family, with a few
trees, largely tropical or at least warm temperate, and a few
perennial herbaceous species. In 1946, Swingle stated there
were 80 genera and 1350 species in the Ericaceae. Good, in
1964, revised this, reducing the genera to 60 but increasing
the number of species known at the time to 2250. In the United
States, Canada, and Greenland, according to Kartesz and Kartesz
(1980) the number is 44 genera and 219 species, in which there
are 63 subspecies and 53 varieties. For these species, there
are 318 synonyms, and 9 hybrids, which add to the confusion.
It is of perhaps some interest that of the manuals commonly
used for plant species identification in the United States,
only Gleason and Cronquist (1963) include *Chimaphila, Moneses,
Pyrola, Monotropa, Pterospora,* and *Monotropsis* in the Ericaceae; Fernald's (1950) (Gray's) Manual, Scoggan (1978), and
Hulten (1968) include them in the Pyrolaceae.

Whatever one prefers in this kind of taxonomic hair-split-
ting, there are evidently five main groups of Ericaceae, and
these are generally considered to be the following:

Arbutoideae--predominantly north-temperate and scarcely
represented in Africa and Australia

Rhododendroideae--similarly distributed, absent from Africa

Vaccinoideae--similarly distributed, in Madagascar but not tropical Africa, in tropical America, Asia, Malaysia.

Ericoideae--confined to Africa and Europe, mostly south of the Tropic of Capricorn

Epicridaceae--principally Australian; one genus in Patagonia

These five groups constitute woody plants for the most part, the most widely distributed of all such plants, and for flowering shrubs, in the words of Swingle (1946), "no family can compare with the Ericaceae. Their fragrant flowers, often in great clusters, and their glossy evergreen leaves give them a peculiar charm."

NORTH AMERICAN HABITATS

The species of tropical and temperate America do not concern us here, but in the northern parts of the North American continent with which we are concerned it seems as though the ranges of many of the ericaceous species are determined by geological and topographic features. They are essentially plants of the bogs, peatlands, and wetlands for the most part, or of sandy woods or openings in the case of a few, but it is of interest that they are almost entirely absent from the unglaciated areas of, for example, the southwestern part of Wisconsin. It was Fassett (1929) who pointed out that this may be the consequence of the fact that both bogs and very dry soils are generally rare in the unglaciated region, but another factor also involved may be the nature of the rocks themselves. The rocks of the unglaciated areas are sedimentary and calcareous, and many of the ericaceous species prefer acid habitats and would avoid soils derived from rocks of alkaline reaction. Northward, where glacial till and kettleholes are abundant, the ericaceous species are the dominants in the acidic bogs and conifer swamps found so commonly throughout the region.

Seeds of many species of the northern regions are dispersed by birds and mammals. It has been noted by botanists (Stebbins, 1974) that the genera of the Ericaceae that have wind-borne seeds occupy a wide variety of habitats, but members of the berry-forming genera such as *Gaultheria* and *Vaccinium* occur chiefly as undershrubs or trailing plants in forests. This apparently indicates an evolutionary shift to dispersal in the digestive tract of animals in association with adaptation to forest conditions. This adaptation is also present in such other genera as *Fragaria, Rubus, Myrica, Empetrum,* and *Gaylussacia*. For many animals, the berries of *Vaccinium* may at times constitute the chief food since they are present in abundance during some years and remain on the bushes for some length of time.

It is evident that at some point during the course of evolution, the ericads developed adaptations fitting them for relatively rapid seed dispersal by animals, as well as preferences for acid soils and dependence upon the symbiotic association of root tissues with mycorrhizal fungi. When these evolutionary events took place is not known; as Stebbins points out, the Ericaceae probably originated on some land mass underlain by acid igneous rocks, but which land mass it may have been, or in what period of geological history, is still a mystery. It remains to be discovered what quirks of physiology make it possible for the Ericaceae to inhabit acid soils where competition from other species is minimal. During the long stretch of geological history, the environments of the continents have changed, probably most appreciably in regard to climate, and we have much to learn about how environment and evolutionary processes led to the myriad morphological and physiological adaptations exhibited by the species of plants inhabiting the earth today.

6 Plant Species of the Bogs—II

The basin or kettlehole bogs of glaciated northern regions
are unique habitats, which differ even from the related marshes and fens in characteristics such as acidity, nutrient mineral content, aeration, temperature, cation exchange capacity,
as well as general chemical composition of the soil. Just as
a habitat is unique, so is its community of plant species; both
bog habitat and plant community are so distinctive that the
sight of one will lead an ecologist to anticipate the other.
What comes to mind initially is the abundance of *Sphagnum* and
other mosses on the surface of the moist peat, an aggregation
of sedge species at or near the edge of any open water, a relatively dense cover of ericaceous shrubs, some bog birch, perhaps a few willows, and a group of other species making up the
bog flora--a flora that is somewhat limited in diversity and
range of morphological characteristics but fascinating for the
adaptations, physiological as well as structural, that fit the
species for this habitat.

Pages could be devoted to descriptions of many of the
plant species, with attention given not only to appearance and
morphology but also to ecology, habitat perferences, physiology,
and biochemistry. For many other species, however, relatively
little is known. They are a blank page in the ecological note-
book, waiting for interested students. Until more is known
about these species, it cannot be said that the ecology of the
bog communities is fully understood.

For our purposes here, it is necessary to compress descriptions of the individual species into a paragraph or two;
students curious about these species have the prospect of a
search--exciting or otherwise, depending upon one's view--
through the botanical literature for more of what is known
about them. Nor will the trees be dealt with here, since much
written on each of the species is readily available in research
libraries. Likewise, such common shrubs as the willows and
alders will be left to the exploratory instincts that libraries
release in scholars. We shall deal, on the other hand, with
the species that for one reason or another seem to characterize

Fig. 1. Andromeda glaucophylla.

the plant communities of the bogs by reason of ubiquity, abundance, or persistent appearance (even if rare) in bog habitats over at least a fairly broad region.

Andromeda glaucophylla (Fig. 1) is a plant found commonly in open bogs, pond margins, and the thickets around the edges of boggy lakes, as well as in the coniferous swamp forests. It is commonly known as bog rosemary and is found rather abundantly in suitable habitats in arctic and boreal eastern North America, from Minnesota and Manitoba to southern Greenland, Labrador, and New Jersey. It contains a toxic compound now known as acetylandromedol. The same poison is found in the Rhododendrons and the Kalmias and a longer exposition of its interesting history is to be found on a subsequent page under *Rhododendron* and *Ledum*. The leaves of *A. glaucophylla* are evergreen, firm, revolute, alternate, narrow, up to 5 cm in length, white and puberulent beneath.

Andromeda polifolia is the northern species found both in open muskegs and spruce forests or treed muskegs, occurring from the foothills of the Brooks Range in Alaska southward and eastward through the Northwest Territories of Canada, to Washington, northern Idaho, Alberta, Ontario, and southern Labrador. It is found also in western Greenland and northern

Eurasia. In North America it generally extends northward somewhat beyond the limit of trees--well into the northern tundra.
Interesting, however, is the fact that the species is very
closely related to *A. glaucophylla,* the latter of more limited
range and confined to eastern North America. It has actually
at times (and still is by some) been considered a subspecies
of *A. polifolia.* In any case, the two hybridize, and intermediate forms are found where the range of the two overlap.
The evergreen leaves of *A. polifolia* are mostly less than 3 cm
long, and are alternate, with a white glaucous coating beneath
and grayish green above. The plant also contains the toxin
acetylandromedol.

   Arctostaphylos (Arctous) alpina and *Arctostaphylos (Arc-*
tous) rubra are closely related northern species, and many
taxonomists have called one or the other a subspecies or have
simply included them together under one name. *Arctostaphylos*
rubra is evidently somewhat more southern, with *A. alpina*, as
the name implies, more northern and alpine in its affinities,
although Polunin (1959) and others have also found what they
considered to be the former in the Arctic. If one chooses to
call them separate entities, then both are wide-ranging in
northern North America and are circumpolar in distribution.
The two species have also been placed in the genus *Arctous* by
some taxonomists--an older name that is still encountered,
particularly since recent work has shown that both species
should probably be separated from *Arctostaphylos* and placed
into a distinct genus, logically *Arctous* (Diggs and Breckon,
1981). *Arctostaphylos (Arctous) alpina* has the common name
alpine bearberry, and *A. rubra,* since it is not considered
especially alpine or arctic in affinities, may be known simply
as bearberry, but this is confusing since *Arctostaphylos uva-*
ursi is also known as bearberry. Some taxonomists have apparently noted certain differences other than color of the berries,
which in the case of *alpina* is considered to be black and in
rubra red; the latter is also purported to have thinner leaves
and more sparingly ciliate margins on the leaves. There is
also apparently some indication that the latter is calcareous
in its soil preferences, while *A. alpina* is more of an oxylo-
phyte. Both, however, are found in a variety of habitats,
ranging from gravel and rocky tundra to moist lowlands and muskegs, and so the preference is not necessarily a highly demand-
ing one nor can it be said to be diagnostic in distinguishing
one from the other. The leaves are considered to be deciduous
or, more accurately, marcescent, which refers to the fact that
they tend to wither but persist in attachment to the stem,
whitening with age.

Fig. 2. Arctostaphylos uva-ursi.

Arctostaphylos uva-ursi (Fig. 2) is known as the common bearberry or kinnikinnick and is boreal and circumpolar in distribution, with a range extending from Alaska to Labrador and to northern California, New Mexico, Minnesota, New England, Greenland, and northern Eurasia. It is essentially a species of dry upland sandy slopes, but it is also found in relatively moist open places southward. The berry is red, dry, and taste-less. If bears indeed eat them, they are probably the only animals that do so.

The designation of subspecies is based upon the presence or absence of pubescence and stalked glandular hairs on the twigs (Rosatti, 1981). The leaves are evergreen and leathery.

It is perhaps of interest that Stebbins (1974) believes that the Arbutoidea (a tribe or subfamily of the Ericaceae) demonstrate adaptive radiation from submesic forms to forms adapted to more arid or more mesic conditions than the ances-tral types. Thus, *A. uva-ursi,* with small sclerophyllous leaves, has increased its leaf surface through evolution of a prostrate creeping habit of growth with elongation of vegeta-tive shoots and an increase in the number of leaves. The same, he says, may be true of *A. (Arctous) alpina.*

Fig. 3. Chamaedaphne calyculata.

Chamaedaphne calyculata (Fig. 3) is another of the ericads that, according to Stebbins, has an interesting evolutionary history, since it appears to be a specialized radiant that
developed originally in intermediate or mesic habitats and now

grows best in wet marshes and bogs. In the somewhat more
southern reaches of its range, it is frequently one of the
dominant species in peaty swales, bogs, pond margins, and the
borders of lakes, often covering an area with a virtually continuous carpet. Known as leatherleaf, it has a tough, thick,
olive-green, almost brown leaf, which during winter actually
does become dominantly brown in color. The leaves remain attached during winter and reportedly are then shed the following growing season; it seems reasonable, however, that some
leaves may persist through more than a single complete summer
of photosynthetic activity. It occurs increasingly rarely to
the north, becoming uncommon at the northern forest border in
Keewatin; it is not common in the Yukon, but is found in some
abundance in at least the forested regions of Alaska and south
to British Columbia and then eastward to Labrador, Newfoundland, North Carolina, northern Europe, and Asia. An older
generic name still in use is *Cassandra,* not encountered commonly today but found in older botanical manuals.

The use of *Chamaedaphne* leaves as tea is discussed later
(see *Ledum* and *Rhododendron*).

Epigaea repens (Fig. 4) is the trailing arbutus of nature
lovers, and is commonly found in coniferous forests and jackpine stands on gravelly acid soils, blossoming in the earliest
days of spring. A prostrate, creeping shrub, with leathery
evergreen leaves, it occurs widely, being found in woods, on
dry rocks, in alpine woods, and in northern bogs throughout
its North American boreal range, Labrador to Saskatchewan, Iowa,
Wisconsin, Michigan, Pennsylvania, Tennessee, North Carolina,
Quebec, Ontario, and Manitoba, with the variety *glabrifolia*
being somewhat more northern in its affinities.

Gaultheria hispidula (Fig. 5) is the creeping snowberry,
known also as *Chiogenes hispidula,* a somewhat older name now
generally in disuse. It has persistent, evergreen leaves mostly less than 1 cm long, with trailing, creeping, barely woody
stems. It is found most abundantly in moist and mossy coniferous woods and has been described as one of the most abundant species of the poorly drained black spruce forests northward in Canada, where it forms large trailing mats on the damp
humus. It is found also on subalpine slopes throughout its
boreal-American range: British Columbia to Labrador, south to
Idaho, Wisconsin, Minnesota, Michigan, and North Carolina.

Gaultheria procumbens is the wintergreen or checkerberry,
a low, creeping, almost herbaceous shrub with evergreen or at
least persistent, alternate, leathery leaves, usually more
than 1 cm long. It is known for the distinctive flavor of its
leaves, namely, oil of wintergreen (now also made synthetically).

Fig. 4.   *Epigaea repens.*

Fig. 5.   *Gaultheria hispidula.*

It is a common occupant of the spruce swamps and is found in boreal temperate America, from Manitoba to eastern Quebec, south to Alabama and Georgia.

Gaylussacia baccata, huckleberry, is found in dry to moist woods, thickets, and clearings with acid sandy soils, from New-foundland to Saskatchewan, barely into southeastern Minnesota and eastern Iowa, and in New England, Georgia, and Louisiana. The leaves are resin-dotted on both surfaces and are deciduous.

Kalmia angustifolia, known commonly as sheep laurel or lambkill, is widely distributed from sandy jackpine forest to spruce woods, alpine bogs, and subalpine forests throughout the region from Ontario to Labrador and south to Michigan and Geor-gia. *Kalmia* was named by Linnaeus for Pehr Kalm, 1717-1779, one of the first professional botanists to study the flora of the northeastern United States and eastern Carada. It has ever-green, mostly opposite leaves, and as inferred in the name lambkill is occasionally eaten by animals, which are then pois-oned by the toxin acetylandromedol. The leaves are tough and leathery, however, and are eaten only when nothing else is available by animals unfamiliar with the effects. In winter or early spring, however, the leaves above the snow may be the only greenery in sight, and sheep are the usual victims since the land on which the *Kalmia* grows is usually given over to sheep rather than other livestock.

Kalmia polifolia (Figs. 6 and 7) or bog laurel is found in bogs, muskegs, and coniferous forests. Known also as Am-erican laurel, it is boreal and arctic American in range, found in Alaska and Quebec and points between, and then southward to New Jersey, Pennsylvania, Minnesota, and California. Porsild (1955) writes that it is: "A plant of northern muskegs that in Keewatin extends some distance beyond the limit of trees; rare in the lower Mackenzie basin, north to Bear Lake and in Central Yukon." It is common only in the northern regions and in al-pine regions southward, and seems to be most abundant near and on both sides of the arctic forest border. It is common local-ly in the alpine areas where it is found.

The leaves are opposite and evergreen, and the plant is poisonous (like *K. angustifolia*), but it grows in places where livestock are rarely grazed or allowed to roam. On high range in the western states, however, it is sometimes a danger to grazing animals.

Ledum groenlandicum, Labrador tea (Fig. 8), is abundant in lowlands southward and uplands northward, often the dominant shrub in bogs and spruce forests. It is arctic boreal American, found in muskegs, forests, and alpine regions, and is usaually the most frequent and abundant plant of the wet black spruce

Fig. 6. Kalmia polifolia (flower).

forests typical of boreal Canada. The distinguishing character is the dense tomentum of the leaves, the lower surface
being completely covered with a long tawny wool; it is evergreen and can be distinguished from *L. decumbens* (also known
as *L. palustre, L. palustre* and *decumbens,* and so on) by its
broader leaves. *Ledum decumbens* also has the peduncle sharply
bent just below the capsule, while *L. groenlandicum* has the
peduncle evenly bent or curved. The plant has evergreen alternate entire leaves, strongly revolute, with rusty wool beneath.

   L. groenlandicum is similar to *L. glandulosum,* a far
western species in North America, known also as trapper's tea,
a somewhat misleading appellation since the plant contains
acetylandromedol and is therefore poisonous. The author once
met a middle-aged couple who had attempted using the species
for a tea substitute over a period of time. They had experienced not only the usually reported symptoms of persistent
weakness and nausea after using it for a time but they also
became exceedingly nervous with trembling limbs and apparently
some disturbance of vision. The Labrador tea, *L. groenlandicum,* apparently either lacks the poison or it is not present
in levels capable producing symptoms since there seem to be
no reports of poisoning. Since the two species hybridize,
however, they must be generally quite similar, and anyone us-

Fig. 7.   Kalmia polifolia (fruit).

ing *L. groenlandicum* for tea should do so cautiously. This is
advisable, since *Ledum decumbens*, the next species described, is
also known to contain a toxic substance, presumably the same one,

Fig. 8.   Ledum groenlandicum.

since all three species are similar in appearance and are tax-
onimically closely related.

   Ledum decumbens, also known variously as *L. palustre* or
L. palustre var. *decumbens,* is a northern species, circumpolar,
found in the barren grounds and the northern parts of the wood-
ed country from Alaska to Greenland and then through northern
Eurasia. It is a common inhabitant of lichen woodlands, spruce
muskegs, rock field tundra, alpine slopes, and dry mountain
ridges.

   The early explorers who reported using this *Ledum* species
for a tea must have been hardy indeed, since they evidently
drank it with relish and in quantity; one must assume, however,
they did not do so very often. Fernald and Kinsey (1958) state
that Palliser wrote in his journal of 1866 that "We...got a
supply of the muskeg tea *(Ledum palustre),* which makes a capital
beverage in the absence of a better." Sir John Richardson wrote
of his drinking both *L. palustre* tea and that made from *Rhododendron lapponicum* during his expeditions in search of Franklin,
indicating that he preferred the tea from *Ledum.*

   Rhododendron canadense, the rhodora, known also in the
older literature as *Rhodora canadense,* is a common shrub in
eastern North American boreal temperate regions. Poisoning

by members of the genus *Rhododendron* in the historical record dates back more than 2400 years; primitive peoples of Europe and Asia knew of the toxic properties of the rhododendrons.

Rhododendron lapponicum, Lapland rosebay, is a northern circumpolar species, wide-ranging in arctic and northern boreal North America. It inhabits dry rocky tundra, stony slopes, sandy swales, and extends southward only a short distance into the northern boreal forest. It is a rare alpine species in the Yukon, but is common locally on the east slope of the Mackenzie Mountains, then to northern British Columbia, and eastward to Labrador, Greenland, and Eurasia.

Vaccinium species with which we are most concerned can generally be distinguished according to the following key:

1. Leaves deciduous
    a. Anthers awned: Bilberries
        1. Flower parts mostly 4, leaves entire, thick.................*Vaccinium uliginosum*
        2. Flower parts mostly 5, leaves serrate, thin.................*Vaccinium caespitosum*
    b. Anthers not awned: Blueberries
        1. Leaves serrate, twigs glabrous............*Vaccinium angustifolium*
        2. Leaves entire, twigs densely hairy........*Vaccinium myrtilloides*
2. Leaves leathery, evergreen
    a. Petals united..............*Vaccinium vitis-idaea*
    b. Petals reflexed, nearly separate....................*Vaccinium oxycoccus*

Vaccinium oxycoccus has evidently been a problem for taxonomists, since it has also often been considered a separate genus, *Oxycoccus.* In any case, *V. oxycoccus* can be distinguished from the common cranberry, *V. macrocarpon,* as follows:
    Leaves ovate, small fruit.........*Vaccinium oxycoccus*
    Leaves elliptical, large fruit...*Vaccinium macrocarpon*

Vaccinium angustifolium (Fig. 9), the low or late sweet blueberry, is the abundant blueberry in the upper Midwest, found in drier woodlands, sandy and rocky openings, and forming extensive patches following forest fires. It is found in peatlands, but is not as abundant there as *V. myrtilloides.* It is boreal eastern American, found from Minnesota to Newfoundland, and is widely distributed from forests to alpine and subalpine slopes. The leaves are finely serrate, with the exception of one variety found in parts of Quebec and western Labrador.

Fig. 9. Vaccinium angustifolium.

Vaccinium caespitosum, the dwarf bilberry, is locally
abundant in northern coniferous forests, subalpine meadows,
forested slopes, pine woods, gravelly or rocky shores, and
other habitats, and it is circumboreal in range, extending in
North America from Alaska to Labrador, south to California and
New York, and ranging along the north shore of the Great Lakes.

Vaccinium myrtilloides, also known as V. canadense, is the
common blueberry of dense dark spruce forests and conifer swamps
It is known as the velvet-leaf blueberry, and is found also,
but less commonly, in such other habitats as spruce lichen woodlands, jackpine woods on sandy soil, and in open areas. It
ranges from Mackenzie to Labrador and south to Illinois, Louisiana, and Virginia. The leaves and twigs are copiously vel-
vety-pilose. The leaves are entire.

Vaccinium macrocarpon, or if preferred, Oxycoccus macrocarpus, is the common cranberry. It is boreal temperate eastern American, found from Minnesota to Newfoundland, Quebec, the
Maritimes, and south to Arkansas, Illinois, Tennessee, Ohio,
and North Carolina.

Vaccinium oxycoccus is a fascinating species, if for no
other reason that it has so confused the taxonomists that it--
or its close relatives--have been accorded a chaotic array of

names, subspecies, and varieties. It is also known as *Oxycoccus,* an old generic name that does nothing to clarify the general state of confusion. There is also another northern species, *V. microcarpus,* or *O. microcarpus,* which does little to help matters.

Fernald (1950), for example, calls *O. microcarpus* and *O. quadripetalus* synonyms, but others, Hultén (1968) in particular, adds variation to the theme by calling them both *O. palustris,* saying it is similar to *O. microcarpus* and giving a variant found in eastern North America the subspecific designation *microphyllum.* Scoggan (1978) considers *O. microcarpus, O. ovalifolius,* and *O. quadripetalus* (as well as *O. macrocarpus*) as individual species, based largely on the pedicels (which are glabrous or pubescent), length of the leaves (*O. microcarpus* being the smaller: 6 mm long and 2 mm broad), and size of the berry (*O. macrocarpus* up to 2 cm thick). He indicates, however, that further studies of these species are needed, and says they might all be included in a group, the *Oxycoccus* or the *V. oxycoccus* complex. Gleason and Cronquist (1963) apparently shed some light on the problem when they indicate that *V. oxycoccus* is synonymous with *O. oxycoccus, O. palustris,* and *O. quadripetalus,* and that it is a tetraploid derived from *V. macrocarpon* and *V. microcarpon* (or *O. macrocarpus* and *O. microcarpus,* since these are synonyms), which greatly simplifies the whole matter. There are then, if this bears out, only two species plus the tetraploid hybrid.

Vaccinium uliginosum is widely distributed in the low-latitude arctic and northern boreal regions throughout the circumpolar land areas; it is alpine in affinities in the more southern parts of its range. As a consequence of its wide range, it has gathered a host of common names, among them alpine bilberry, bog blueberry, bog whortleberry, arctic bog bilberry, alpine bog bilberry, and arctic-alpine blueberry. It is a deciduous species and is apparently better protected from winterkill than evergreen species in areas where snow cover is sparse or where winds remove the snow from upland barrens. It is found from the foothills of the Brooks Range in northern Alaska south to northern California, east to Quebec and Newfoundland, the mountains of New Hampshire, and then to Greenland and Eurasia. It is most frequent generally in moist lowlands, but it is also found on boulder fields, granite cliffs, and rocky ridges and shores. In the central United States, it extends into the extreme northeastern corner of Minnesota along the shore of Lake Superior. Northward, it occurs in a great variety of habitats.

Vaccinium vitis-idaea, like the *V. uliginosum,* has a variety of common names, including rock cranberry, cowberry, lingen, lingberry, red whortleberry, lingonberry, and mountain cranberry. It is wide-ranging, circumpolar, alpine, as well as boreal, and it is found in the subarctic from British Columbia to Newfoundland, Ontario, northeastern Minnesota, Manitoba, and northern Michigan, and then to Europe and Eurasia. It has evergreen leaves, shiny, thick, leathery, and coriaceous, obovate in shape, with heavy cuticle, and revolute, slightly revolute, or marginally reflexed leaves. It is generally low-growing, with red berries that are easily recognized. It is without doubt one of the most common and best known of the northern *Vaccinium* species, used for jellies and jams as well as for the pemmican of days now long past.

Pyrola asarifolia, the pink pyrola, a species of moist woods, is found throughout boreal America. There are evidently two varieties, variety *purpurea* being the transcontinental northern one and variety *asarifolia* the one commonly found in more southern parts of the range.

There are other *Pyrola* species, probably none of which should be dealt with in more than summary form here since they are not generally abundant and cannot be considered common or dominant species in any community. They are: *P. chlorantha* (also *P. virens*), *P. elliptica, P. grandiflora, P. minor, P. rotundifolia,* and *P. secunda.*

Chimaphila umbellata, pipsissewa, is a low, semiherbaceous shrub, with leathery, evergreen, sharply serrate leaves, found in dry, sandy, acid soils. The species is boreal, circumpolar, and found in conifer woods.

Moneses uniflora, the one-flowered *Pyrola,* is a boreal circumpolar species, found from Alaska to Labrador, south to New Mexico, Pennsylvania, and New England, and then to Eurasia. It is one of those unusual species that lack chlorophyll, are brownish or pasty-white in appearance, and live as saprophytes or root parasites, and hence usually in soils with a thick surface humus.

Pterospora andromeda, pinedrops, is temperate American, found usually on deep humus in coniferous forests, extending from British Columbia to eastern Quebec, then south to New York, Michigan, California, and New Mexico. It is a purplish-brown, root-parasitic herb with scales in place of leaves, and lacks chlorophyll.

Monotropa hypopithys, pinesap, is found in conifer woods throughout temperate boreal North America, from Newfoundland to Alaska, south to Mexico and Florida, and then to Eurasia.

It lacks chlorophyll and is variously yellow, tan, pink, or
red in color. It is also known as *Hypopithys monotropa,* an
interesting reversal.

Monotropa uniflora, Indian pipe, is the better known of
the relatively rare species that lack chlorophyll. It is a
circumpolar inhabitant of conifer woods, and is found in boreal
North America from Alaska to Newfoundland, to California, Mexico, Florida, thence to Asia, India, and Japan.

Empetrum nigrum, crowberry or curlewberry, is another of
the widely distributed and well-known arctic-alpine species,
with purplish black fruits that are fairly juicy and sweet but
that contain several large, hard seeds. It is found in sandy,
rocky, acid soils, and it is circumpolar, ranging in North America from the Arctic south to Newfoundland, Maine, northern
Michigan and Minnesota, and south along alpine slopes and ridges. It is reportedly favored by Eskimos and northern Indians,
and it is likely a source of vitamin C, as are the berries of
V. vitis-idaea. Thus it perhaps served as a source of this
vitamin during winter months in arctic regions. The name *E.
nigrum* s. l. includes the varieties *hermaphroditum, sibiricum,
androgynum,* and *arcticum* (see Polunin, 1959), all based on variations in certain morphological characteristics. It inhabits
rather dry heathy areas, sand, gravel, dry peaty soils, the
sands of eskers, and it is common in boreal spruce woods--in
short, it has a wide latitude of tolerance for habitat conditions, from dry eskers in the Arctic to subarctic forests and
bogs of northern Minnesota, Michigan, southern Ontario, and
Maine, as well as islands in Lake Superior where it grows in
bogs and muskegs or even on wave-swept ledges. It is tolerant
of fire and regenerates quickly in areas that have burned.

Rubus chamaemorus, one of the few members of the family
Rosaceae found in bogs and conifer swamps, is known as the
cloudberry or the baked apple berry. It is found throughout
the northern circumpolar regions, but interestingly is apparently absent from east Greenland. It is found on moist peaty tundra, acidic boggy areas, and in conifer swamps and forests.
Although it is deciduous, it leafs out rather late in the spring,
and in this sense can be said to possess xeromorphic adaptations
since it avoids winterkill in early spring. The adaptation
thus is phenological rather than morphological. The berry is
a favored fruit of the Eskimos, who are reported to preserve
it in seal oil.

Potentilla palustris, marsh cinquefoil or purple cinquefoil, is found in aquatic or marshy areas, wet meadows, and
the margins of streams and ponds. It is in southern portions

of all sectors of the Arctic (except evidently western Europe),
and in North America is found south to Newfoundland, Nova Scotia, Pennsylvania, Ohio, Indiana, Illinois, Wyoming, and California.

Sibbaldia procumbens, the procumbent *Sibbaldia,* is also
a member of the Rosaceae, but it is arctic and northern boreal
and does not range southward except in alpine regions. It is
found on alpine gravels and in meadows, south to Newfoundland,
Quebec, Colorado, Utah, and California. It is found on the
turfy sides of snowdrift areas and in heathy bogs in the mountains southward.

Many other species can be described and discussed in relation to their adaptations to the arctic, subarctic, and boggy
environments in which they are found. Their adaptations to
the arctic very closely resemble the adaptations characteristic of the common bog plants--particularly in respect to their
leaf structure--but we cannot deal with them in detail here.
The interested botanist must seek out the information elsewhere.
Names of some of the species that might be mentioned as being
of particular interest include *Cassiope hypnoides, Cassiope
tetragona, Diapensia lapponica, Loiseluria procumbens, Phyllodoce coerulea, Phyllodoce empetriformis, Phyllodoce glanduli-
fera.*

Native orchids found in the bogs are never numerous but
they are an interesting group and a few species occur in sufficient abundance to reward the botanist who makes a careful
search. Others, however, are quite rare and probably on the
verge of extirpation in at least some regions. Those that a
bog ecologist might be most apt to see are listed in Table I,
with some indication of the parts of North America in which
they occur.

Perhaps the most unusual species possessing a high degree
of fidelity to the oligotrophic bog environment are the insectivorous plants, species with characteristics that have fascina-
ted biologists since the purpose of their unusual morphology
was first correctly interpreted in the mideighteenth century.
The pitcher plant *(Sarracenia purpurea),* for example, catches
insects in a tubular-shaped leaf that is partially filled with
water. Stiff hairs along the inner walls of the leaf point
down, thus preventing escape of any insects that are captured.
The sundews *(Drosera* species) have a rosette of small leaves,
with thick glandular hairs that have a drop of highly viscous
fluid at the ends. When an insect is trapped on the hairs, the
leaf slowly encloses the hapless creature and it is digested
by proteolytic enzymes. The bladderworts *(Utricularia* species)
are aquatic, and usually present in open pools in the bogs;

Table I.   Rare Native Orchids of North American Bogs

Species	Occurrences
Cypripedium arietinum	Eastward, rare
Cypripedium acaule	Eastward
Cypripedium reginae	Eastward
Orchis rotundifolia	Northern, rare
Habenaria clavellata	Eastern, rare northward
Habenaria hyperborea	Wide-ranging, rare southward
Habenaria dilatata	Wide-ranging, rare southward
Habenaria obtusata	Wide-ranging, rare southward
Habenaria ciliaris	Eastern, rare northward
Pogonia ophioglossoides	Eastward, rare northward
Calopogon pulchellus	Eastward, rare northward
Arethusa bulbosa	Eastward, rare
Spiranthes cernua	Eastward, rare northward
Listera cordata	Wide-ranging
Malaxis unifolia	Westward
Liparis loeselii	Eastward
Calypso bulbosa	Wide-ranging, rare

they possess hollow leaves with an opening and trigger hairs at one end. When a protozoan or mosquito larvae trip the hairs, the leaf expands, sucking the animal into the interior.

The presence of such adaptations is usually explained by the low available nitrogen content of the peat soils, and hence the need for additional nitrogen is met by digesting the proteins of the trapped animals. The digestive glands of these species, as well as those of the butterwort (Pinguicula vulgaris), another common insectivorous species, have been studied by Heslop-Harrison (1976), who has found that in some of the species the discharge of digestive enzymes from the leaf glands is stimulated by the chemical compounds present in the prey. The enzymes are then flushed onto the leaf, and the digestion products are absorbed by the leaf through the same glands. The whole mechanism is beautifully developed and renders the plants truly carnivorous in their habits and capabilities.

7   Character Sketch
of Marshland Species

Undrained depressions and marshy ground in northern circumboreal regions, including northern Minnesota, Wisconsin,
Michigan, as well as areas of southern Ontario, Manitoba, New
England, and the Maritime Provinces of Canada, occur on land
areas covered with glacial till or with outcropping Precambri-
an bedrock over the landscape. These have long held a fascination for ecologists, and the reasons are manifold. For one
thing, the region possesses an aggregation of plant species
with unusual morphological structures and physiological characteristics that fit them for life in bog, swamp, and marshland
environments. In some species, leaves possess such interesting adaptations as traps for catching insects, others have
needlelike evergreen leaves, and there is a rather larger and
equally interesting group of species with leaf adaptations that
to early-day botanists seemed paradoxical because in general
morphology they closely resemble the leaves of plant species
native to hot, dry, desert regions. These characteristics are
collectively termed *xeromorphic*, and the plants that possess
them grow in swamps, bogs, and other wet habitats, in direct
contrast to hot, dry, desert habitats, where plants with xeromorphic features are plentiful.

   That there are special plants favoring the swamplands is
an idea evidently as old as the historical record. The Kale-
vale, the national epic of the Finns, dating to about 900 B.C.,
depicts the godlike figure Pellervoinen sowing the seeds from
which the earth's vegetation sprang:

> Seeds upon the land he scatters,
> Seeds in every swamp and meadow...
> In the swamps he sows the birches,
> On the quaking marshes alders...
> In the moist earth sows the willows...
> On the banks of streams the hawthorne,
> Junipers on knolls and highlands...

The vast heaths of Scotland were early accorded place in English literature, and for what are perhaps very obvious reasons Macbeth shouts when all is turning against him, "This blasted heath..."

More recently, botanists have described the swamps of northern North America in some detail, beginning with Whitford, who in 1901 described, as he termed them, the "swamp societies" characteristic of the topography of areas of postglacial drift:

> One of the most characteristic features of a young glacial topography is the large number of lakes... Some find outlets and ultimately pass out of existence through the normal stages in the life-history of a river. A larger number, however, never find outlets, but are silted up by the wash of the surrounding soil, and by the accumulation of vegetation. Thus swamps are formed.

Thus it is evident that the outlines of Pleistocene continental glaciation were well incorporated into the common body of scientific knowledge by the turn of the century. Half a century before this, as we shall see, Agassiz (1850) had traveled along the north shore of Lake Superior and recognized the same signs of glaciation here that he had seen in Europe. For an overall view of the vegetation of the region, however, there is no better brief description than that of Crum (1976) in his manual for the identification of the mosses of the Great Lakes region:

> This is a land of lakes. The most beautiful habitats are the many peat bogs at the edges of pot-hole lakes, eventually transforming them into black spruce muskeg, the forest climax on acid peat. Our bogs, fed by ground water and therefore minerotrophic, are more properly considered rich or poor fens, depending on the stage of succession toward drier and more acid conditions. Succession is often cyclic rather than directional, and so the story-book progression from open water to muskeg is, more often than not, only a theoretical possibility. *Sphagnum* creates an acid habitat and controls the vegetation of bogs at every stage of development.

On surrounding uplands, fire and windthrow reduce the chance that any uniform blanket of vegetation will ever be achieved over a large enough area to consider it the regional climatic climax. So also, in the case of the swamp forests of the Great Lakes region, succession beyond a certain point seems never to occur. There is a cyclic repetition of decadence and regeneration that appears to recur with no trend discernible over the span of years that it has been possible to observe these forests--both within historical time and into the past as far as can be inferred from pollen analysis.

The wetlands, to view them in relation to the other communities, are at one extreme end of a scale that runs from wet,
through mesic, to dry, with light conditions forming a second
axis, as shown in Fig. 1.

One of the more characteristic morphological traits of the
species that make up the communities of the bogs and conifer
swamps is evergreenness. The fact that a plant is evergreen
evidently indicates that this characteristic has developed during a long period of evolution in which it was necessary to
accommodate to growing seasons of short duration and to soils
low in nutrients. Under these conditions, the opportunity to
produce organic material by photosynthesis is minimal, and the
plants have evolved in such a way that they can make and save
as much of the organic material as possible under conditions
present in the habitat. Thus, retention of leaves through the
winter saves both nutrients and time in early spring. This
means, however, that the evergreen plants may often be subject
to the very thing that deciduous species are equally adept at
avoiding--winterkill. Deciduous trees and shrubs shed leaves
in fall to avoid desiccation during winter when evaporation
(sublimation) from leaves could occur, but when roots and stem
are frozen and are incapable of replacing lost moisture. This,
at least, is a conclusion one can draw from the fact that they
indeed lose the leaves, and that they are, moreover, rarely
killed by late or early frosts in spring and fall, respectively.

In evergreen species, during warm spells in winter and
during spring and fall, leaves and other plant parts in sunlight
will be warm and metabolic processes such as photosynthesis,
respiration, and transpiration can occur. Roots, however, are
encased in frozen soil, and thus are incapable of meeting the
plants' requirements for water. The result is winterkill.

Bog plants often resemble xeromorphic desert plants in
that they possess leaf structures evidently capable of reducing
water loss through evaporation and transpiration, including
thick leathery leaves, thick shiny waxey cuticle over leaf surfaces, and a thick mat of tomentum over the undersurface of the
leaves where stomata are located. This latter thick matrix of
hairlike structures reduces air movement over the leaf, slows
down evaporation of water through stomata, and thereby reduces
the rate of passage of water vapor from within a leaf to the
atmosphere outside. The stomata in some species are located
in deep pits, and we infer that the pits serve the same purpose as the covering of tomentum. In some other species, along
the underside of the thick leaves are grooves in which the
stomata are located and presumably protected from wind.

Another leaf structure that evidently is xeromorphic in
character is the hypodermis, a layer of thick-walled cells

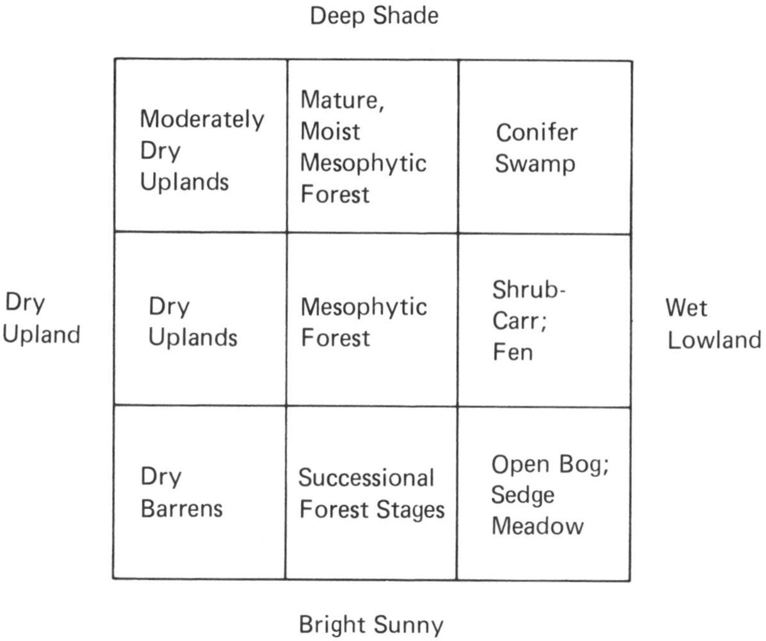

Deep Shade

Moderately Dry Uplands	Mature, Moist Mesophytic Forest	Conifer Swamp
Dry Uplands	Mesophytic Forest	Shrub-Carr; Fen
Dry Barrens	Successional Forest Stages	Open Bog; Sedge Meadow

Dry Upland (left)   Wet Lowland (right)

Bright Sunny

Fig. 1. Community relationships.

located beneath the epidermis. These cells serve to check water movement to the epidermis, where it would evaporate. The cells also form a rigid tubular structure that, like the body of a modern aircraft, is hollow but very strongly resists bending or, in the case of the leaf, wilting or shrinking when dry.

The needles of species in the genera *Pinus, Picea, Abies,* and *Larix* all possess xeromorphic characteristics. Looking at cross sections of the needles under a microscope will reveal what are considered to be typical xeromorphic characteristics--they are thick, with cuticle, a hypodermis, and stomata sunk into pits or grooves, and the triangular or hemispherical needle shape conserves water better than, for example, the flat wide leaves of deciduous species. Of the more common bog and swamp species that possess exceedingly hairy leaf undersurfaces, one that comes readily to mind is *L. groenlandicum,* Labrador tea. The leaves of this plant also have revolute borders that curl around (Fig. 2) and partly over the hairy underside of the leaf--in effect, a windbreak. Even on exceedingly windy days there must be very little air movement over stomata located beneath the thick tomentum surrounded by the revolute leaf margin.

*Fig. 2. Tomentum on underside of leaves of L. groenland-
icum. The leaves are dried herbarium specimens. Note revolute
borders.*

Still other bog species, among them *C. calyculata,* also
known as leatherleaf, and *K. polifolia,* swamp or bog laurel,
possess a heavy cuticle over the leaves. This is covered with
a layer of waxy material sufficiently thick to give the underside of the leaf a white polished sheen. The conclusion that
one naturally draws from observation of these unusual morphological traits is that they developed during evolution of these
species as a way of conserving water and protecting internal
tissues of leaves from desiccation.

In what might well be considered a classical demonstration
of the effectiveness of xeromorphy in reducing water loss by
transpiration, the Norwegian plant physiologist Hygen (1953)
measured transpiration rates in the leaves of a number of species of the genus *Vaccinium* as well as other northern plant species. He found that the species with the lowest transpiration
rate was *V. vitis-idaea,* lingonberry or rock cranberry, and
this was also the species possessing the most pronounced xeromorphy of all the plant species tested. Hygen used a simple
device to quantify the transpiration rates of the plants he
tested. He measured the rate of transpiration in water-satura-
ted leaves under standard conditions with the stomata open (E_S)

and when stomata closed (E_c), then multiplied E_s and E_c to produce an index number that characterized the species, an index,
in a sense, of xerophytism. The comparisons are shown in Table
I. Some of the species are European rather than North American
species, but they are so closely related to the North American
plants that leaves are virtually identical.

As Hygen concludes from his study, significant differences
in transpiration rates can be demonstrated among the different
species, and even between samples of the same species taken
from different habitats. The differences, he adds, appear
closely related to differences in the morphological structure
of the leaves. These are the consequence, on the one hand, of
hereditary constitution and, on the other, of phenotypic variation resulting from environmental influences upon growth and
development.

Table I.   Transpiration Rates (E_sE_c) of Species[a]

Species	E_sE_c	Range[b]
Xeromorphic leaves		
Empetrum nigrum	0.2	NA, EU, EA, A
Vaccinium vitis-idaea	0.3	NA, EU, EA, A
Mesomorphic leaves; dry end of scale		
Saxifraga aizoides	1.0	NA, EU, EA
Maianthemum bifolium	1.3	EU, EA, A
Vaccinium myrtillus	1.8	EU
Saussurea alpina	2.5	EU, EA
Antennaria dioica	2.8	EU, EA, A
Alchemilla alpina	2.9	EU
Calluna vulgaris	3.0	EU, EA
Mesomorphic leaves; wet end of scale		
Viola palustris	3.3	NA, EU, EA
Salix herbacea	4.0	NA, EU, EA
Sibbaldia procumbens	4.9	NA, EU, EA
Alchemilla glabra	5.0	EU, EA
Vaccinium uliginosum	5.3	NA, EU, EA, A
Hydromorphic leaves		
Rubus chamaemorus	6.4	NA, EU, EA, A
Alchemilla glomerulans	11.7	EU, EA
Potentilla palustris	13.0	NA, EU, EA, A

[a] From Hygen (1953).

[b] The regions are as follows: NA, North America; EU, Europe;
EA, Eurasia; A, Asia.

In species with xerophytic adaptations, stomatal closing
can greatly reduce transpiration. In *Antennaria dioica, Calluna
vulgaris, Empetrum nigrum,* and *V. vitis-idaea,* for example,
stomatal closing will reduce transpiration to 5-10% of the rate
under conditions in which stomata are open. In mesophytic
species such as *Alchemilla alpina, Alchemilla glabra, Maianthemum bifolium,* and *Saussurea alpina,* the corresponding figure is 10-20%. In plants growing in places with a constant
and ample water supply, the transpiration rate through the leaf
cuticle (with stomata closed) is 25-40% of the rate with stomata open. Species characteristically showing this latter value
include *Alchemilla glomerulans, Potentilla palustris, Rubus
chamaemorus,* and *V. uliginosum.*

Subsequent research has shown that Hygen's results may be
somewhat misleading, in that other workers have not always
been able to discern real or striking differences between transpiration rates of plant species with xeromorphic leaf characteristics and those without. We deal with some of these in
greater detail in subsequent chapters. It is still possible,
however, to assert that Hygen's experiments were significant,
in the sense that they were well thought out and represented
an attempt to demonstrate by experimental means what intuitively seemed a reasonable explanation of the xeromorphy of bog
plant species. The results of the experiments may, moreover,
be ultimately confirmed if future work reveals that transpiration rates are, in fact, reduced in the bog plant species.

In any case, some simple observations that can be made
easily without special equipment reveal that certain species,
among them *C. calyculata,* the common leatherleaf, possess leaves
with unusual capabilities for water retention during winter
months.

The leaves of *C. calyculata,* (Fig. 3), as can be inferred
from its common name, leatherleaf, are distinctive for their
tough and flexible qualities--although these are not the only
characteristics that make them unique. Under the microscope,
the upper surface resembles a kind of variegated ruddy brown
porcelain tile, polished and shiny, with a lighter-colored
caulking between the individual tiles of various shapes. The
under surface of the leaf is even more distinctive, so much so
as to be difficult to describe. It is particularly noteworthy,
however, for being covered with a multitude of reflective amber
disks, spangles one might say, that appear to be flat round
resinous plaques of obscure purpose but probably impermeable to
moisture and hence a device for preventing unduly rapid loss of
water from the leaf by evaporation or, perhaps, transpiration.
That the leaf is capable of retaining its moisture is readily
demonstrated by a very simple experiment. During the winter,

if twigs bearing the evergreen leaves are brought into a warm
room, the frozen tissues quickly thaw and the leaves are as
tough and flexible as they were during the summer, even though
it is apparent that the ground in which the plant is growing
is frozen solid and no uptake of soil moisture is possible.
The leaves, hence, have retained the moisture they had when
the plant was initially frozen at the onset of winter. The
leaves retained moisture throughout the freeze-thaw cycles of
late fall and through the months of snow cover during winter.

Even the leaves that are not covered with snow, but protrude above the surface in full sunlight, retain their flexi-
bility and resilience, indicating that moisture in some abundance is retained in the leaf tissues. The proof of this comes
when the leaves are exposed in a warm room for a matter of days
or a week. They then become dry and brittle, indicating beyond
doubt that they contained abundant moisture at the time of thaw-
ing. Obviously they were prevented from losing water while
frozen, but the hot dry air of a room in winter is too much for
even the protective resinous coating on the upper and lower leaf
surfaces.

Fig. 3. A leaf of C. calyculata is greenish brown and
has a tough outer covering of cuticle.

Leaves beneath the surface of the snow are, of course, closely packed with abundant water in frozen form, and vapor pressure of water sublimating from snow crystals is relatively high. Under such conditions a leaf retains moisture and will even absorb water from the atmosphere if the tissues are sufficiently desiccated. A leaf in air and sunlight, however, will ordinarily lose some water slowly by evaporation directly from the frozen tissues and this is probably also true in the case of *Chamaedaphne*, but the loss occurs at a slower rate than in most species. The *Chamaedaphne* leaf, so distinctive in appearance beneath a microscope, has somehow the ability to conserve water under conditions that would dry out any leaf of deciduous structure in a few weeks or even a few days in winter.

These are some of the more obvious of the morphological characteristics that give the bog plant species their unique ability to survive in the unusual habitat provided by the kettleholes of the northern glaciated regions. There are other advantages that these xeromorphic structures confer upon the plants, and combined with certain physiological adaptations they give the species a competitive advantage over others in the unique environment of the northern bogs. Some of these are considered in greater detail in subsequent chapters.

8   Where the Bogs Are Found

In terms of geological time, the bogs with which we are to be concerned are exceedingly youthful--on the order of a dozen or so millenia, a consequence of the fact that the region in which they are found was beneath the ice of vast continental glaciers for long periods of time during what is known as the Pleistocene Epoch. As the last of the melting ice dwindled away, it left a reasonably flat landscape in the sense that it was not mountainous but rolling, at times fairly rugged, dotted with innumerable pits and hollows that have come to be known as kettles or kettleholes. In these, ground water was near or at the surface, or even slightly above, creating a great number of wet areas or shallow lakes that were available for colonization by plant species adapted to such habitats. Where the kettles were deep there remain today the many lakes that give parts of the region their distinctive quality and exceptional beauty--as can be noted by the idiomatic names they have been given, the "Lake Country," "Lakeland," and so on.

This is not to say that plant species inhabiting the bogs are equally youthful; they are, in fact, much older, having evolved in some cases evidently as far away as the distant Himalayas, but of their origins little is known except that when the ice vanished the plants were there along the fringes, in the so-called periglacial areas, ready to move into wetlands left in saucerlike depressions once occupied by huge chunks of glacial ice. Scientific study of these unique and distinctive features of the landscape in North America is relatively recent, one of the first comprehensive reviews of knowledge available at the time being that written by Transeau in 1903 (see Fig. 15). He stated:

> In order to obtain a better understanding of data on the geographical distribution of bog plants...the number of species would have to be limited and...only those which are characteristic of these situations across northern North America could be considered....Beginning with those which first find a foothold in such depressions and continuing

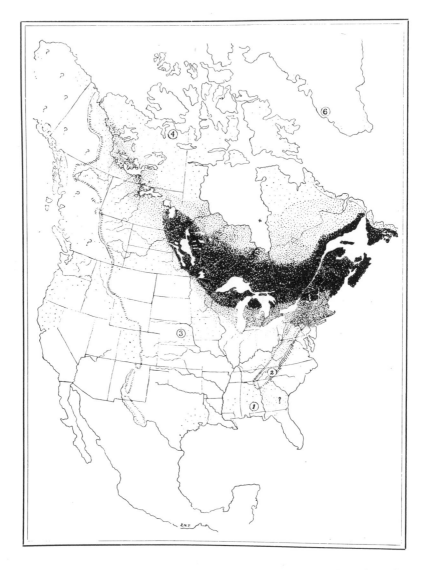

Fig. 1. Transeau's map of 1903 shows the distribution of
the genera of common bog plant species. The numbers designate
the area within which particular genera are found. The region
of darkest stippling is where all genera are present and where
bogs are most numerous. The genera indicated by the numbers
are (1) Drosera, Dulichium; (2) Sarracenia, Drosera, Dulichium,
Eriophorum, Chamaedaphne; (3) Dulichium, Menyanthes; (4) Drosera, Potentilla, Menyanthes, Eriophorum, Ledum, Andromeda;

in their approximate order of advent, they are: *Menyanthes trifoliata, Dulichium arundinaceum, Comarum palustre, Scheuchzeria palustris, Eriophorum polystachyon, Drosera rotundifolia, Sarracenia purpurea, Oxycoccus Oxycoccus, Chiogenes hispidula, Andromeda Polifolia, Chamaedaphne calyculata, Ledum groenlandicum, Kalmia glauca, Betula pumila,* and *Larix laricina.* *

It should be noted parenthetically that some of the botanical names used by Transeau, as well as the quaint capitalization in two of them, are now out of date, changed for reasons known to taxonomists and not important to us here, but the species are all so distinctive in their preference for bog habitats that any botanist shown a list of these names would know at once the kind of place in which the plants might be found.

Many of the species are circumpolar in distribution, meaning they are found around the world--in North America, Europe, and Asia--and many of those restricted to one continent have counterparts elsewhere so closely related that were they growing together one might easily be considered subspecies of the other. Transeau goes on:

Of these fiften species, three, *Dulichium, Sarracenia,* and *Kalmia,* are endemic. The larch and birch are represented in the Old World by closely related forms, while the remaining ten occur in similar habitats in Europe and Asia. This naturally points to their origin, and certainly indicates their preglacial distribution to have been in the circumpolar regions of both continents. It also implies that these great land masses must have been connected for a long time during the Tertiary period, so that migration from one to the other was by no means difficult. Whether these forms originated in a single polar area is of little consequence. They may have arisen partly in America, partly in Eurasia, but they were essentially the products of similar conditions and by migration came to be associated.*

(Continued, Fig. 1)

(5) Drosera, Potentilla, Menyanthes, Eriophorum, Oxycoccus, Andromeda, Ledum, Kalmia, Chamaedaphne; (6) Menyanthes, Oxycoccus, Ledum, Andromeda, Kalmia.

* Reprinted by permission of The University of Chicago Press.

It is perhaps interesting that here, in 1903, we have an early hint of the concept--one taking many decades to be finally accepted--that the continents were once joined, all in a single great Pangaea that has since been fragmented, Laurasia being the primordial section that became North America, Europe, and Asia, and Gondwanaland the section that has become South America, Africa, India, Arabia, New Guinea, Australia, and Antarctica.

Transeau (1903) again, speaking of the species' distribution (Fig. 1):

> But the map has still greater significance. The dark area represents the region in which most of the plants attain their highest physical development. Those who have seen the magnificent groves of tamarack in the north, attaining a height of thirty meters and a bole diameter of a meter, will appreciate this fact when they compare them with the stunted groups of the larch in the bogs near the southern and northern limits.

> Again, within this same belt, at least eight of the plants, the buckbean, cranberry, snowberry, rosemary, leather leaf, labrador tea, birch, and tamarack, are not confined to bog areas. They may be said to have there a wider life-range and are to be found in a variety of habitats. The tamarack, for example, is found on the hills and most of the streams. With the black and white spruce and pine, it makes up a large part of the forest. Here, too, the buckbean, leather leaf, Labrador tea, and birch occur along slow streams, and the rosemary, snowberry, and cranberry in moist ravines and rich woods.*

The ultimate geographical limits to the range of each of these species seems to be established by climate, each encountering conditions at some point to the east, west, north, and south beyond which it is prevented from migrating because of conditions inimical to its survival. This, too, was realized clearly by the turn of the century, as witness again Transeau's (1903) description of the climatic limits to the range of the species:

> On the south and southeast, while the rainfall and relative humidity are favorable, the intense insolation of the summer months seems to be the controlled factor. The northern boundary coincides with that of the northern limits of dense forests...controlled by the amount of snowfall, exposure to dry winter winds, and the length of the growing season. There does not appear to be any relation between the distribution of this group of plant societies and the "life zones" distinguished by Merriam.

* Reprinted by permission of The University of Chicago Press.

Within the belt of optimum conditions the climate is characterized by great range of temperature, both daily and annual. As we go toward the east from the Mackenzie basin, this is modified by the increase in relative humidity. The summers are short, bright, and warm, with abundant rainfall, principally in the form of thunder showers. The winters are long, and extremely low temperatures may occur. The snowfall increases from a foot or two in the western part to several feet in Ontario and the St. Lawrence basin.*

If climatic conditions limit the range of these species today, one might readily ask the question: "What were the conditions during the glaciations of the Pleistocene, and how did these plants manage to survive the harsh conditions that must have prevailed throughout northern regions at that time?" Transeau(1903) also asked that question and provided this answer:

In order to get an idea of the distribution of the boreal plant societies during the maximum glaciation, let us try to picture what would become of these same societies if a similar period of glaciation were to come upon them now. A sufficient time has probably intervened since the last glacial epoch to allow of almost perfect climatic adjustment on the part of the tundra and conifer societies, so that the climate now most favorable for their development may well have characterized a zone just beyond the ice margin....According to Chamberlin, the climatic conditions prevailing about the margin were intermediate between those of Greenland and Alaska at the present time. In the former case the vegetation is sparse and of a tundra type, in the latter the forests occur on the stagnant ice margin. It would appear then that the glaciers would not affect the tree distribution at any great distance from the ice front. But there are other factors which would affect the breadth of the zone of conifer dominance. As we may learn from their present distribution, a dry climate, a youthful topography in which erosion is active, high elevation and sterile soil, all of which imply great variations in temperature and relative humidity, are more favorable to conifers than to broadleaved deciduous trees.
Now as to the bog plants: since under favorable conditions they may occupy other habitats than undrained depressions, they probably existed on the borders of the heavily loaded streams, in ravines and moist situations generally along the whole ice front. It is to be noted that practically all of the existing small lake areas of the northern states were covered by the ice during the maximum extension of the Wisconsin ice sheet...it follows that the bog societies must have occupied other habitats.*

* Reprinted by permission of The University of Chicago Press.

By this time, the critical observer will have noted that
while bogs are prevalent and readily recognized features of
the regional landscape, there are other wetlands that cannot
properly be called bogs. Over large areas, instead of deep
accumulations of peat on which are growing the typical communities of bog species, there are also marshy, swampy wetlands,
often persistently ankle or knee deep in water, on which grow
sedges, rushes, cattails, and other emergent aquatic plants
altogether different, and growing under altogether different
conditions, than the typical bog plants found on the peat bogs.
Transeau (1903) had an explanation for this also:

As we know from the various physiographic studies that
have been made of glacial basins, many of the lakes were
formerly much larger than at present. Some of them in
early postglacial times had steep banks, which were unfavorable to the development of shore vegetation. But
by the lowering of the water level consequent upon the
cutting down of the outlet, the shore line at present is
a gradually sloping one, and supports a "drained swamp"
flora. In other cases, irregular arms, extending away
from the main body of the lake and protected from wind
and wave action, doubtless supported a bog vegetation
during the tundra dominance. Since then they have been
separated from the main lake by a lowering of the water
level. Today we find in many such cases the bog vegetation still persisting in the depressions which were
formerly arms of the lake, while on the shore of the
main body, which came to be swampy at a much later period,
the so-called "drained swamp" flora occurs.... Without
multiplying examples, the relation of these two groups
of swamp societies seems to depend largely upon the time
when the swamps came into existence as swamp habitats.
If they have existed since the days of tundra conditions
they may show a bog flora today. If they are of recent
origin, the plants will correspond to the normal swamp
plants of the present climatic conditions. If of intermediate age, we may have various mixtures of the two...
The preservation of the bog societies in poorly drained
situations down to the present time seems to be due (1) to
the lower temperatures prevailing there, (2) to the sterile
nature of the substratum, (3) to the completeness with
which the substratum is occupied by the bog plants, and
(4) to the fact that most bog habitats are associated with
lakes, whose basins must be entirely filled with debris,
before the drainage conditions will be naturally improved
and made more favorable for the coming in of other plant
societies.

To account for the xerophytic character of many of the bog plants, experiments now being carried on seem to indicate that differences of temperature between substratum and air are adequate. But the presence in many of our bog habitats of swamp species which show no xerophytic adaptations suggests that such xerophytic structures may be unnecessary under present conditions in *this* region.*

The emphasis in the last sentence is Transeau's, and here we have a clear statement of the question that has puzzled plant geographers and ecologists for decades, and which now appears to be in the process of being answered in a satisfactory way: "Why should the plants of the northern bogs have, in many cases, ranges that extend far north into the boreal forest of Canada and beyond, and why, moreover, do they so often resemble morphologically the plants of dry regions or savannas in so many ways?" To the answer of this question we shall devote many pages in subsequent chapters. For the moment, we simply summarize what Transeau (1903) wrote of the bogs and swampy wetlands so long ago, in his own words:

> The bog societies are typical of the colder portions of North America and are closely related to the bog societies of Europe and Asia...
> They show an optimum region of dispersal having a moist climate, subject to very great temperature extremes. Within this region the plants have a greater range of habitats and an increased physical development...
> As we go away from this center, either north or south, the first forms to show the effect of climatic change in diminished size and frequency of occurrence are the arborescent species. The species which extend furthest from this optimum range are herbaceous forms...
> The bog societies are normally related to the conifer forests in their development to a climax tree vegetation... Where surrounded by oaks and hickories, or in general when conifers are absent, they show no order of succession to the forest societies...
> Present bog habitats are continuations of similar habitats which existed in early postglacial times, when tundra conditions and tundra vegetation were dominant...
> The temperature phenomena of undrained depressions, containing deposits of peat, are favorable to the preservation of these types...
> The bog societies are composed of boreal species and...must be considered as relicts of former climatic conditions. The swamp societies, made up of more southerly forms, must be considered as the normal hydrophytic vegetation of the present climatic conditions.*

* Reprinted by permission of The University of Chicago Press.

Perhaps the most interesting aspect of this is the fact that Transeau's statements remain valid close to a century later. Only details have been added, and only to this extent can we say that our understanding of the bogs is greater than it was in Transeau's time. However, in regard to the details, we have a vastly greater knowledge than did Transeau. Probably no one would read the modern scientific literature dealing with the boglands with greater enthusiasm, or with greater satisfaction, than Transeau, were he able to do so today.

9 Some Reflections on the Species

The common bog species in the region with which we are concerned were listed in the selections from the writings of Transeau presented in Chapter 8. The statement was also made that these are species with northern affinities--a phrase used by botanists to mean that they range far north into boreal and tundra regions. Since they are not very common in places other than bogs in the southern portions of their geographical range, an obvious question to ask is "How, then, do these species fare in the boreal and arctic regions to which by inference they are better adapted?"

The species referred to are mostly ericads, members of the family Ericaceae, as interesting a group of plants as can be found anywhere. The Ericaceae are a large family, with genera widely distributed throughout the world, and so the species referred to here are but a small portion of the total. However, these are of special interest to us because of their importance in the bog communities, as well as in the boreal forest regions northward. The species that are not ericads, but are nevertheless bog plants of widespread occurrence, have interesting adaptations of their own, as we shall see.

The species that might be said to be of greatest interest to bog ecologists are as follows:

Bog ericads: *Chamaedaphne calyculata, Andromeda glaucophylla, Kalmia polifolia, Vaccinium oxycoccus* (or often called by the name *Oxycoccus oxycoccus*), *Vaccinium microcarpon* (or *Oxycoccus microcarpon*), *Ledum groenlandicum.*

Ericads growing more often on uplands: *Vaccinium angustifolium, Gaultheria hispidula, Gaultheria procumbens, Arctostaphylos uva-ursi,* the *Chimaphila* and *Pyrola* species, as well as the unusual *Monotropa* and the *Moneses,* which if not ericads are at least closely related.

Species abundant northward but only barely reaching as far south as the region concerning us here: *Vaccinium vitis-idaea,* and *Empetrum nigrum.*

Northern ericads closely related to the southern ones or of
    sufficient interest to include here: *Vaccinium uliginosum,
    Ledum decumbens, Loiseleuria procumbens, Phyllodoce coerulea,
    Rhododendron lapponicum,* and *Cassiope tetragona.*
A group, not closely related but of interest because they are
    bog plants--and insectivorous: *Drosera, Pinguicula, Utricu-
    laria,* and *Sarracenia.*

A broad summary of the extent to which some of the southern
bog species range northward is given in Table I.

It is evident that some species are very wide ranging and
occur in abundance in the north. Others decline in significance northward, and some that are absent or very rare southward become of great importance throughout boreal forest and
tundra. It should perhaps be mentioned that the northern forest
edge crosses southern Keewatin, and so the species found in
northern Keewatin are tundra species without question.

The species that decline in importance northward have their
places taken in northern boreal forest and tundra by other
species often closely related to them; thus *L. groenlandicum,*
which is wide ranging in the boreal forest, is increasingly
rare northward in the tundra, but the genus is still represented northward by the closely related *L. decumbens,* primarily a
tundra species although it does extend a short distance into
the northern fringe of boreal forest. There is, on the other
hand, another group of ericads with purely arctic affinities,
and these are exceedingly interesting in their own right. We
shall not be much concerned with them later, but their habitat
preferences are such that they throw light on what might appear otherwise to be inexplicable characteristics of the bog
plants of northern Minnesota, Michigan, Wisconsin, and eastward; thus it will be profitable to discuss them briefly here.

These far northern ericads such as *Rhododendron lapponicum*
and *Loiseleuria procumbens* are all upland species, found on
open ridges and slopes, dry eskers, on rocky or gravelly sites,
in full sunlight, exposed to winds and, in winter, the strongly
abrasive effect of driven snow. None stand tall, but all are
short, hard, smooth, and tough, adapted to an environment that
few other plants could survive for a single summer. But just
as other plant species are poorly adapted to conditions that
these northern ericads survive with ease, so are the northern
ericads unable to adjust to what might be considered more com-
fortable conditions. They cannot compete against species
adapted to more temperate climates, and they probably could
not live in warmer climes even if there were no species there
to compete with them.

Table I. Species Presence by Area[a]

	Minnesota, Michigan, Wisconsin	Northern Ontario	No. Central Manitoba	Keewatin Southern	Keewatin Northern
Chamaedaphne calculata	X	X	X	R	
Ledum groenlandicum	X	X	X	X	
Kalmia polifolia	X	X	X	X	X
Andromeda glaucophylla	X	X	X		
Vaccinium oxycoccus	X	X			
Vaccinium microcarpon		X	X	X	X
Vaccinium myrtilloides	X	X	X		
Rhododendron lapponicum	R[b]	R[c]	R	R	X
Rubus chamaemorus		X	X	X	X
Vaccinium vitis-idaea	R[b]	X	X	X	X
Vaccinium uliginosum			X	X	X
Eriophorum angustifolium	X	X	X	X	X
Sarracenia purpurea	X	X	X	X	
Drosera rotundifolia	X	X	X	X	
Menyanthes trifoliata	X	X	X	X	
Potentilla palustris	X	X	X	X	

[a] R = rare.

[b] One or a few collections in early days.

[c] Locally in James Bay.

Of the northern species rare or absent in the south, one of the most ubiquitous in boreal and low-latitude tundra regions is *Vaccinium vitis-idaea*. This is a most interesting species, for reasons other than the fact that its berries are edible and high in vitamin C--an attribute that made it unknowingly of great value to Indians who pounded the berries into meat prior to drying, thus preparing pemmican, a dry winter food. It keeps for long periods of time without spoiling, and undoubtedly it effectively prevented scurvy, especially during long winters when fresh food was unavailable. The berries are known as lingon berries in Europe, and are used in jam and jelly.

From the point of view of the plant ecologist and physiologist, however, *Vaccinium vitis-idaea* is interesting for other reasons. Most plants have a preferred habitat and will, for example, grow well in only pine woodlands, spruce forest, wet meadow, or open bog, and so on, entirely or almost always avoiding habitats very different from the preferred one. Not so with *V. vitis-idaea*. It grows everywhere. It attains greater densities in preferred habitats, that is true, but it rarely if ever avoids any given kind of environment entirely. Thus, it grows in the low meadows and the rock field uplands of areas near the northern Arctic coast; it grows in white spruce and black spruce forests throughout the boreal region; and it is found in pine woods and recently burned areas, as well as feathermoss forests and leatherleaf bogs as far south as northern Minnesota.

Why then, when *V. vitis-idaea* grows in so wide a range of habitats over so wide a range of latitude, from the Arctic coast southward to northern Minnesota and the north shore of Lake Superior, does it not grow even farther to the south? No one knows the answer to this question. It was found at one time in Wisconsin, around Lake Superior, but it occurred rarely even then. It is a northern plant and it obviously will not grow farther south, at least on its own initiative, but the reasons are obscure, just as they are with the range limits of the other species with which we are to be concerned.

Another northern ericad, this one extending not as far south as *V. vitis-idaea,* is *Andromeda polifolia,* found in acid peat bogs, pool margins, and spruce woodlands in the boreal forest regions and in tundra northward where it occupies meadows and muskegs to the Arctic coast. It extends southward to southern British Columbia, Alberta, Saskatchewan, nearly to Duck Mountain in Manitoba, to Fort Severn on Hudson Bay, as well as in southern Labrador, and it is found also in northern Eurasia. *Andromeda glaucophylla,* the bog rosemary, is, on the other hand, found only from Minnesota eastward to the Atlantic, overlapping the range of *A. polifolia* in northeastern Ontario and in Quebec.

The species evidently hybridize where they are both available to do so. They are quite similar, although *A. polifolia* is smaller, shorter, and obviously better equipped to survive in the far north than is the bog rosemary.

Another species pair should be discussed. They are members of the Betulaceae, the birch family. *Betula glandulosa* is northern and *Betula pumila,* is southern. They produce hybrids where they overlap in range. The first is called dwarf or scrub birch, the second low or swamp birch, the former is found from Alaska to Baffin Island and northern Ungava-Labrador. The latter is found from southern Yukon, across to Manitoba, Quebec, and central Labrador. There are, moreover, three or four other *Betula* species, one of them paper birch, *Betula papyrifera,* all of which are apparently capable of hybridizing with one another. The picture of the birches is not as clear as it is with species of *Andromeda*. The swarms of hybrid birch have puzzled botanists for years, and the difficulties in their identification are so great that no definite statements can be made about them. In his "The Flora of Canada," Scoggan devotes five pages to descriptions of the dozen or so birch species, one of which is given over entirely to a simple listing of the reported hybrids among them.

Another of the wide-ranging species that comes southward is *Empetrum nigrum,* crowberry or curlewberry, found abundantly in a wide variety of habitats, from low wet meadows to rock fields in northern tundra, in lowland spruce forests and upland pine woods of the southern boreal regions, as well as bogs and muskegs. It has been found on the south shore of Lake Superior, although it is quite rare. It was collected in 1831 at the Pictured Rocks by Douglass Houghton, who appreciated its rarity at the time. It is now considered a threatened species in Michigan, as well it might, but along the north shore of Lake Superior it is found in favored places, on a few islands, and from there northward it becomes more and more abundant, without doubt one of the more common species throughout the boreal forest and northward to the Arctic Archipelago, although at this extreme latitude it again becomes scarce. In the boreal forest, however, it is often one of the dominant species in a variety of communities.

The three ericaceous plant species that commonly dominate bogs in northern Minnesota, Wisconsin, Michigan, as well as eastward and westward from this center are *C. calyculata, L. groenlandicum,* and *A. glaucophylla.* Of these, the latter two have closely related species more northern in affinity with which they overlap in geographical range. The species paired with *A. glaucophylla,* as mentioned above, is *A. polifolia,* the latter northern and wide-ranging. In the case of this species pair, however, one member of the pair, *A. glaucophylla,* is

only eastern in its range, evidently finding its western range
limit somewhere in Manitoba. This is not the case with L.
groenlandicum and L. decumbens (or L. palustre), the former
more southern, the latter northern in range, both of which extend across the continent from Alaska to Labrador. The difference in their range is that L. decumbens extends southward into the boreal forest for only a short distance and only in few
places as much as 300 or 400 miles--a little south of Great
Slave Lake, for example, but farther south of treeline in
Alaska. Ledum groenlandicum, on the other hand, is found
throughout the boreal forest, a short distance northward into
tundra in many areas, and southward into the bogs of the northern United States. Ledum decumbens extends farther south into
forest in the far west than in the central and eastern parts of
North America, but this may be influenced by the mountainous
terrain. Thus, it extends throughout most of Alaska, the Yukon,
and southward into the northern British Columbia, where it is
found in heaths, barrens, and dry rocky places, mostly at higher
elevations. Across the vast interior northern plains of Canada,
however, L. groenlandicum overlaps the range of L. decumbens
only in a fairly narrow ribbon that marks the northern edge of
the boreal forest.

The southern member of this species pair, L. groenlandicum,
occupies the forests of black spruce and white spruce all
across the continent, one of the ubiquitous species so familiar
to plant ecologists. The leaves of both are quite similar:
those of L. decumbens are somewhat narrower and more closely
rolled, but both are soft leaves and velvety, with a thick
rusty-woolly tomentum beneath. Ordinarily, L. decumbens lives
up to its name; it is short and sticks close to the ground--
habitually decumbent in growth form. In places, however, it
grows as tall as L. groenlandicum, in which case it is distinguished by its more narrow leaves. One wonders if these
two species do not hybridize more than is usually considered
to be the case. Around Fort Providence, at the western end of
Great Slave Lake, some high Ledum shrubs have typical or nearly typical L. decumbens leaves, and this would be a good region
to investigate the possibility. Savile (1969) says that the
two species hybridize in the far west, but just how widespread
the phenomenon is, we do not know.

Other than V. vitis-idaea, the Vaccinium species of interest
to us here are the common blueberries of the south, V. myrtilloides and V. angustifolium, the former found in wetter sites
and the latter in pine and aspen woods, openings, drier sites,
and somewhat more southern in general affinities. Northward,
V. uliginosum, the bilberry, is generally wide-ranging in
boreal forest and low-altitude arctic tundra. It is found from
low meadows to rock fields in northern Keewatin, in black spruce

and white spruce forests in the boreal regions, and southward to the north shore of Lake Superior.

Other wide-ranging ericads are *Arctostaphylos (Arctous) alpina, Vaccinium microcarpus (Oxycoccus microcarpus), Cassiope tetragona, Rhododendron lapponicum,* and a species closely related to the ericads, *Diapensia lapponica.* The ericads are not the only species with wide ranges throughout the boreal regions and northward into tundra, but the others are so numerous that they cannot be discussed in detail here. They do not extend southward into the region of the bogs of northern United States and southern Canada, but often in morphology and other respects they resemble the evergreen sclerophyllous ericads. They include *Rubus chamaemorus, Dryas integrifolia, Salix arctica, Salix herbacea, Oxytropis arctica,* and *Polygonum viviparum.* Certain of the ericads are of special interest since they are strictly arctic in affinities but extend southward in rather unusual sites far removed from arctic regions. *Rhododendron,* for example, is found southward to the edge of the forest in some areas, notably around Fort Reliance at the eastern end of Great Slave Lake, but it is also found-- or was found at one time--on cliffs of the Dells of the Wisconsin River in south central Wisconsin and also along the Mississippi River, far disjunct from its main present-day range. *Polygonum viviparum* is found on cliffs along the north shore of Lake Superior, also far disjunct from its range in the arctic regions.

Many of the ericaceous species, or other species closely resembling them in morphology, are as wide-ranging as *V. vitisidaea, V. uliginosum,* and *L. decumbens,* etc. but generally range farther northward. At the extreme southern fringe of boreal forest and from there southward into the boreal outliers that we term the ombrotrophic bogs are found the typically southern boreal ericaceous species, *C. calyculata, A. glaucophylla, K. polifolia,* as well as *K. angustifolia* in the extreme eastern United States and Canada, with *Phyllodoce caerulea* and *Rhododendron canadense* also found in the eastern parts of the continent.

Thus, in summary, the common, distinctive, dominant species of the ombrotrophic bogs are mostly wide-ranging, evergreen, sclerophyllous perennials, which if themselves not wide-ranging northward often have counterparts of the same genus that do extend far into boreal and tundra regions. Other nonericaceous genera such as *Betula, Empetrum,* and *Salix* have northern species often with many characteristics resembling, in one way or another the ericads, although their southern representatives may have broad, soft, deciduous leaves quite unlike the leaves of many of the arctic species. These relationships present some interesting questions in regard to the evolutionary history of the distinctive species of the ombrotrophic bogs, and discussion of some of these questions will be undertaken in somewhat greater detail in subsequent chapters.

10   More Reflections on the Species

The members of the Ericaceae that make up such an interesting and important group inhabiting the bogs of the Great Lakes
region are actually one of three distinctive aggregations of
northern evergreen ericads. Many of the species in these groups
are circumpolar in range--or there are at least very closely
related species in Europe and Asia--and so they may be said to
be both important and cosmopolitan over large areas of both
continents in boreal and arctic habitats. There are three
groups of northern evergreen ericads:

1. species that inhabit bogs in the Great Lakes region and
from there range northward, often becoming upland species in
northern boreal and arctic regions;
2. species with the southern edge of range north of the
Great Lakes region. Some of these are closely related to
similar species of the same genus found in the group listed in
(1);
3. evergreen ericads that inhabit upland areas, woodlands,
in the Great Lakes region and range northward into boreal and
arctic regions.

The first group includes *L. groenlandicum*, which is certainly a ubiquitous, wide-ranging species, in many ways virtually
typical and representative of the ericads in the group. It is
certainly a typical member in terms of the extreme distinctive-
ness of its leaves, despite the fact that they may be considered persistent rather than evergreen since they are leathery in
texture (coriaceous) and tend to turn brown in the fall and do
not retain a green color that would be necessary to be considered a true evergreen. The fact that the leaves are never a very
bright green even in summer perhaps can be considered a somewhat mitigating factor and Labrador tea is, indeed, evergreen
if one accepts the fact that it is not bright green.
Chamaedaphne calyculata is another member of the group; it
too is abundant in the bogs of the Great Lakes region and has

rather brownish green leaves that turn dark bronze rather than
remaining green through the winter, gradually restoring the
deep green coloration in spring as leaf tissue regenerates
chlorophyll needed for summer photosynthesis. This, as in
Ledum, is a minor color variation in the evergreen habit and
not sufficiently pronounced to keep these species from being
full-fledged members of the evergreen bog ericads. They are
both so abundant and so strongly characteristic in other ericaceous traits that their place in the group cannot be questioned.

Two other species are somewhat confusing in their Latin
scientific names, since both possess the same specific name:
Kalmia polifolia and *Andromeda polifolia,* the latter also known
in the Great Lakes region by its subspecific name *A. polifolia*
spp. *glaucophylla* or, as many people prefer, by a name that
accords it full species status in its own right, *A. glaucophylla.* Most of the botanical guidebooks, in fact, consider *A.
glaucophylla* a separate species in good standing; only Eric
Hulten in his "Flora of Alaska" (1968) accords it subspecific
status. In the Great Lakes region, both *K. polifolia* and *A.
glaucophylla* are found commonly in the bogs, wide-ranging and
ubiquitous, though never as abundant as *Ledum* or *Chamaedaphne.*

Kalmia has leaves that are bright green and shiny above,
fairly flat or at least more so than *Ledum* or *Andromeda.* The
latter have strongly revolute borders, are in-rolled, and are,
moreover, never as brilliantly green as *Kalmia,* which appear
to have been enameled. The undersides of the leaves of both
Kalmia and *Andromeda* are also very distinctive, being a polished white, a characteristic quite distinct from the leaves of
Ledum or *Chamaedaphne.* *Kalmia* and *Andromeda,* like *Ledum* and
Chamaedaphne, inhabit bogs and other peaty sites in the Great
Lakes region, showing a somewhat greater preference for upland
habitats toward the northern portions of their range. *Kalmia*
is found from the Great Lakes region westward into northern
Mackenzie and to an area in central and western British Columbia. It does not reach the Bering Strait in the west, although
eastward it extends to the Atlantic coast in Canada and New
England.

Andromeda polifolia and *A. glaucophylla* possess quite distinct ranges, although they overlap in a rather narrow band,
and this can probably be cited as another reason for considering them distinct species, in addition to the fact that they
are sufficiently different in appearance to be distinguished
upon observation. There is, for example, the fact that *A.
glaucophylla* has somewhat longer leaves (up to 5 cm in overall
length) and the flowers have pedicels less than 1 cm long and
are in nodding clusters. On the other hand, the leaves of
A. polifolia are usually less than 3 cm long. The flowers are
on pedicels up to 2 cm long and are in erect clusters. There

is no problem with identification west of Manitoba, or in southern Ungava and southeastern Quebec; *A. glaucophylla* and *A. polifolia* overlap in range only in a band stretching through central Ungava to central Manitoba. *Andromeda glaucophylla* is the only one in the Great Lakes area; *A. polifolia* is north of this, extending across the continent to Alaska and thence across northern Eurasia. Hybrids are reported from the band in which both occur, and so there is perhaps some problem with identification in this area.

Vaccinium vitis-idaea, like *A. polifolia*, ranges through northern Canada and Eurasia, and is joined in this wide range by another interesting species, *Empetrum nigrum*. The latter is not a member of the Ericaceae but rather has a family of its own, the Empetraceae, which is sufficiently like the ericads to have been previously considered as such. It is a member of the same order, the Ericales, which also includes such evergreen genera as *Pyrola* and *Diapensia*, which are discussed later. Both *V. vitis-idaea* and *E. nigrum* are considered here as members of the bog communities largely with an honorary status--they occur in these communities only in the very northern extremity of the region, for example, along the north shore of Lake Superior, but they are so interesting and in morphology so revealing of some principles that we are to discuss that they must be included. There are records that both have been collected in Wisconsin, around the west end of Lake Superior and in Michigan at the tip of the upper peninsula. They are still to be found in northern Minnesota but they usually escape notice.

Both *V. vitis-idaea* and *E. nigrum* are of interest because they range far northward into the Canadian boreal forest, and beyond that into the tundra, much farther than the northern limit of such other Great Lakes region bog species as *C. caly-culata, A. glaucophylla, L. groenlandicum,* and *V. macrocarpus,* as far, in fact, as most of the species mentioned above in group (2), the latter group made up of the northern ericads that do not extend as far south as the Great Lakes region.

THE NORTHERN ERICADS

The first group of evergreen ericads, as discussed above, is made up of species with the southern edge of their range in the Great Lakes region or southward, where they primarily are occupants of bogs and swamps. They range northward, finding more upland habitats increasingly suitable as the latitude increases.

The more northern group (group 2 listed above) is made up of evergreen ericads that are of interest because many belong

to the same genera as the evergreen ericads of group (1).
These members of group (2), however, range through arctic and
northern boreal regions, seldom if ever reaching as far south
as southern Canada. The point in mentioning them is simply
that in many ways they resemble the species in group (1)--they
have many morphological traits in common with the first group:
they have tough leathery leaves, often shiny or with an almost
lacquered bright green; the margins of leaves are rolled over
the underside of the leaves to a greater or lesser extent in
all of the species; and they are all small woody shrubs. The
members of this northern group are *L. decumbens* (with persistent leaves), *A. polifolia* (noted in connection with *A. glaucophylla*), *V. microcarpus* (*O. microcarpus*), *Loiseleuria procumbens*, *Phyllodoce coerulea*, *A. (Arctous) alpina* (marcescent
leaves), *Cassiope tetragona*, and *Diapensia lapponica* (closely
related to ericads).

It is significant that while the range of these northern
species does not extend southward into the Great Lakes region,
some do extend southward along the Rockies and the Appalachians,
thus leading to the interesting conclusion that they are un-
compromisingly adapted to the cold and dry arctic or alpine
environment, unlike the members of group (1), which occupy bogs
southward as discussed above.

Thus, *A. alpina*, *L. procumbens*, *P. coerulea*, and *D. lapponica*, for example, extend into New England along the Appalachian
summits, and the first two are found in the Canadian Rockies,
their southernmost latitude. Otherwise their range extends
entirely northward, never south of James Bay, stretching westward across the continent in a (sometimes broken) arc to the
Bering Strait and then into Siberia. In the case of *A. alpina*
and a subspecies of *D. lapponica* the range extends into northern Eurasia. *Rhododendron lapponicum* would be a member of the
group were it not for the fact that it is not evergreen; it is,
however, an ericoid of northern affinities, and it extends south
into New England along the mountain ridges.

Other members of the second group, however, are such confirmed northerners that they do not extend southward even along
the mountain chains; these include *L. decumbens* and *A. polifolia*.

OXYCOCCUS

In terms of the taxonomic problems created, probably the
genus *Oxycoccus*, a complex of species that often have been
lumped under the name *V. oxycoccus*, can be said to have easily
achieved first place. The *Oxycoccus* genus has been shifted in
and out of the Vaccinaceae, the blueberry family, as often as

the Vaccinaceae have been shifted in and out of the Ericaceae, perhaps more often. Every taxonomist apparently has given the matter some rather intense study and has come up with an arrangement different from that of anyone else. There are thus three names of long standing for the commonly recognized species--which it now turns out is not a species at all but a tetraploid hybrid. The various hybrid mixtures have understandably been the source of endless confusion for anyone trying to make sense of the bewildering array of morphological characteristics found in the group.

It was clear from the beginning that *V.* (or *O.*) *macrocarpus* (or *macrocarpon*) and *V.* (or *O.*) *microcarpus* (or *microcarpon*) could easily be distinguished from one another. The first is a southern bog inhabitant, the common cranberry. The second is found only in the far northern regions of boreal forest; it possesses much smaller, pointed, ovate rather than elliptical leaves, and there is not much difficulty identifying these two species, all the more so since their ranges do not overlap, at least to any significant extent. Between the two, however, and also very common is another entity, overlapping in range with both of them, and one given several different names over the years, of which the most common are *V. oxycoccus, V. oxycoccus* var. *ovalifolium, O. ovalifolius, O. quadripetalus,* and *O. palustris,* the latter derived from the similar (identical?) species in Europe. Moreover, there was evidently no end to the varieties that could be recognized if enough specimens were available for study, and such subspecific or varietal names as *intermedius* and *microphyllus* were applied with either hope or desperation to the plants that showed, or seemed to show, some recognizable patterns of similarity in the array of morphological characteristics exhibited by the specimens.

The mystery was evidently solved with the discovery that *O.* (or *V.*) *macrocarpus* (or *macrocarpon*) and *V.* (or *O.*) *microcarpus* (or *microcarpon*) are diploids and the other species are tetraploids. It became apparent that *O.* (or *Vaccinium*) *ovalifolius* and *O. quadripetalus* were members of a species complex that could all be lumped together; they were the consequence of hybridization, and the strange and confusing array of characteristics such as pedicels hairy or glabrous, short or long, leaves flat or revolute, ovate or elliptical, bracts scaly or leaflike, red or green, all occurring in a chaotic melange of illogic, were simply the result of a random drifting about of genes among the hybrids. There is nothing really to be gained in trying to make sense of such a mix, or to sort out the various names that now grace the genus *Oxycoccus* or the subspecific and varietal names for *V. oxycoccus* in the botanical manuals, and it is probably adequate for most purposes to simply use *microcarpus* for the northern species, *macrocarpus* for the common cranberry, and any name one likes for all of the rest.

GROUP THREE

Three groups of evergreen ericads were mentioned at the start, and two have been discussed. There is a third, and for most individuals these species will be the easiest to recognize and to find in their natural habitat. They do not grow in the far northern regions or in inaccessible bogs and swamps, but in the forests--hardwood or conifer stands or mixtures of the two found throughout the Great Lakes region, especially northward. Most of the species are easily recognized, at least to the genus to which they belong. They are, in most instances, common species that everyone remembers once they have seen a specimen.

This third group of species includes the following: the species of *Pyrola*, of which there are a half dozen; the single species of *Moneses,* two of *Monotropa,* as well as *Arctostaphylos uva-ursi, Chimaphila umbellata, Epigaea repens, Gaultheria procumbens,* and *Gaultheria hispidula*.

Other members of the Ericaceae that inhabit woodlands and should be mentioned because of their interest, in particular their gastronomic attributes, are the blueberries, *Vaccinium angustifolium* and *Vaccinium myrtilloides,* the former preferring more or less dry sandy uplands and the latter somewhat moister sites. *Vaccinium vitis-idaea,* which has already been mentioned as a member of group (1), can also be thought of as a member of this group; it is, moreover, truly evergreen, and while it is found only northward of the extreme northern rim of the Great Lakes region and in northern Minnesota, it ranges north, east, and west to the shores of the continent, being able to find suitable living conditions in a variety of habitats, from bogs to uplands, preferring the latter northward. It should probably be mentioned that not all taxonomists have agreed to place the blueberries in the ericads, some preferring to give them a family of their own, the Vaccinaceae, but agreement is general that on the basis of flower structure they are surely closely related to if not members of the Ericaceae.

There are a half-dozen species of *Pyrola* in eastern North America. It is not necessary to distinguish between them here since all of them commonly inhabit upland forests and are readily recognized by their basal rosette of a few rounded leaves and by their single flowering stalk or peduncle with a few (3-4) to several (10-12) flowers nodding from short pedicels located mostly at the upper terminus in a form that is termed a raceme. They are perennial herbs, evergreen, and rather

frequent and easily recognized members of the forest communities. *Pyrola,* like *Vaccinium,* is often placed in a separate
family, the Pyrolaceae, shinleaf family, along with *Moneses*
and *Chimaphila,* but they are also, on the other hand, often
included in the Ericaceae by other taxonomists and they are
in any case similar. *Moneses uniflora* closely resembles the
species of *Pyrola* except that, as the name implies, it has but
one flower at the tip of the peduncle.

Monotropa is a distinctive genus of the northern woods,
but notably colorless in more ways than one because of its
total lack of chlorophyll. It has been variously described as
being parasitic on roots or soil fungi, or saprophytic on decomposing organic material. It is obviously one or another of
these, since it has no chlorophyll of its own and must draw its
sustenance from organic compounds manufactured by green plants.
It possesses no leaves but only stalkless scales, which are
deciduous, on the single stem, the latter with an equally colorless flower or group of flowers at the tip. One of the two
species, *M. uniflora,* is known commonly as Indian pipe, and
has, as the name indicates, a single flower just as a pipe has
a single bowl. The other species, *M. hypopithys,* pinesap,
resembles Indian pipe but often is darker or reddish in contrast to the customary waxey white of *M. uniflora* especially
when it is young. The pinesap possesses more than one flower,
held together in a tight bunch at the top of the leafless stem.

Five other species in the last group should be mentioned
since they are usually fairly common in most upland woods, are
evergreen, and are readily recognized: *A. uva-ursi*, bearberry;
G. hispidula, snowberry; *G. procumbens,* wintergreen; *E. repens,*
trailing arbutus or mayflower; and *C. umbellata,* pipsissewa.
The bearberry is also known as kinnikinnick. This is a good
chance to mention the dangerous confusion that occurs when one
goes only by the common names of species. *Pyrola* is known
commonly as shinleaf, but another common name is wintergreen,
the same common name as that given to *G. procumbens.* If it
were not for the scientific name, one would not know which
species was meant when the name wintergreen was used. This
happens so frequently in the common botanical terminology that
it is always best to avoid common names when possible and to
use only the scientific names. This is the reason why botanists
use the latter almost exclusively, often to the annoyance of
persons to whom the names are unfamiliar. It is in the interests of scientific accuracy that the scientific name be
used whenever possible. The problem is much greater than most
people realize, because the same name in different parts of
the country often refers to different species entirely, and
at times the same name is given to two different species that

grow in the same area, such as the case with wintergreen, *Pyrola* and *G. procumbens*.

All of these species of the third group are found in the forests of the Great Lakes region and tend to prefer somewhat dry sites, often woods in which jack pine is commonly an associate in the arboreal stratum, but areas where other tree species are also present. In other words, they are found in relatively young successional forest stands with a fairly rich mixture of species both in the overstory of trees and the understory of herbs and shrubs.

ORIGINS

A branch of the science of botany known as paleobotany has developed in response to the question that ultimately will always be asked in regard to the different distributions and habitat preferences of the plant species: "How did this all come about?"

The answer, of course, is that no one knows for sure, and it is perhaps unlikely that sufficient knowledge will ever be derived from the study of the few fossils available, or inferred from the present-day geographical distribution of the species, to answer the question with certainty and in great detail.

The studies conducted on the origin of the Ericaceae, however, point up some interesting and plausible possibilities and it is perhaps pertinent to discuss them at least in outline here so that curiosity can be satisfied to a degree, or, on the other hand, larger measures of curiosity might be inspired in those whose interests are such that they might pursue the matter further.

For the purposes of studying the evolutionary development of groups of plants, it has become the custom to gather together the genera that seem to be closely related to group them into subfamilies. The relationship is based largely on the characteristics of the flowers, the most complex of the plant organs, which apparently follow rather easily discernible trends in evolutionary development from less to more advanced. It is possible, by looking at a series of related species, to deduce which have been derived from others and which are the oldest from the standpoint of evolutionary time. In the common ericads of north central and northern North America, the species have been assigned to three subfamilies, the Rhododendroideae, the Arbutoideae, and the Vaccinoideae.

Many years ago, Hiden T. Cox (1949) studied the phylogenetic relationships of the Ericaceae, taking them as groups or subfamilies, one of which, the Arbutoideae, includes genera that have been mentioned above--*Cassiope, Andromeda, Epigaea, Chamaedaphne, Gaultheria, Chiogenes* (which has been included often in *Gaultheria; G. hispidula* is synonymous with *C. hispidula)* and *Arctostaphylos.* It should perhaps be noted that this arrangement is not one followed by all taxonomists, and Fernald (1950) in the eighth edition of "Gray's Manual of Botany," considers these species to be members of tribes in the subfamily Rhododendroideae; in his view, the tribe Andromedeae comprises all but one species above, and the Arbuteae takes in *Arctostaphylos.* These are details, however, that concern us only to the extent that the difference of opinion is noted, should anyone consult "Gray's Manual of Botany" with the thought in mind of verifying or making some additional study of the subfamilies of the Ericaceae. The issue probably reveals more of the penchant taxonomists have for disagreement than any really basic issue in the classification of plants. Cox employs a rather large number of tribes to encompass the subfamilies; others do not. It is largely a matter of temperament, perhaps, or convenience. Of concern here is the history of the ericads as presented by Cox and the general avoidance of taxonomic confusion.

We must at once concede to the conservative view that Cox's deductions are pure speculation, since the real nature of ericad history remains, and probably will remain, virtually unknown. There is, nevertheless, enough logic and rational supposition in Cox's analysis to furnish at least an idea of what the ericaceous history is, and if it is not an accurate one, then the real history must have been similar in outlines if not in particulars.

The species of the subfamilies Rhododendroideae and Arbutoideae (Cox's grouping) that seem closest to the ancient, primitive, and now extinct ericad ancestors are found in the Himalayan Mountains and in southeastern Asia in general. It is logical to conclude, says Cox, that the primitive ancestor (or ancestors) was also native to the region. It is probable, he adds, that this primitive ancestor gave rise to the ancestors of the various tribes of the Rhododendroideae, Arbutoideae, and Vaccinoideae that now occupy northern North America, and that these migrated into the regions occupied by these ericads today, notable Siberia, northern Europe, and northern North America, the latter by way of the Bering Strait if it existed at that far distant time. Members of other tribes or of other subfamilies of the Ericaceae, those now occupying tropical or temperate regions of the southern hemisphere, spread south from the Himalayan center of origin.

In some instances the migrating species left populations in the wake of their migration, and the path can be followed by means of these historical traces. Thus, in the tribe Gaul-

therieae, the genus *Diplycosia* is the most primitive. It is
found in the southeastern Himalayas and from there into the
Malay Peninsula. As Cox states, the logical hypothesis is
that a recent descendant of *Diplycosia* also gave rise to *G.* (or
C.) *hispidula* and then to *G. procumbens*. The former can be
found along the path of its migration in Japan, northern North
America, and from Newfoundland south to North Carolina. On
the other hand, *G. procumbens,* which arose later from *G. hispidula,* or perhaps from *Diplycosia* or some other ancestor, is
largely North American and has moved south along the eastern
mountain ranges as well as along the western ranges into Central and South America. Some species of *Gaultheria* still remain along the route from the Himalayas to Japan, and other
species are found in Australia, New Zealand, and Tasmania,
relics of another migration in this southern direction.

The tribe Andromedeae is another example. Members of the
most primitive genus, *Andromeda,* are found from the Himalayas
northward to Japan and the circumpolar regions. Evidently,
Chamaedaphne arose from *Andromeda,* and it is now found in
northern Europe, northern Asia, and northern North America, as
well as southward along the Alleghenies.

In the case of most if not all of these species, the intermediate ancestors linking them to original subfamilial ancestors have become extinct without leaving a trace, and so
the actual course of paleogeographic history is lost and is
probably irrecoverable. Most of the groups are more complex
in their phylogenetic relationships than *Gaultheria* and *Chamaedaphne,* so that logical conjectures are more difficult to come
by, and it must be said again, even in the case of the latter
genera, that the outlines of evolutionary progression are dim
and any theories concerning the region of their origin must
clearly be labeled as speculative. The only really dependable
fact is that they originated somewhere, and just as clearly
they must have migrated into most of the regions they now
occupy. The events must have followed a pattern that at least
resembles that described above. This evolutionary history has
been influenced, too, by continental drift, changes in climates
over the continents as a consequence of drift or other causes,
and by the great continental glaciations. But these are influences that have occurred largely beyond the reach of historical record, and so these, too, will remain a mystery. Almost everything in this realm of botany must be considered
speculation.

11 Origins of the Ericaceae

Inferences from phylogenetic relationships among the various genera of the Ericaceae, as can be drawn from the similarities and differences in flowers and other organs, has led to the conclusion that they originated in southeastern Asia, for here the most primitive forms are to be found today, and that they spread from there to present distributions throughout the world. The ancestors of what are now the modern species migrated to northern areas in Asia, then spread east and west from there into Europe and North America. The species of the Great Lakes region, then, have a history dating back to the beginnings of the Tertiary or earlier. When someone picks a blueberry along the shores of Lake Superior he is holding a bit of history that began millions of years ago in southeastern Asia.

Louis Agassiz was at the head of an expedition that canoed along the north shore of Lake Superior in the summer of 1848. The expedition consisted of 16 instructors and students from eastern universities, two physicians, plus a dozen canoemen who were Indian, French Canadian, or half-breed, all initially to be crammed with their supplies into one large (18 foot) mackinaw boat and two canoes; that is, until it became evident, as one might readily infer, that one more canoe was needed to accommodate the overflow. At the helm of this powerful force, Agassiz worked his way along the north shore from Sault Ste. Marie to Fort William, observing the geology of the region as well as the fish, birds, insects, reptiles, mollusks, and plants, the latter collection of which included the following species: the blueberries, *Vaccinium* species; *Andromeda polifolia* and other members of the Ericaceae; the insectivorous species *Drosera rotundifolia* and *Drosera longifolia* as well as *Pinguicula vulgaris*; arctic species such as *Polygonum viviparum, Saxifraga aizoon*, and *Scirpus caespitosus, Empetrum nigrum*, as well as such other interesting things as *Linnaea borealis* and *Goodyera repens, Shepherdia canadensis, Comandra livida*, and *Clintonia borealis*, the last three endemic to North America. All the rest were those that Agassiz had seen before in Europe (or at least they are very close relatives of the European plants). In his report, published in 1850, Agassiz wrote:

> The vegetation of the northern shores of Lake Superior agrees so closely with that of the higher tracts of the Jura, which encloses the lower and middle zone of the subalpine region, that...it is another proof that the vegetation of the two continents becomes more and more homogeneous the more we advance northwards.

Writing of the Ericaceae in particular, he says:

> No family is more homogeneous in its distributions, or more equally spread in the North of America and Europe, than that of the Ericaceae, which characterizes rather the region of the pines than the subalpine flora; for these species follow the pine forests in their more or less elevated stations. The Equisetaceae, the ferns, and the Lycopodiaceae of Lake Superior are almost absolutely the same species as those of the subalpine region of Europe... Thus the Lichens and Mosses are already entirely the same species here as in Europe, and it will be sufficient to make a single list of them, without indicating the corresponding European species since all are identical.

Equally significant were Agassiz's observations of the landforms along the Lake Superior shore, for they confirmed his interpretations of what were in reality the markings of a great continental glaciation, similar to those he had seen in Europe--grooved rocks, outwash deposits, erratic boulders, sand and gravel hills and hollows, all the work of a vast continental glacier.

The continental glaciation, as well as what preceded and followed, has a profound bearing upon the present-day distribution of plant species in northern North America. Why this should be so is examined below.

TERTIARY, PLIOCENE, AND PLEISTOCENE

Fossil collections reveal that in the first half of the Tertiary period, roughly from 65 to 25 million years ago, plants with tropical adaptations inhabited middle latitudes in the Northern Hemisphere. Plants characteristic of regions farther north, in what we call arctic and northern boreal zones, possessed morphological characteristics that now are associated with plant species growing in temperate latitudes.

This latter vegetation has been termed the *Arctotertiary forest* for obvious reasons, since it existed in Tertiary time and in what are now arctic regions; many of the fossils from this forest are of plants that resemble, and are perhaps truly members of, genera to which species living today belong.

By the end of the Tertiary period, however, the global scene was changing markedly. The closing epoch of the Tertiary is known as the Pliocene, and during the 10 million years or so of the Pliocene there were shifts in the global climate, the cause of which is still a matter of speculation. The close of the Pliocene is marked by the beginnings of glaciation of the northern parts of the Northern Hemisphere. The great continental ice masses, covering large parts of North America and Eurasia, expanded and retreated time and again during the Pleistocene epoch, which precedes the Holocene of the present day. There were at least four and possibly more major advances in the Pleistocene, separated by periods of retreat, over a time span of at least two and perhaps as long as four million years or more in North America, the ice at one time or another covered a region extending south to New England, Ohio, Illinois, Iowa, Nebraska, the Dakotas, northern Montana, and Washington. This vast layer of ice did not form overnight, for obvious reasons, but was built slowly over a period of thousands of years by gradual accumulation from snow, more of which must have fallen in winter than could melt in summer. The ice front advanced slowly during the episodes of glacial growth and retreated slowly during the interglacials. In North America, the last of the great advances is known as Wisconsin, corresponding to the Würm in Europe. The Wisconsin ice front, reaching its maximum extent just south of Lake Michigan and then extending northwest across Wisconsin and central Minnesota, began its retreat some 10,000-12,000 years ago, the last vestige remaining in north central Canada until perhaps 6000 years ago or thereabouts in an area now known as the Keewatin Ice Divide. We are now in the post-Wisconsin interglacial. When it will end, we do not know, but predictions are that no one need worry over another glacial advance for perhaps 23,000 years.

The Arctotertiary forest obviously could not survive this inundation of snow and ice. The rich and varied assortment of species that had been part of the vast vegetational cover over the northern parts of North America was pushed southward in a great slow migration. The fossil evidence is scanty, since most of it was destroyed by the glacial advance, but at the edges of the glacier are found fossils that show the kind of vegetation existing when the ice reached its southernmost extent. Jack pine, tamarack, spruce, and cedar were found in Arkansas and Illinois, and extinct species of muskox, reindeer, and mammoth were found in what are now warm temperate regions. Such arctic plants as *Betula nana* (dwarf birch), *Salix herbacea* (least willow), and *Dryas octopetala* (mountain avens) were found also in temperate regions.

The species ancestral to those that now make up at least much of the ericaceous component in the arctic and boreal flora obviously were forced southward along with the rest of the living organisms making up the biota of northern North America, and they lived out the long periods of glaciation in suitably cool refuges near the ice front. Much of the history of the glaciations is known in quite surprising detail, as a consequence of intensive studies of geological deposits, of plant and animal fossils, and of pollen preserved in sediments existing in parts of Canada and the United States. To go into the history in greater detail here, however, would serve no purpose for we are to be preoccupied with what has happened subsequent to the retreat of the ice.

12 Post-Glacial Migrations

In the millenia immediately following the great glacial epoch known as the Pleistocene, the region of Alaska and eastern Asia known as Beringia--the land east and west of the Bering Strait--takes on great importance, because of two aspects of glacial history. First, much of Alaska and Siberia escaped glaciation; the higher mountains possessed an ice cover during the glacial epochs, but lowlands and many of the upland areas remained ice-free. Second, there were, at times, ice-free corridors between Alaska and central North America, and there were, in addition, times even during the height of the Wisconsin glaciation, for example, when the level of the sea declined sufficiently to establish a land bridge across what is now the Bering Strait, joining eastern Siberia and western Alaska at the same time that an ice-free corridor existed between Alaska and central North America.

These events have been summarized on the basis of rather detailed geological and paleontological evidence that we cannot go into here, but there existed a refuge into which plants and animals retreated to escape the great refrigeration that accompanied the glacial epochs. There was a route south, and many of them took it. At these times the ice-free Beringian land was almost certainly tundra, and the species that were inhabitants of the Alaskan forests and not adapted to the severe cold of the tundra could move southward. Those that were capable of arctic survival, perhaps with some need for accommodating adaptations that could be accomplished in relatively short periods of time, remained in the Beringian tundra. Those plants that were inhabitants of the great forests stretching across Canada were, of course, forced to retreat southward before the advancing ice. Whether there were refugia in the Arctic Islands for the ericads and other plants adapted to arctic conditions is uncertain, although there is some evidence that at least parts of the Queen Elizabeth Islands could have provided unglaciated refugia for species capable of surviving cold, long winters, short growing seasons, typical long summer days, and the harsh abrasive effects of

wind-blown snow in winter. Floras existing in the high latitudes prior to the Pleistocene are known only poorly, if at
all, but it seems virtually self-evident that far northern
lands must have harbored cold-adapted antecedents of what are
now high arctic species. Other species, along with what are
now boreal species, must have moved south, either along the
ice-free corridor from Alaska or simply directly south before
the advancing ice across Canada and the northern United States.

When the Wisconsin ice retreated, the plants that had
adapted to high arctic latitudes again moved northward across
the newly opened land of Canada. Likewise, the boreal species,
including the boreal trees such as spruce and tamarack, as well
as the boreal herbaceous species and the shrubs, including the
ericads, moved north in the wake of the retreating ice front.
Arctic species that survived the Pleistocene in Beringia were
now able to move eastward into formerly glaciated northern
Canada. Thus, today, in northern Canada are found species with
southern limits far north of the Great Lakes region, and this
group of species includes *L. decumbens*, *R. lapponicum*, *L. procumbens*, *P. coerulea*, *C. tetragona*, *A. polifolia*, *A. (Arctous)
alpina*, *V. uliginosum* subsp. *microphyllum*, *O. microcarpus*, as
well as *Diapensia lapponica*, *Dryas integrifolia*, *Pyrola grandiflora*, *Saxifraga oppositifolia*, and *Saxifraga tricuspidata*.

South of these far northern regions, in the boreal forest
of Canada and extending southward into bogs and swamps of the
upper Great Lakes region in the United States, are the southern
boreal species such as *L. groenlandicum*, *C. calyculata*, *K.
polifolia*, *A. glaucophylla*, *A. uva-ursi*, *V. vitis-idaea*, *V.
uliginosum* subsp. *alpinum*, *O. quadripetalus* (or *V. oxycoccus*),
as well as *Empetrum nigrum*, *Pyrola minor*, *Pyrola asarifolia*,
Pyrola secunda, and *Moneses uniflora*.

That some of the northern species survived south of the
ice, in regions that are now parts of the United States, is
clear from fossil evidence obtained from Minnesota bogs. There
was a late-glacial flora in the region that included such high
arctic-alpine species as *D. integrifolia*, *S. herbacea*, *R. lapponicum*, *P. nivea*, and *C. capillaris*. A spruce-dominated
assemblage characterized the first forest in the Great Lakes
region following the wasting of the Wisconsin ice, and plants
that today have widely separated ranges--members of one group
now in the arctic and those of the other now found in boreal
regions--were in late-glacial times growing together near the
edge of the glacial ice front in Minnesota.

It perhaps should be stated that while such trees as spruce
and pine leave abundant fossil pollen in the sediments of lakes
and in the accumulated peat strata of bogs, the ericads are
less productive of those most useful bits of microscopic evidence. The reason is simple. Spruce and similarly anemo-

philous species produce large amounts of pollen since they depend on air currents to transport the pollen grains to the female flowers, and large amounts must be produced to ensure adequate pollination. On the other hand, the ericads and many other plant species are entomophilous, depending on insects to pollinate the flowers, and there is much less chance that pollen grains in large numbers will find a way into a lake or bog where they constitute an archival record for all who wish to know the kind of vegetation that occupied the region at various periods in the past.

The fossil pollen and bits and pieces of plants found in lake sediments and the peat strata of bogs, however, are not the only evidence that arctic and boreal plants occupied areas around the Great Lakes and southward during late-glacial time. There are what might be termed living fossils that furnish evidence that the plants once occupied the land in reasonable abundance. Along the north shore of Lake Superior, Agassiz discovered such far northern arctic species as *Saxifraga aizoon, Polygonum viviparum,* and *Scirpus caespitosus,* found elsewhere today only in arctic regions and with a wide gap between Lake Superior and the Arctic within which no specimens have ever been found. It is apparent that these plants survive because they have the special habitats afforded by rocky ledges along the north shore of Lake Superior where the microclimate must resemble that of the Arctic. They have been extirpated in the vast expanse of spruce forest between Lake Superior and the Canadian Arctic by the entirely different environmental regime of the forest.

Other species of arctic affinity found along the north shore of Lake Superior in favorable arctic-like habitats, usually north-facing cliffs rising sheer from the water's edge, include *Sagina nodosa, Loiseleuria procumbens, Pinguicula vulgaris, Tofieldia pusilla, Poa alpina, Potentilla tridentata, Carex scirpoidea,* and *Trisetum spicatum.* These species were discovered in Old Woman Bay, in Lake Superior Provincial Park, by Soper and Maycock (1963), and in their report they write that the cliffs of the area furnish a microclimatic environment sufficiently resembling the Arctic to permit survival of a community made up of arctic-alpine plant species. It is even possible, according to other observers, that the steep cliff faces were unglaciated, protruding from the ice cover during glaciation, permitting survival of plants *in situ* even through the glacial epochs.

Equally interesting is the case of *D. integrifolia.* Across North America, the southern limit of range for *D. integrifolia* is the southern edge of the open tundra (the northern edge of the boreal forest), and from there it extends northward to the

northernmost islands of the Arctic Archipelago. Within its
range it is common wherever soil conditions are suitable. As
Porsild (1955) points out, in some parts of the Archipelago it
is by far the most common and widespread of all flowering plants.
It is absent entirely from the southern boreal forest, having
never been collected in the vast expanse of land between the
northern edge of the forest and Lake Superior, except at one
place along the northernmost part of the north shore of Lake
Superior, and another southern point where it has been collected at Lake Mistassini in Quebec. Both this site and that along
the north shore of Lake Superior are separated from the main
range of the species by a broad belt of forest. Like the other
species found by Soper and Maycock along the north shore of
Lake Superior, *D. integrifolia* must have survived the Pleistocene in close proximity to the ice front, reoccupying the area
vacated by the retreating ice, only to be extirpated by the advancing spruce forest.

One other point of interest in regard to the arctic flora,
is its evident youth in terms of evolutionary time. It must,
in short, have occupied the Arctic fairly recently, geologic-
ally speaking. The reasons for this conclusion are summarized
by Good (1964), who points out that there are few endemic arctic species. Endemic species are those found in a given region
and nowhere else; an endemic species is one of relatively restricted range, found only in a relatively small area; it
seems obviously to have evolved in the area where it is found
and to have migrated no great distance from that area. Since
the proportion of species endemic to a region is directly pro-
portional to the length of time the region has been occupied
by the flora now there, it follows that the arctic flora must
be very young, perhaps the youngest in the world. Good adds
that the arctic flora is not isolated--it is made up simply of
the most climatically resistant species from the northern temperate flora or of readily adaptable species that have evolved
from ancestral species of an ancient northern temperate flora.

The latter, for example, is probably the case with the endemic northern North American species *D. integrifolia*; it
probably originated in North America from another *Dryas* and
has not yet had time to expand its range into other regions.
It reaches east Greenland but not Iceland, northwestern Europe,
or northeastern Asia. It is a plant of the open arctic tundra
and is intolerant of shade such as it would encounter in a
forested region.

All of these plants have a similar evolutionary history in
that either they or their ancestors, during the long Tertiary,
were members of a high arctic or at least northern boreal flora,
adapted to exceedingly harsh conditions of life. During the
glaciations of the Pleistocene they moved southward in front

of the advancing ice and then probably retreated northward
again during at least the four known interglacial intervals.
Those adapted to the dryest, coldest, and most difficult conditions have now recolonized the far northern regions, joining
other species that have moved eastward from refugia in Beringia
or perhaps southward from the most northern reaches of the
Arctic Archipelago. Only a few have left small surviving rem-
nant colonies along the north shore of Lake Superior. Those
species adapted to intermediate but still cold northern boreal
regions moved northward into what is now the boreal forest,
with southernmost outliers in the bogs and swamps of the regions around the southern shore of Lake Superior and the other
Great Lakes, as well as in New England and along the mountain
chains southward.

13 Some Speculation on Sclerophyllous Matters

We pursued the topic of sclerophylly to some extent in
Chapter 12, in preparation for what is to follow: some amiable
thoughts and conjectures on the sclerophyllous bog ericads, not
only what some nice plants like these are doing in such low
places as swamps and bogs but what they are doing so far to
the north in such inhospitable places as the dark boreal forests
of Canada, remote tundra regions extending into the Canadian
Arctic, and, in fact, into Siberia. They inhabit the Arctic
of not only North America but Europe, Eurasia, and Asia, and
that far northern outpost of the United States, Alaska, and the
Aleutians as well. They inhabit bogs and marshlands along the
southern fringe of their range, but northward they are found
also in muskeg, spruce forests, and upland tundra, only the
first of which is as wet as the bogs and marshlands of the southern parts of their range. The uplands in the spruce forest and
tundra are, in fact, exceedingly dry as habitat for plant life,
and, were it not for the fact that summers are so cool that
evaporation is very low, they would be considered deserts on
the basis of the annual amounts of precipitation they receive.
At Ennadai Lake, for example, a few miles north of the northwestern corner of Manitoba, at the northern edge of the boreal
forest in Canada, the annual precipitation is something between
nine and ten inches, with an inch or more received in each of
the four months that are not winter, June through September.
The rest of the year, by temperate zone standards, can hardly
be called summer, since the mean daily maximum temperature in
the warmest month, July, is only a little more than 60°F. It
is this low temperature, however, that permits the soil to remain reasonably moist throughout the summer and not to become
a parched desert pavement such as is invariably found in regions with warmer temperatures and the same sparse input of
moisture. In fact, the moisture received in rain and snow
evaporates so little that the cold clear streams, lakes, and
rivers that exist in great abundance over the Keewatin landscape are almost always full and flowing, the water from rain
and snow taking this course of travel out of the country rather

than the more traditional mode in temperate regions, evaporation.

The streams and rivers in the Keewatin region flow north and east, into an even colder climate than exists at Ennadai, and so the moisture dropped on the land in this region, for the most part, never does vanish into the atmosphere but rather is transported to Hudson Bay or, in the case of the rivers of eastern Mackenzie and northern Keewatin, into the Arctic Ocean far to the north.

Diversions aside, however, we find that the map (Fig. 1, Chapter 8) of the range of the bog plants presented by Transeau in his most interesting paper of 1903, "On the Geographic Distribution and Ecological Relations of the Bog Plant Societies of Northern North America," is not as clearly defined as it might be although it was surely an exceptionally cogent interpretation of the knowledge available in that day. Indeed, much of the information presented is quite accurate, especially concerning the southern edge of the range of the species, and it is for this reason still useful today.

Transeau indicates that species of the genera *Drosera, Eriophorum, Ledum,* and *Andromeda* are encountered most abundantly in wetlands along the southern edge of their range and then northward tend to occupy progressively more upland sites. At the northern edge of their range, the bog ericads become confined almost exclusively to what are often termed the dry upland barrens--rocky or sandy tundra of southern Keewatin in the case of the central portions of northern Canada.

As an example, *V. vitis-idaea*, a species known variously as lingonberry or mountain cranberry, is found in northern Minnesota locally abundant in cranberry bogs. It is rare in northern Wisconsin and upper Michigan, but relatively abundant in the lands around the northern shore of Lake Superior and from there northward. In these areas, and in northern Manitoba, Saskatchewan, Alberta, and the Northwest Territories, it is found over a wide range of habitats, from spruce woods to muskegs and bogs. At the northern border of Manitoba, it is found on the dry rocky barrens. At Ennadai Lake, it attains its greatest abundance on dry sandy esker ridges, in spruce stands found in sheltered ravines, on upland rock fields, and the summits of tussocks in so-called tussock muskegs.

This is not to indicate that *V. vitis-idaea* is invariably found only in these preferred habitats at the southern and northern edges of its range. In Minnesota and the western Great Lakes region, it is found, for example, most abundantly in bogs, but it is also found on granitic ledges along Lake Superior. At the north end of Ennadai, in a far northern portion of its range that is mostly tundra, it is found abundantly on dry sandy eskers. Only in much reduced numbers does it occur in the wet

meadows that are found at Ennadai in the lowland areas that are
the topographic equivalents of the bogs of northern Minnesota
and the other Great Lakes states.   There obviously is a marked
shift in preferred habitat for *V. vitis-idaea* between the southern and the northern parts of its range, and obviously it is
able to compete most effectively against plants of other species
in the extreme lowlands at the southern edge of its range and
on upland summits at the northern edge of its range.   Since
topographically there are no great differences between these
areas, both of which are covered largely with glacial till, and
since the parent material for the soils is much the same at
both locations, one can infer only that factors related to the
climate, length of growing season, or perhaps day length, and,
consequently, the amount of energy available for growth, determine the preferred site on the which *V. vitis-idaea* will grow
over the entire latitudinal extent of its range.

      These same variations in preferred habitat over the extent
of geographic range is also evident in the other bog ericads
and not only *V. vitis-idaea*, but we need not go into each one
in detail.   Suffice it to say that the same general rules hold
true for such species as *C. calyculata*, *A. glaucophylla* (which
grades into *A. polifolia* in northeastern Canada), *K. polifolia,*
L. groenlandicum, and the other species that are commonly associated with the bog ericads such as *Betula glandulosa* (and the
closely related forms and subspecies and hybrids).   Subsequently
we shall deal with reasons for these shifts latitudinally in
habitat preference, and with some morphological characteristics
of plants, many of which are broadleafed evergreens, that may
account for the unusual capabilities of these species to survive in such harsh and inhospitable environments as bogs of the
Great Lakes region and summits of ridges in the far northern
tundra of Canada.

CONDITIONS OF LIFE FOR ERICADS

      Many of the ericads of the Great Lakes region inhabit bogs,
while others inhabit the forests, and these latter species are
joined by plants belonging to such genera as *Pyrola* and *Moneses,*
which have leaves and flowers resembling in many respects those
of the plants placed today in the family known as Ericaceae, to
which they have at various times in the past been assigned by
some taxonomists.

      Conditions of life in the Arctic apparently require special
morphological adaptations, at least in most or many species,
and these morphological characteristics are also often found in
the evergreen ericads inhabiting bogs of northern Minnesota,
Michigan, and Wisconsin, eastward through New England and south-

ern Canada, and down the Appalachian mountains. It seems reasonable to believe that the bog species evolved in the Arctic during Tertiary time or before, then moved south during the Pleistocene glaciations, and now remain in such environments as bogs and other sites furnishing conditions resembling those of the Arctic in which they originally developed the characteristic morphological structures.

Some species apparently must have become adapted to forest conditions, and this is the case with species of *Pyrola, Moneses,* and *Chimaphila.* If they were not already adapted to forest conditions at the beginning of the Pleistocene glaciations they became so later. Two interesting species, *V. vitis-idaea* and *E. nigrum,* are somewhat more abundant in forested uplands along the north shore of Lake Superior, for example, than in the lowland bogs and muskegs of the region, although they are found in both habitats. *Vaccinium vitis idaea, E. nigrum,* and *A. uva-ursi* are, indeed, rather interesting because of the wide range of habitats they are capable of occupying persistently and with obvious competitive success. They all inhabit forests, bogs, and recently burned regenerating areas, apparently without noticeable preference for any special soil conditions or for sunny or shaded sites, as so often is the case with many other species. They also grow in other regions with seemingly equal abandon, occupying mountains in low alpine and subalpine zones. *Vaccinium vitis-idaea* and *E. nigrum* range northward much farther than *A. uva-ursi,* however, occupying the shores of the Arctic Ocean across Canada and all Eurasia.

Whatever individual preference for latitude or for one kind of habitat or another demonstrated by the evergreen ericads and other species, all of these plants have certain morphological characteristics in common, characteristics that derive from long adaptation to the arctic environment. There are also many physiological adaptations to the arctic, invisible but just as significant as the morphological adaptations, and in fact related to them since they involve photosynthesis, respiration, and manner of reproduction.

What are the environmental conditions in arctic regions to which these plants have developed specialized adaptations through the long expanse of Tertiary time? First, and probably individually most important, is low temperature in both summer and winter. Plants must grow during the cold summers, even enduring intermittent freezing during the growing season, and they must withstand the severe cold of winter. They must, in addition to the cool temperatures of the growing season, somehow manage to surmount the added disadvantage that the summer season is not only cold but very short--no longer than June to August at most. There are, in addition to these two deficiencies in the environment, such added hazards as strong winds

that whip sand and snow to velocities causing abrasion of leaves
and stems, low light intensities since the sun never rises very
high in the sky even in midsummer, low nitrogen supplies in most
soils, and levels of precipitation so low as to be characteristic of desert regions--indeed, the Arctic would be a very dry
desert were it not for the fact that cold temperatures reduce
evaporation to equally low levels.

Abrasion by wind-driven snow is a source of continual injury to arctic plants, and the winds also have a desiccating
effect, extracting moisture that cannot be replaced until soil
thaws in spring--which occurs long after leaves have warmed in
the sun and begun photosynthesis and respiration.

MORPHOLOGY OF THE NORTHERN PLANTS

What are some of the morphological adaptations in plants
of northern regions that appear to have developed in response
to the harsh environmental conditions of arctic and boreal
environments? Among the most readily apparent are the tough
and shiny evergreen leaves characteristic of many of the species, leaves with an outer coating of a waxy protective material covering a thick layer of cutin. The species with leaves
of this kind include *V. vitis-idaea* and *E. nigrum*. The former
has small rounded bright green leaves perhaps a quarter of an
inch long, curved so that the lower surface is concave like a
spoon with a partition running down the middle. The latter has
needlelike leaves of about the same length, and these make the
twigs of *Empetrum* look like miniature branches of spruce trees.
Both of these species are low and decumbent, and unless covered with snow will be subjected to severe abrasion by wind-driv-
en snow particles. For this reason it seems fairly logical to
assume that the tough shiny leaf is an adaptation enabling the
plant to withstand snow-blasting with some degree of impunity.
Other species with leaves similar to *V. vitis-idaea* and *E.
nigrum* in that they possess a shiny covering of what is apparently a waxy cutinous material include *K. angustifolia*, *K. polifolia*, *P. coerulea*, *L. procumbens*, and *A. uva-ursi*. A somewhat
different leaf structure is characteristic of the other evergreen ericads and related species: tough leathery leaves, often
somewhat darker in color than the bright green of *V. vitis-idaea*
and *E. nigrum*, but covered nevertheless with a fairly heavy
waxlike coating and with a dense collection of hairs known as
tomentum on the underside (see Fig. 2, Chapter 7). This leaf
is characteristic of *L. groenlandicum* and *L. decumbens*, the
former a common species of bogs in the Great Lakes region as
well as spruce forests of boreal regions, and the latter a
species of the far northern forest and the tundra. A common

species of the Great Lakes bogs and swamps often found in
association with   *L. groenlandicum* is *C. calyculata,* with an
upper leaf surface somewhat resembling that of *Ledum* in color
and texture, but with an undersurface bare of tomentum and
covered instead with a mottled waxy coating that is most interesting to observe under a microscope and most difficult to
describe with words.

There are many other morphological characteristics more or
less peculiar to the ericads and other northern species, and
the leaves of such species as *L. procumbens, O. microcarpus,
P. coerulea,* and *R. lapponicum, Saxifraga aizoon,* and *Saxifraga tricuspidata,* all arctic species, make them easy to
identify on sight. Similarly, the boreal species such as
Linnaea borealis and the *Pyrola* species make them among the
best-known of the plants of the southern boreal regions because
they are easy to identify and are well known by sight.

It seems evident that all of these adaptations are the result of evolutionary development that produced leaf structures
with peculiar capabilities for serving two main purposes--they
resist physical damage from high winds and other harsh climatic
forces so obviously part of the northern environment, and,
equally important, they reduce loss of water by transpiration,
this being of very great importance in regions where soil
water supplies usually are minimal and where plant roots are
often still encased in ice when leaves are beginning to photosynthesize in spring, a process in which leaf stomata must be
open and respiration in the leaves under way. The latter processes require open stomata, which then permit an unavoidable
loss of water from the leaves by evaporation. This water loss
must be made up, or the leaf will become wilted, but whatever
can be done to reduce water loss as much as possible is also
helpful. This must be one of the purposes of the shiny waxy
coating on the leaves and, in certain species, the undercoat
of thick tomentum that keeps air movement in and out of stomata at a minimum. Leaves lacking tomentum on the underside
usually have revolute margins and a thick layering of waxlike
material, often shocking white in aspect, on the underside of
the leaf, evidently also designed to reduce transpiration and
water loss. This is of particular importance in early spring
when the leaves are beginning to photosynthesize and respire
in the warm sunlight of the long days in June when roots are
still solidly frozen in the soil of the arctic regions.

The evergreen leaf, it should be mentioned, is capable of
beginning photosynthetic activity early in spring, taking advantage of as many days as possible in which temperatures permit growth. This has long been considered to be the obvious
advantage of evergreenness in northern plants, growing as they

Fig. 1. *Surface of the so-called wintergreen or evergreen (semievergreen) L. groenlandicum leaf.*

do where the warm season is short and cool. Some of the species, such as *L. groenlandicum* and *C. calyculata,* do not have leaves that are truly evergreen but rather are what is known as wintergreen, or semievergreen (Fig. 1). In this form of leaf adaptation, the leaves remain on the plant for a year or two following the summer they are produced, and the supposition is that these leaves, like those that are truly evergreen, permit the plant to begin photosynthesis as soon in spring as the daytime temperatures rise and snow melts sufficiently to expose the plants to adequate warmth and sunlight.

The coniferous trees that inhabit the conifer swamps and the bogs of the Great Lakes region, and that dominate the vegetation of the spruce forest in the circumboreal regions, are also revealing of the origins of characteristic leaves of northern plants, in this case the highly cutinized needlelike leaves of some of the northern plant species. The origins of the evergreen coniferous trees also demonstrate the principle that species need not have evolved in the region where they are now found; we have seen this to be the case with the Ericaceae, which are believed to have had their origin in southeastern Asia and to have migrated from there, evolving as they moved, northward into Siberia and from there east and west across the globe. Other species of the Ericaceae, of course, went in other directions, and ericads are now found in the southern as well as the northern hemisphere.

So it is with the northern evergreen conifers. At the present time, the largest number and greatest abundance of coniferous trees are found in middle and low latitudes, especially in southeast Asia and Australasia, in this respect resembling the Ericaceae. Since the evergreen needle leaf is also found in abundance in the trees of lower latitudes in Europe and the Mediterranean region, perhaps it originated somewhere in that general part of the world, where it represents, interesting enough, an adaptive response to minimal seasonal changes in climate and where extreme lack of water and cold temperatures do not occur.

In China, too, as well as Formosa and the subtropics in general from the Philippines to New Caledonia, there are conifers with needles closely resembling those of the trees of northern regions. The species of the southern latitudes are much more numerous than those of the north. In the boreal forests of the northern hemisphere, there are only the species of *Picea* and *Pinus,* of which only two each are very common in North America, along with *Abies,* with one species that does not range very far north or into western North America, and with *Larix,* the tamarack, interesting because it is a species that ranges far north, as far as any of the spruces, but which is a deciduous needle leaf conifer (Fig. 2), losing its needles every fall in a golden avalanche of surprising brilliance. The species of the northern forests make up in vast numbers what they lack in variety of species, however, and the dark coniferous forests of North America, made up of *Picea mariana,* black spruce, *Picea glauca,* white spruce, *Abies balsamea,* balsam fir, and *Pinus banksiana,* jack pine, are familiar to all who have traveled northward into Canada or Alaska or who are acquainted with the writing of Jack London and other bards of the far north. The firs, spruces, and larches dominate the northern forests around the globe in the far north and to high elevations in the mountain ranges of the middle latitudes--the Rockies, the Appalachians, and the Himalayas.

It is possible that this kind of foliage is an adaptation to drought, but it is also at least not a serious disadvantage in other environments, as can be seen by the fact that *A. balsamea* and other needle leaf species throughout the world are found where neither drought nor severe cold occurs. Douglas fir (*Pseudotsuga menziesii*), for example, is a common tree of wet temperate forests in northwestern North America and does not range as far north as southern Alaska. It is, in fact, intolerant of cold arid conditions, more so than many boreal deciduous species. Moreover, to complicate matters, some other

Fig. 2. Needles of L. laricina, a deciduous needleleaf conifer.

needle leaf species in various parts of the world are actually intolerant of arid conditions.

Another example might be that of jack pine, a species that is thought of as colonizing dry sites with poor sandy soils in the Great Lakes region. It is also found, however, in bogs, often springing up in considerable numbers in a habitat that ordinarily is thought to be the exclusive province of black spruce and tamarack. On such sites, there is obviously no advantage served by the lowered rates of transpiration supposedly conferred by needle leaves since water is in abundant supply; just as obvious, however, is the fact that the needle leaves are here no disadvantage. They simply appear to have no special adaptive significance whatsoever.

It is thus apparent that no general rules can be drawn from the xeromorphy of the evergreen needle leaf. The different species bearing the needles of this type appear to have a wide range of environmental tolerance--or perhaps one could say preference--for conditions from wet to arid, and in this respect are no different from deciduous broad-leaved plant species.

Appearances are thus deceptive. To return briefly to the matter of the ericoid leaf, it must be said in conclusion that there is no final evidence yet available that the small, shiny, tough, evergreen leaves of the members of the Ericaceae family are a particular adaptation to the environment in which the species are found growing today. It merely appears that this must be so, but this view is derived from inference and not from demonstrated fact. These adaptations undoubtedly contribute in some way to the survival of the plants, since the plants do, indeed, survive in cold harsh environments, but perhaps these characteristics evolved earlier in an altogether different environment from that in which the species are now found. The characteristics may have had pronounced survival value in the former environment, but they may be of indifferent significance at present.

In the case of the arctic ericads, as in that of the evergreen needle leaf trees, we must keep in mind the possibility that they survive where they do today despite, not because of, their distinctive morphological characteristics. This may, in fact, be the case with *L. groenlandicum* and *C. calyculata* in the bogs of the Great Lakes region. Their adaptations may be for cold, dry, upland sites farther north, and they survive in the bogs at the south edge of their range because they have no real competition from any other species for such wet ombrotrophic sites. In fact, a study by Monk (1966) has shown that in the southeastern United States, the percentage of evergreen species with tough leathery leaves increases on dry infertile sites, with deciduous species predominating on mesic sites with rich soils. Monk concludes that the evergreens conserve resources better than deciduous species and thus are better able

to survive on nutrient-poor sites. This factor may be more involved in survival than the fact that the leaves are tough and
leathery.

The same conclusion may apply to the wintergreen *Ledum* and
Chamaedaphne in bogs of the Great Lakes region; it is not so
much that the leaves are leathery and resistant to rapid transpiration as it is that they conserve nutrients, which are always in short supply on the ombrotrophic sites. There is, in
fact, usually ample moisture in the bogs, and so transpiration
losses should be of no significance since water can be absorbed
in unlimited quantities at any time. On the other hand, there
are nutrient deficiencies in bogs, and these may give the
wintergreen ericads the competitive advantage required for them
to be the dominant species in the bog communities.

At this point it should be apparent that a number of possible alternative explanations have thus been developed to explain the characteristic structure of the ericoid leaf. It is
the development of these differing views that will be explored
in the next few chapters.

14   Acidity, Minerals, and Sclerophylly

In swamps and bogs, acidity of the water is often intense, indicating that organic acids are present and probably some inorganic acids as well. The soil moisture thus is not pure water but contains a wide variety of other compounds. If these entered a plant unhindered, toxic amounts would soon accumulate. Plants, as a consequence, have developed structures and physiological mechanisms that prevent the root tissues from indiscriminately sweeping up dissolved materials in the soil water. Under conditions in which there is a high concentration of solutes in the soil water, the amount of nutrients and other compounds accumulating in leaves and stems of plants is often much less than would be expected considering the amount of soil water absorbed by roots and transpired by leaves. There is obviously some method by which a root screens out at least a large proportion of these materials from the water absorbed. Not all solutes can be excluded, however, particularly when the concentrations are high, and there are limits to the concentration of solutes that any plant can tolerate without developing toxicity symptoms. There is also the so-called osmotic effect, in which the soil solution is so concentrated that water itself resists absorption by roots. Existence of these conditions in varying degrees of intensity long ago led plants that grow in environments of this type to evolve structures that reduce the rate of water loss. Such structures include the well-known xerophytic morphological characteristics of desert plants, which evidently are also useful adaptations to the cold dry environments of arctic regions, or are at least not a handicap. The desert plants apparently are so adapted because water is in short supply, although in deserts there may also be high concentrations of alkali salts in soil water. Looked at in a somewhat different way, water supplies may also be difficult of access even in wet bogs and swamps. These sites are usually wet, but the water frequently is very cold, and roots are apt to be unable to absorb moisture rapidly because of these low temperatures (Dalton and Gardner, 1978), a situation similar to the conditions existing in soils where alkali salts are present.

In any case, low temperatures frequently prevail, in spring and fall as well as in winter, and it seems reasonable to conclude that xerophytic adaptations have a competitive, and hence selective, advantage in cold habitats; whether plants evolved these characteristics as a result of adaptation to bog conditions, or whether they are coincidentally able to survive in bogs is still an open question.

It is obvious, however, that *V. vitis-idaea* and *E. nigrum* can survive both on very dry sandy uplands and in wet swamps and bogs. This is true also of a wide range of other species, including trees such as spruce, jack pine, and a rather large group of other species with what is termed a bimodal distribution, i.e., species that are found in both wet and dry but not intermediate habitats. Among species found in abundance in boreal forest communities in northern Wisconsin and Michigan, Maycock and Curtis (1960) found that the following were bimodal: *G. procumbens, L. groenlandicum, V. angustifolium, V. myrtilloides, Polygala paucifolia, Rubus pubescens,* as well as *Acer rubrum* and *Betula papyrifera,* although the latter two species were less so than the others. It is perhaps particularly interesting that jack pine, which is usually considered a tree adapted to dry sandy uplands, can be seen pioneering bog habitats wherever nearby sources of jack pine seed have been available. Thus, in northern Wisconsin, in such sandy regions as the Northern Highland State Forest, jack pine saplings can occasionally be found growing in an open bog, a somewhat surprising sight for students who have been taught that jack pine is a species of dry sandy flats. Xerophytic adaptations of the jack pine have obviously not prevented the tree from growing in bogs, but they probably grow there slowly and with greater chance for mortality than spruce, for example. It is unlikely that they will persist very long after spruce or other bog-adapted species reach a height at which the jack pine saplings or seedlings are in deep shade, for they are successful only in places where bright sunlight reaches the branches. On occasion other species of pine also grow in bogs.

It has been found that increased sclerophylly is a phenotypic response to low availability of certain nutrient mineral elements (Loveless, 1961), and so it is perhaps reasonable to infer that genotypic sclerophylly associated with xerophytism is the consequence of evolutionary selection for morphological characteristcs that protect plants from nutrient shortages. Permanent enhancement of xerophytic traits, through their incorporation into the genotype as found in pines, spruce, as well as the Ericaceae, will result from selection for these characteristics that lend the members of these groups a competitive advantage in bogs and marshlands. It is also reasonable to expect that there will be eventual development of ecotypes suited to bog habitats on the one hand and to dry upland sites on the other. This is, then, at least one post hoc explanation of sclerophylly, as well as of bimodal distributions in species, that should be considered. Another, of course, is simply that the bog ericads of northern regions are the product of evolution in higher latitudes, where they acquired these characteristics that confer also an ability to survive in bog habitats.

The bogs of Minnesota, Wisconsin, and Michigan, as well as of New England, are at the southern edge of the range for most of the species involved. Many bog ericads found in the northern United States have a much more extensive range farther north, and if it is assumed that species are best adapted to conditions in the central portions of their range, it can be inferred that bog habitats for these species are a special niche inhabitable at the southern edge of their range; for the most part they are upland or at least mesic species northward. If we look at the adaptations required for upland species in the northern regions, we find that xeromorphy is one of them. The evolutionary means by which xeromorphy became part of the genotypic heritage of northern species is, however, not clear, and all inferences must be provisional at this stage. Evolution is not always, perhaps not ever, a straight-line affair, and characteristics needed for survival in one region may well fit a plant for life in habitats that seem unusual for it in other regions. The bimodality in habitat preference shown by some species--not all of which possess xeromorphic leaves--is also an interesting evolutionary occurrence, for it seems rather incongruous that a species could undergo selection for characteristics that adapt it more effectively to both wet and dry habitats than for the habitats between these extremes. It is perhaps possible that, in the process of evolving characteristics permitting effective survival in wet areas, the plants also acquired characteristics fitting them for survival in dry areas; we have offered some explanations (see above) for why this might have been the case. And, too, in the case of the bog ericads, adaptations making the leaves of the plants resistant to wind-driven snow abrasion may also have yielded adaptations to bog habitats at the southern edge of their range where they benefit from the fact that tough leaves are unpalatable to grazing insects and animals.

There are thus alternative explanations that can be invoked to explain the apparently ambiguous environmental conditions under which bog species can be found throughout their entire range. Moreover, the plant species that appear to be inhabiting dichotomous environments may actually be diverging in evolutionary development; they may be developing distinct ecotypes each adapted to quite different habitats. The bimodality may represent the beginning of an advance toward development

of two species from one--two species that will be still related
morphologically. One species, however, will eventually become
an inhabitant of uplands, the other of bogs and lowlands. It
would be expected that progressively diverging morphological
and physiological characteristics would, at some point in the
future, result in development of two distinct species, such as,
for example, *L. groenlandicum* and *L. decumbens*.

As Stebbins (1974) points out, specialized xeromorphic
adaptations are, however, not in any case an evolutionary cul-
de-sac, but represent instead a high degree of specialization
to factors of the environment, and species possessing them can
continue adaptive radiation, as it is termed, to adjust better
to one habitat or another existing within the range of the species. It is possible, too, for the species to adapt to other
regions into which it is possible for it to migrate.

In terms of evolution, xerophytic adaptations are reversi-
ble, requiring only mutations that result in the loss of certain morphological or physiological traits, which, in Stebbin's
words, "inactivate the pathways leading to the elaboration of
complex structures or the synthesis of special chemical compounds." There may also be "increases in vigor and fecundity,
which can be elicited with relative ease by selection for·mu-
tations that promote greater meristematic activity."

In the Ericaceae, for example, the genus *Arctostaphylos*
appears to be derived phylogenetically from mesophyllic *Arbutus*-like ancient stock. Some of the present-day species of
Arctostaphylos are more xeric in adaptations, with thick sclerophyllous leaves, small flowers, and coalescence of carpels to
form a single hard stone, while other species are more mesic,
with broad, thin leaves, and other adaptations to mesic conditions. *Arctostaphylos uva-ursi* has fairly small leathery leaves
but each plant has many of them as a consequence of its long
creeping stems that grow and produce many leaves rapidly, with
the result that the leaf surface area of each plant is as large
as that of many plants that would, at first glance, appear to
be more mesophytic in adaptations. This seems to be a reversion
toward mesophytism of a species that at one time was more xerophytic than it is at the present time. *Arctostaphylos (Arctous)
alpina* may have done essentially the same thing; it has not,
however, developed the long, prostrate, creeping stems typical
of *A. uva-ursi*.

MINERALS AND SCLEROPHYLLY

While low summer temperatures and the desiccating influences
of the winter environment upon leaves have often been invoked
as factors to which xeromorphy and sclerophylly are an adapta-

tion, little attention is given other possible environmental conditions that could lead to virtually identical morphological characteristics. The mineral nutrient content of the peat soils of bogs is one such possibility. Comparisons of data on the mineral nutrient content of the peat in bogs with that of the humus layer in forest soils is difficult because of the variations in methods employed by those who have conducted the few studies available. There are studies, for example, of boreal forest soils that give the content of nitrogen, phosphorus, potassium, and other nutrient elements, but these values are given in kilograms per hectare in one study, milliequivalents per 100 g in another, and parts per million in a third. This renders comparison difficult, not only because of the difficulty of converting the values from one to another but because of the different techniques of analysis employed and the possibility that they yield somewhat different results. In one study, however, parts per million have been employed, and the data, although scanty, are used here in comparison with other values obtained in a study of the mineral contents of foliage in native plants (Gerloff et al., 1964, 1966) and of representative soils (Damman, 1971) shown in Tables I and II.

In comparing the data of Tables I and II, it is seen that both nitrogen and phosphorus in the Ericaceae are at levels a third below what is generally considered adequate for growth of most species. Average levels, when all bog plants are considered together, are perfectly adequate, but this is the result of higher than average levels in several species, including those in the genera *Alnus, Betula, Dryopteris,* and *Smilacina,* none of which are ericaceous. The boreal group averages somewhat below the level of adequacy, the result of the fact that *Picea glauca, Abies balsamea,* and *Rubus* have low levels of both nitrogen and phosphorus. As Gerloff et al. (1964, 1966) point out in their discussion, other species in the boreal forest group are amply supplied with both nutrients, with *Aster macrophyllus,* for example, possessing 1.90% nitrogen and *Athyrium filix-femina* 0.40% phosphorus. *Aster macrophyllus* and *Hepatica* have higher than adequate amounts of potassium, and *Corylus cornuta* and *P. glauca* lower than adequate by relatively large amounts.

Perhaps most interesting is the content of manganese. As Gerloff et al. (1966) indicated (Table III), variation in content of manganese is one of the most striking features of native plant species. It is apparent that individual species have inherent characteristics that render them capable of either excluding or of accumulating manganese:

Table I. Mineral Content of Leaves: Comparison of Average Mineral Content of Leaves (Plus Stems) of Specimens of Cornaceae, Corylaceae, and Ericaceae[a] and Similar Comparisons between Communities[b]

Group	Percent				Parts per million[c]			
	N	P	Ca	K	Fe	Mn	Cu	Zn
Cornaceae	1.49	0.26	1.12	0.89	160	74	4.3	29.7
Corylaceae	1.87	0.15	0.93	0.64	177	1062	6.6	65.8
Ericaceae	1.02	0.12	0.51	0.46	181	984	5.2	30.3
No. mesic forest	1.79	0.26	1.21	3.81	217	391	5.5	99.2
Boreal forest	1.36	0.24	0.86	1.91	149	398	5.1	42.8
Northern bog	1.66	0.27	0.54	0.94	154	926	5.9	47.1
Adequate level[d]	1.50	0.20	0.50	1.00	100	50	6.0	20.0

[a]Numbers of specimens by species in each group: Cornaceae--Cornus canadensis, 1; C. racemosa, 3; C. rugosa, 1; C. stolonifera, 1. Corylaceae--Alnus rugosa, 1; Betula nigra,1; B. pumila, 1; Corylus americana, 2; C. cornuta, 1; Ostrya virginiana, 2. Ericaceae--A. glaucophylla, 1; C. calyculata, 2; Epigaea repens,1; G. hispidula,1; G. procumbens,1; K. polifolia, 2; L. groenlandicum,2; V. angustifolium, 2; V. myrtilloides,1; V. oxycoccus, 1. Northern mesic forest-- one specimen each of Aralia nudicaulis, Aster macrophyllus, Clintonia borealis, Gymnocarpium dryopteris, Polygonatum pubescens, Smilacina racemosa, Streptopus roseus, Uvularia grandiflora, Taxus canadensis, Trillium grandiflora, Tsuga canadensis, Viola pubescens. Boreal forest--one specimen each of Abies balsamea, Apocynum androsaemifolium, Aster macrophyllus, Athyrium filix- femina, Corylus cornuta, Diervilla lonicera, Fragaria virginiana, Hepatica americana, Pteridium aquilinum, Rubus strigosus, and two specimens of Picea glauca. Northern bog--one specimen each of Alnus rugosa, Betula pumila, C. calyculata, Cornus canadensis, Dryopteris cristata, G. his- pidula, K. polifolia, Larix laricina, L. groenlandicum, Smilacina trifolia, V. myrtilloides, V. oxycoccus.

(Table I continued)

Values for individual species do not as a rule vary greatly from averages for the group, although there are exceptions (some of which are discussed in the text), and the values here are used to demonstrate a trend rather than to define the characteristics of individual species.

[b] Species selected were those commonly found in the indicated communities in northern Wisconsin. Data from Gerloff et al. (1964, 1966).

[c] Percentage of oven dry weight and parts per million of oven dry weight, respectively.

[d] These are levels of the indicated nutrients that are generally considered to be adequate for normal nutrition and growth. The data are from Epstein (1972).

Table II. Mineral Content of Soil: Comparison of Average
Mineral Content of Upper Levels of Soil in Various Northern
Community Types[a]

| Forest type | Mineral nutrient[b] | | | | |
	N (NH$_4$)	K	Ca	P	Fe
Balsam	103	878	1162	87.3	0.43
Black spruce	79	705	639	68.9	0.67
Kalmia heath	36	335	739	44.0	0.50

[a]*Values are averages of three samples in litter layer and three in humus layer. Data are from Damman (1971).* In the case of P, the adequate level for most crop plants is considered to be 50-60 ppm in the soil.*

[b]*Values in ppm dry weight. For Fe, values in percentage dry weight.*

species collected from environments which would not be expected to be particularly high in manganese vary tremendously in manganese content and...some species from these environments have extremely high manganese contents. Furthermore, some species from environments which are very high in manganese have relatively low manganese contents. These are very interesting examples of selective uptake and exclusion of an element...

The very high manganese content of the plant tissue samples obtained from bog plants indicates that the high manganese availability is one of the primary features making the bog environment unusual from a nutritional standpoint. In fact the concentrations in the tissue are so high that tolerance to this element could well be a factor determining which plants are able to survive the bog environment.

Even in communities other than the open bog, there were a number of species with very high concentrations of manganese. In addition, there was a tremendous range in manganese concentration in samples from the sample site. Since native plants so frequently occur in strongly acid soils, it would seem well worthwhile carrying out nutrient experiments on the manganese uptake and tolerance of some of the native species analyzed in this study.

Table III.   Manganese Content of Plant Species Collected from the Same Site in Wisconsin[a]

Date sampled	Sample site	Plant species	Mn content (ppm)[b]
8-07-58	No. 6, pH	Aralia racemosa	128
6-18-59	5.1	Cornus racemosa	71
6-18-59		Corylus americana	1487
8-06-58		Helianthus strumosus	258
6-18-59		Prunus serotina	585
6-18-59		Quercus alba	1374
6-18-59		Quercus rubra	1736
6-18-59		Rubus allegheniensis	932
7-29-61	No. 67, pH	Carya ovata	727
7-29-61	6.5	Morus alba	53
7-29-61		Pyrus ioensis	20
7-29-61		Quercus rubra, Var. borealis	849
7-12-59	53-a, pH	Chamaedaphne calyculata	772
7-12-59	4.0	Cornus canadensis	149
7-12-59		Dryopteris cristata	426
7-12-59		Gaultheria hispidula	2999
7-11-59		Kalmia polifolia	116
7-22-61		Larix laricina	310
7-11-59		Ledum groenlandicum	888
7-12-59		Smilacina trifolia	1288
7-12-59		Vaccinium myrtilloides	2177
7-12-59		Vaccinium Oxyococcus	1340

[a] From Gerloff et al. (1966).
[b] Parts per million dry weight.

It was also pointed out by Gerloff et al. (1966) that other factors influence the mineral content of plants, including site conditions, soil pH, and the age of plant tissues, but by far the most important factor is the capability of the species under consideration for excluding or accumulating the various mineral nutrient elements. Potassium and zinc were the most important elements showing wide variation in concentration in plant tissues. The potassium content of some species was extremely high, more than 6%, and this was characteristically the case in all of the different samples taken of the same species wherever it may have been found growing.

Selective uptake of zinc by Nemopanthus mucronata is also unusual. The zinc content of leaves and stems of N. mucronata ranged from 327-711 ppm, compared to samples from other

species growing at the same sites, which showed less than
50 ppm zinc content. Other species also demonstrated selective
uptake of zinc, but not to the same extent, and these include
Populus deltoides and *Betula nigra*. Another genus reported to
show the same ability is *Ilex*.

The relative availability of the essential elements may
very well be a factor determining the distribution of native
plants, Gerloff *et al.* point out, but it is difficult to determine whether a particular element is important in a given
situation. Moreover, there is still great uncertainty over the
particular metabolic factors involved in poor growth of crop
plants on very acid soils, and so interpretations of the effects
of acidity upon native bog plant species must be put forth with
caution. Gerloff *et al.* (1966) summarize their study:

> In comparison with crop plants, the concentrations of the
> essential elements in native plants are low. The manganese
> content is a general exception to this, and there are many
> exceptions involving individual species...
> Nitrogen and phosphorus supplies are the nutritional fac-
> tors most often considered limiting factors for plant growth
> in soils. A striking feature of the native plant analyses
> is the low nitrogen content of many samples. Only in about
> 6 percent of the samples was the nitrogen content within
> the range of 2.2 to 2.7 percent which has been stated as
> optimal.... Individual samples were low in phosphorus, be-
> low 0.1 percent. Nevertheless, there were more indications
> that nitrogen supply was likely to be limiting growth than
> was the phosphorus supply, and in many cases nitrogen actual-
> ly seemed to be a growth limiting factor....
> The concentrations of the bases, calcium, magnesium, and
> potassium were not as low as might be expected in view of
> the low pH of the soils from which many of the samples were
> collected. In fact, the calcium contents of the bog samples
> was surprisingly high even thought the pH was approximately
> 4.0.
> There were several significant features of the analyses
> for trace elements. For example, the molybdenum and the
> copper contents of many samples were not only low but below
> the contents considered minimal for optimum crop plant
> growth. The copper contents in a number of cases were even
> below the concentrations considered adequate for animal
> nutrition. On the basis of these analyses, further consider-
> ation of the possibility that copper or molybdenum supplies
> might be limiting the growth of some species in particular
> environments seems justified.

It is possible from this discussion to infer that a suggestive
coincidence exists between the xeromorphy and sclerophylly of

the bog plant species and nutrient contents of the tissues, but at present it is not possible to extrapolate much beyond this statement. The subject is one that we return to in subsequent pages, but before doing so there are other factors that bear on the xeromorphic and sclerophyllous characteristics of the bog plants, which are discussed next.

15   More on Sclerophylly and Xeromorphy

Sclerophyllous evergreen leaves are characteristic of many of the plant species that make up the arctic and alpine flora as well as the common flora of the bogs in the northern parts of the United States and the bordering regions of Canada. The evergreen characteristic is evidently an adaptation to particular conditions in bogs and marshes, as well as in arctic and alpine habitats. Another characteristic of the leaves of these species is as ubiquitous as evergreenness and is commonly associated with it. This is sclerophylly, mentioned before as a trait often associated with xerophytic species--a term employed to species with tough, waxy, leathery leaves common to many bog plants as well as to those of arctic, alpine, and desert regions.

It was noted long ago that xeromorphy is characteristic of plants of dry regions, and it has also been long realized that species with xeromorphic characteristics are found in great abundance in regions of high latitude and high altitude. For example, Shaw (1909) wrote of the Selkirk Mountains in western North America:

> In ascending beyond about 1,600 meters, the balsams (*Abies lasiocarpa*) and spruces (*Picea Engelmanii*) which are the dominant species of the sub-alpine forest, begin to appear in little groups separated by shrubs (*Azaleastrum albiflorum, Vaccinium membranaceum*). Higher up this tendency becomes more pronounced; the intervals are occupied by heather plants (*Cassiope, Phyllodoce*) till finally at 2,000 meters, more or less, one emerges into open alpine fields dotted with scattered clumps of spire-shaped trees.

Thus it is shown that at higher altitudes the evergreen needle leaf coniferous trees dominate up to treeline, and beyond this the species of plants in the community covering the ground--a sclerophyllous and xeromorphic aggregation--include *Cassiope* and *Phyllodoce,* both arctic and alpine in habitat preference, along with a number of other lesser known species with tough, leathery, often evergreen leaves.

124

A few years after publication of Shaw's discussion, Gates
(1914) reported on a detailed study of some of the common evergreen ericads found growing in Michigan. Gates' treatise can
justifiably be regarded as an early classic. Although his description of the causes of sclerophylly contains some assumptions
that today cannot be regarded as entirely tenable, he asked the
important questions. His conclusions establish a framework
that much subsequent research has confirmed. Moreover, 1914
was evidently a time in which space in botanical journals was
unlimited, and writers were allowed to discourse at length on
topics of interest. As with much ecological writing of that
day, Gates treats the subject as one commanding literary skill
as well as enough descriptive detail to furnish readers with a
full understanding of the implications of the topics under discussion. Gates began:

> Of late years some considerable attention has been drawn
> toward the apparently anomalous conditions of several plants
> with obvious xeromorphic modifications living in bogs with
> an apparently unlimited water supply. Many explanations of
> this apparent anomaly have been attempted. It was with a
> desire to obtain further knowledge upon the question that
> the author entered upon this piece of research work in the
> Botanical Department of the University of Michigan in the
> fall of 1910.... Although a living plant is always the ex-
> pression of the integration of environmental and hereditary
> factors, the most important single factor in the environment
> is the physiological water supply. The modifications of
> plant structure which lead to the conservation of water are
> termed *xerophytic adaptations* or *xerophytic reactions*. The
> presence of xerophytic adaptations does not necessarily
> predicate that the amount of water used by the plant is
> relatively small, but that the ratio of the amount used to
> that which the plant obtains tends to become less than unity.
> Some so-called xerophytic plants use as much or more than
> ordinary mesophytic plants, as [is] the case with *Larix
> decidua*. They are xerophytic, however, because they cannot
> absorb a large amount of water in proportion to that which
> they could otherwise transpire.
>   This is particularly true in the summer, when plants have
> their transpiring organs. The loss of leaves during winter
> is quite rightly regarded as a xerophytic adaptation. The
> bog ericads which were investigated, however, retain their
> leaves during the winter. This opens at once the question,
> are these plants xerophytes because of their summer or their
> winter environment? As it may be safely assumed that the
> evergreen habit is hereditary in these ericads, the reaction
> to the environment necessitates the xerophylly.

It would seem at first glance that plants which grow in
bogs, where there is an obvious physical water supply, would
not be restricted in its use, but the various xerophytic
adaptations argue for the conservation of water in the plant.
This fact led investigators to ask why the plants could not
make full use of the water present. Many answers have been
attempted, and it seems quite likely that the true answer
is a combination of the different reasons rather than any
one. The problem presents an obvious result obtained from
a bewildering mass of causes, whose interactions are not
yet known.

Gates summarizes the reasons for limited ability on the
part of the plants to absorb water as follows: poorly developed
shallow root systems, low oxygen content of the soil water as
a result of low aeration, root excretions of an evidently toxic
nature, other toxins formed in bog peat, the absence of the
mycorrhizal fungi required by roots of some species, low temperature of the soil water, and high acidity of the soil, although the latter was not responsible for the poor growth of
all species:

> Much stress cannot be laid upon the acidity of the soil,
> as has been done by Schimper, because of the findings of
> later investigations....That acidity is a necessary factor
> in the soil for the growth of trailing arbutus (*Epigaea re-
> pens*) and of the blueberry (*Vaccinium corymbosum*) was most
> admirably demonstrated by Coville...who found that poor
> aeration was usually the real cause for poor growth and not
> acidity. Acidity, however, may be inimical to certain crops.
> Sampson and Allen...found that, as a rule, some of the common
> acids accelerate transpiration, and that weak solutions often
> produce as marked effects as strong ones.

Three evergreen ericad species, all with tough, leathery,
sclerophyllous leaves, were studied by Gates, who describes
their condition during the seasons in these words:

> During the winter the leaves of all of the evergreen
> ericads--*Chamaedaphne calyculata, Andromeda glaucophylla,*
> and *Vaccinium macrocarpon*--are upright, a position in which
> they receive a minimum of direct sunlight. The leaves are
> dark red or brown in color. With the coming of spring the
> old leaves curve outward or downward, resulting in an in-
> crease of the direct sunlight which they receive. At the
> same time the leaves become dark green in color. The season
> growth of young leaves takes place soon after flowering. At
> first the young leaves are upright, but in a short time they
> bend outward. As soon as the young leaves are fully develop
> ed, the old leaves gradually drop off. In the case of *Vac-*

cinium macrocarpon, however, some of the leaves may be retained for two or three years. With the coming of the next
winter, the leaves of these plants gradually bend up into
an upright position and their color changes from bright
green through dark green to shades of red and brown. The
color changes begin at the margins of the leaves and work
toward the midribs. In a mild winter, the basal portion
of midribs of *Chamaedaphne* may remain green the entire winter. *Vaccinium* and *Andromeda* are usually protected by a
covering of snow, but they exhibit these changes of position
and color irrespective of that fact.

In the course of his study, Gates compared the three sclerophyllous evergreen species with deciduous trees, shrubs, and
herbaceous plants, described as follows:

> The seasonal history of the herbaceous bog plants follows
> two general lines: the plant which has developed during the
> growing season may die down completely before winter, leav-
> ing seeds to reproduce it the following year, or it may die
> down to the ground and be vegetatively reproduced the follow-
> ing year from underground stems, bulbs, rootstocks, or buds.
> Any of these ways is an absolute xerophytic adaptation on
> account of winter conditions, but does not interfere with
> summer development.

The study by Gates was exhaustive and detailed, as thorough
as could be accomplished with the relatively simple and un-
sophisticated techniques available at that time. Those interested in the observations made by Gates must seek his paper,
published in the *Botanical Gazette* in 1914, for our interest
here is limited to the conclusions to be derived from the comparisons made between the sclerophylls and the species with
other kinds of leaves.

His studies of the microscopic structure of the leaves of
the sclerophylls led him to describe them in the following
terms:

> Although the external appearance of the leaves of various
> peat bog plants is very different, the general internal
> structure is more nearly similar, and that of the various
> ericads is still more alike. Several well marked xerophytic
> adaptations are present, notably the strongly cuticularized
> epidermis, absence of stomates on the upper surface, a well
> developed palisade layer one to three cells thick, frequent-
> ly sunken stomates, and coatings of wax, bloom, hair, or
> scales. Mechanical tissue is present and accounts for the
> suppression of the ordinary symptoms of wilting. Usually
> the leaves are at least slightly revolute, those of *Andro-
> meda* and *Salix candida* strongly so. The leaves are usually

dark green in color, but often reddish at the beginning and
close of the vegetative season. The abundant presence of
cutin in the evergreen ericads is an efficient xerophytic
adaptation against loss of water at all times, but especially in winter...

There is, Gates concludes, no such phenomenon in the northern freshwater bogs as that described as "physiological drought"
in which the plants, while growing in very moist conditions,
are deprived of water in summer because of factors that limit
their ability to absorb it. Gates measured the rate of transpiration in ericads from the peat bogs and found that there
was no restriction of transpiration such as would occur if the
plants were in an environment were "physiological drought"
would occur if such a thing existed.

It is the conditions in late fall, winter, and early spring,
said Gates, that may be the critical ones in making xeromorphy
of adaptive significance in the bog plant species. He cites
the response of the plants to the cold seasons as follows:

No experimentation was performed upon herbaceous plants
during the winter, for it is known how exceedingly small is
the amount of water loss from seeds, and as the vegetative
means of reproduction employed by other herbs are under-
ground and thoroughly protected from exposure, no comparison
could be made with the ericads which retain their plant body
subject to constant exposure throughout the winter.

The purpose of the winter experimentation, therefore, was
to obtain a knowledge of the transpiration of several of the
shrubs and trees, and compare that of the leaf-retaining
ericads with that of the deciduous shrubs under winter conditions outdoors and under laboratory conditions which simu-
lated the severest conditions which could obtain in nature
during the winter. Experimentation was carried on both
with the potted plants and with cuttings indoors and outdoors...

Consideration of these data clearly indicates that the
transpiration of these bog plants is very low in winter.
Furthermore, with scarcely an exception, the rate of water
loss is much greater (2-15 times) in the evergreen ericads
than in the leafless shrubs and trees. When the very much
more exposed position of the deciduous trees and most of
the deciduous shrubs is taken into account, the difference
in the rate of transpiration in nature is accentuated. The
mere position of the ericads near the ground serves to reduce water loss. This same relation holds among the ericads
themselves, namely, that the greater the rate of transpiration under given conditions, the more protected is the position in which the species grows. For example, *Chamaedaphne*

transpires at a lower rate than *Andromeda* and *Vaccinium;*
and *Chamadephne,* because of its higher growth, is more exposed...

To bring these points together, Gates summarizes his observations in the following words:

That the different ericads experimented with differed
among themselves in their transpiring ability with their
degree of protection from excessive evaporation during the
winter, and that *Chamaedaphne,* the least protected, transpires considerably more than the leafless shrubs and trees,
indicates both the effectiveness of the deciduous habit as
a xerophytic adaptation and the necessity of there being
other xerophytic modifications in the case of the ericads.
Added to this, the difficulty of absorbing water is apparent,
due, if for no other reason, to the colder temperature of
the bog soil in winter, and the necessity of xerophytic
modification. The presence of so many of the usual xerophytic modifications in these peat bog ericads is noteworthy.
The thick cuticle, dense palisade layer, more or less sunk-
en stomates, hairs, scales, bloom, and waxey coverings,
resin, and the upright positions of the leaves are all indications of this xerophylly, this necessity of keeping the
transpiration within the limits of absorption and conduction.

In short, there are advantages to the sclerophyllous evergreen leaf, but disadvantages, too, and xeromorphic adaptations are needed to counteract the impact of the disadvantages
inherent in the evergreen habit. Gates summarizes as follows:
"The xeromorphy of these plants is real xerophyty, occasioned
fundamentally by the necessity of protection when exposed to
winter conditions and used advantageously by these plants during the summer."

There are thus morphological similarities between desert
plants and many plants found in arctic and alpine environments.
Why this should be so is not entirely clear. One favored explanation, as we have seen, is that the xerophytes originated
in early Tertiary time or before, as a consequence of their
evolutionary adaptation to cold and dry habitats. Some of
these xerophytic species, or their descendants, have since that
time become adapted to present-day arctic and alpine conditions,
the result of having been forced to move into these areas by
the great continental glaciations or other fortuitous events of
geological history. Other explanations seem almost if not
equally plausible, and whatever thesis may be put forward one
fact remains: the plants survived because the xerophytic morphology was effective in ensuring survival in arctic and desert
environments as well as the bogs and marshlands of the Great
Lakes region.

SCLEROPHYLLY AND XEROMORPHY

In his classic work entitled (in English) "Physiological
Plant Geography" Schimper (1898) noted that there seemed to be
an interesting discrepancy in the leaf structure of bog plant
species. The leaves were sclerophyllous and hence xeromorphic,
yet the plants grew in sites where water was in ample supply.

As we have seen, Gates (1914) concluded that both summer
and winter conditions were such that a sclerophyllous xeromorphic structure was required in the evergreen ericads. The
idea that the xeromorphic bog plants are adapted to conditions
in which physiological drought somehow is a factor affecting
growth has nevertheless retained some favor despite rejection
of the theory by Gates, and even today it has not been totally
discredited. It is held, for example, that the peat in bogs
is so cold, in spring particularly, that absorption of water
by roots is restricted, and hence leaf xeromorphy becomes a
necessity. There are also, as Gates affirmed, winter conditions under which transpiration occurs, however slowly, without sufficient absorption of significant amounts of water by
roots to replace that lost. These are explanations for the
existence of xeromorphic structures that seem intuitively to
be true as well as verifiable by observation and experiment.

As always, however, there are some anomalous instances in
which plants and environment tend to show that these conclusions
cannot be valid, or at least that they cannot be true in all
cases or in all environments. One such anomalous habitat was
one studied by Caughey (1945)--the bogs of the southern coastal
plains of the United States known as pocosins. Caughey wrote:

> The pocosins, or broad-leaved evergreen shrub bogs,
> constitute one of the most distinctive plant communities of
> the southeastern coastal plain. They occupy flat, poorly-
> drained areas where the soil is frequently water-logged for
> long periods of time, but where surface water seldom stands
> to a depth of more than a few inches, and then only for
> comparatively short periods. The water relations of the
> plants growing in pocosins present an interesting problem
> to the plant physiologist because structurally the leaves
> of many of the species resemble those of plants growing in
> a dry habitat rather than those of plants in wet places.
> The shrubs have simple, more or less elliptical leaves
> which are rather thick, leathery, and heavily cutinized.
> The leaf structure is of a type generally believed to have
> a low rate of transpiration, but there is never a lack of
> soil water except during severe summer droughts.

Caughey points out that Schimper's theory of physiological drought is based on the idea that absorption of water is hindered by humic acids and soluble salts released during decomposition of the organic matter. According to this notion, the sclerophyllous leaves prevent excessive water loss from the plants. This theory of physiological drought was generally accepted in Schimper's time, but early botanists continued to speculate as to the cause, suggesting, for example, that it was the result of periodic droughts, lack of oxygen in bog soils, or toxic compounds from incomplete decomposition of organic materials in soil deficient in oxygen.

The theory of physiological drought was developed to explain xeromorphy in the plants of bogs in cool climates, but it was also extended to the southern bogs or pocosins where, as Caughey points out, low soil temperature could not be a factor. Early ecologists, realizing this, believed that in pocosins the toxin theory perhaps applied, and that low soil oxygen also perhaps prevented good root growth. In such conditions the coriaceous leaves of the bog plants protect them from excessive water loss.

Soon, however, a few experiments eliminated the idea that the southern bog habitats were physiologically dry for any of these reasons--since they were not dry at all in terms of the transpiration rates maintained by the plants without noticeable wilting.

Caughey, in fact, found that transpiration in a pocosin was not notably different from that in upland forests. There was thus no evidence supporting the notion that coriaceous leaf structure in pocosin evergreens is an adaptation needed to slow down the rate of transpiration in the plants. The common pocosin species, such as those of *Clethra, Gordonia, Ilex,* and *Myrica,* all have transpiration rates at least as high as that found in white oak, eastern red oak, and tulip poplar. The species of *Gordonia* and *Ilex*, in fact, had higher rates than any of the forest species. It was evident that at least some plants with xeromorphic leaves commonly had high transpiration rates.

The coriaceous, xeromorphic structure of evergreen-leaved plants in the pocosins could not thus be explained as adaptations to unusual water relations in the southern bogs. Caughey wrote:

> It appears that these concepts have outlived their usefulness and could well be discarded. It will be possible to explain the physiology of the plants in our pocosins only after the accumulation of more experimental data, unhampered by traditional views.... The pocosin habitat is probably not physiologically dry so far as the pocosin

plants are concerned, and these plants are not xerophytes
in the sense of having low transpiration rates. No clear
explanation for their xeromorphic appearance can be offered.

Since it is obviously unlikely that adaptation to cold
soils such as those prevailing in northern regions in spring
and fall could account for the competitive success of plants
with evergreen sclerophyllous leaves in the southern pocosins,
what other factors might be involved? Efforts to answer this
question have revealed some other interesting and perhaps significant correlations between certain environmental factors
and the morphology of the leaves of the bog plant species.

Evergreen species survive where it is cheaper in terms of
energy expenditure to maintain leaves through the winter than
it is to grow them anew every spring. Only deciduous species
survive where it costs more to retain leaves through winter
than to grow a new set annually. This, however, is a broad
generalization that must be supported with more detailed correlations between plant morphology and habitat characteristics.
There are, it seems, other factors also involved--factors that
might very likely be missed by ecologists depending solely
upon field observation for the data from which to draw conclusion. Let us look at one such factor.

SCLEROPHYLLY AND NUTRIENTS

Investigations have largely discredited the concept of
physiological drought, but water uptake by bog plants may be
severely restricted under some conditions--particularly where
the soil is cold during a large part of the year. It seems,
as a consequence, that xeromorphic leaf structures may have
at least some limited survival value for bog plants on occasions
when the roots are cold or frozen and the plant is otherwise
in sunlight and warm. Despite the amount of study given to
the subject, however, questions concerning the adaptive advantage of xeromorphism in bog plant species remain unanswered
and the problem of why the same specialized type of leaf
should occur in plants growing in both dry and wet habitats
continues to resist the ingenuity of botanists.

A study by Loveless and Asprey (1957) of sclerophyllous
vegetation on limestone hills of Jamaica suggested that phosphate deficiency might be an important factor in sclerophylly.
Citing one of the basic principles of plant ecology that "it
is the most severe conditions of habitat rather than average
that mainly determine the characteristics of communities,"
Loveless (1961) concluded that phosphorus content shows "the
greatest relative variation between the low and high ends in

the range of sclerophylly...constitutes the factor that is in 'relative minimum' at the sclerophyllous end of the series."

Loveless concluded that the extreme soil factor, apart from dryness, is phosphate deficiency, and this may furnish the explanation for the presence of sclerophyllous vegetation in the area. The same association between sclerophylly and phosphate levels in soil has been noted in other regions. He added, moreover, that phosphate deficiency also characterizes organic soils in areas of high rainfall; phosphorus in organic combination is not readily available to plants. "In this context," Loveless added, "it is relevant to mention that Caughey (1945), after an intensive study of the water relations of shrubs characteristic of bogs, suggested that their sclerophyllous appearance might be determined partly by mineral deficiencies."

In a subsequent paper, Loveless (1962) presented supporting evidence for this hypothesis from North America, Africa, and India, putting forth the idea that sclerophyllous leaves are "the expression of a metabolism found in plants that can tolerate low levels of phosphate.... Phosphate deficiency, either alone or more usually associated with nitrogen deficiency, is characteristic of the soils, dry or wet, which carry sclerophyllous vegetation."

In reference particularly to the bog ericads, Loveless wrote:

> These conditions (i.e. acid soils in areas of high rainfall) constitute precisely the habitat of moorland and bog vegetation which includes, amongst other life forms, the characteristic *bog sclerophylls*. Thus it is reasonable to suggest that phosphate deficiency is the factor common to both dry and wet habitats which explains the presence of the same specialized leaf type in such apparently different habitats.

THE ERICOID LEAF

The sclerophyllous leaf of the ericads (Fig. 1) may be taken as the typical example of this distinctive form. It has rolled edges, which act as a kind of wall around the lower surface of the leaf. The latter usually bears a tomentum or a waxy surface or both, and the stomata are often in grooves or pits. This leaf structure, one senses intuitively, is designed to reduce water loss through transpiration; it is not surprising that plants of arid regions often possess leaves of this type. On the other hand, many ericads are confined to northern bogs or moors with moist organic soil, as we have seen, and thus the sclerophyllous leaf cannot be considered

Fig. 1. A typically sclerophyllous ericad leaf; this one
is K. polifolia.

an indication of the kind of climate to which the plant species
is adapted. Sclerophyllous evergreen foliage is not an infallible indication that the plant possesses adaptations that
render it drought resistant. This is seen to be the case also
when the transpiration rates of the northern bog plants are
measured; transpiration is often as rapid in plants with sclerophyllous leaves as in plants with mesomorphic leaf structures.

One of the first hypotheses to treat this paradoxical
morphological characteristic was that of Pearsall and Wray,
(1927), who published an interesting study of *Eriophorum* (Fig.
2) stating more or less in passing:

> The physiological peculiarities of moorland plants are
> also indicated by their ability to grow on soils of high
> hydrogen-ion concentration and in media containing toxic
> peaty substances, either of which are [sic] toxic to the
> majority of plants. The general position, therefore, seems
> to be that the moorland plants possess an all-round ability
> to thrive under a variety of conditions which are separate-
> ly unfavorable to the majority of normal plants. When these
> conditions, low calcium, high hydrogen-ion concentration
> and peaty toxins are present together, and often also, it
> must be remembered, in conjunction with nitrogen and oxy-
> gen deficiency and with low soil temperatures, the net

Fig. 2. A species of Eriophorum, this one E. spissum, common in bogs from the United States northward into Canada.

results may well be to exclude every other type of plant on one or more grounds.

It is thus apparent that, as Shields (1950) points out:

> No direct correlation exists between drought resistance
> and the water requirement of plants, xeromorphic leaves
> being spendthrifts where water loss is concerned. Survival
> depends upon the ability to withstand desiccation without
> permanent injury.... This resistance develops as a result
> of purely physical conditions in the plant and soil...and
> is explained on the basis of changes within the cells,
> such as increase in osmotic pressure, decrease in cell
> permeability, and modifications in the protoplasm which
> increase its water-holding capacity. Structural changes
> which may or may not further effect the conservation of
> water are merely the manifestations of these more funda-
> mental physiological changes...

The same general conclusions can be derived from studies
of evergreenness by Monk (1966), who found that the percentage
of species with evergreen leaves that dominated 158 forest
stands in north-central Florida ranged from 0 to 100, and in
general the evergreen species were more important on the dry
sterile sites and the deciduous species on the mesic fertile
sites.

These early studies by Monk and others inspired Ernest
Small (1972a, b, c) to begin investigations on the level of
critical nutrient elements in the foliage of northern bog
plants, in an effort to test the hypothesis that the high degree of evergreenness and sclerophylly is an adaptation to the
conditions of nutrient deficiency prevalent in the bogs. "Phosphorus and nitrogen were selected," he wrote, "for analysis
since previous studies indicated that these two elements are
predominant in importance insofar as nutrient deficiency is
concerned."

In Small's study, the concentrations of nitrogen, phosphorus, manganese, and aluminum in the plants of two bogs and
four adjacent upland areas were examined. He found that the
foliage of the bog species actually was lower in content of
nitrogen and phosphorus than the foliage of plants of the
other habitats and that this is apparently a response to the
paucity of available nitrogen and phosphorus in the peat soils.
It was also interesting that the evergreen bog plants appear
to manufacture more photosynthate per acquired unit of nitrogen or phosphorus than do deciduous species, primarily the
result of the longevity of the evergreen leaves. Small (1972a)
added in summary:

> The high occurrence of evergreenness in infertile en-
> vironments may therefore reflect a decreased need to acquire
> N and P from a substrate deficient in these elements. Mn

and Al contents were comparable in the bog plants to plants
of other habitats, despite potentially toxic levels of these
elements in acid bogs. Apparently many bog plants selectively exclude Mn and Al.... Apparently, because of their
longevity the evergreens examined have the capacity to
manufacture about 50% more photosynthate on a leaf area per
unit N or P basis, and about twice as much photosynthate on
a dry weight per unit N or P basis, compared to the deciduous species.... In an environment in which nitrogen and
phosphorus are extremely difficult to extract, evergreenness may have a considerable advantage in terms of maxi-
mizing production per acquired unit of these elements.*

The fact that evergreen plants do not lose all of their
leaves in the fall is most likely important in two ways. First,
the minerals in older leaves can be translocated directly to
new growing leaves, eliminating any losses that might occur
if nutrients were moved first into storage over winter (in
stems and roots, for example) and then again to new leaves
during the flush of spring growth. Second, the losses that
would occur from the soil (due to washing by rainwater) are
reduced, since the minerals released by decay of leaves dropped continually can be reabsorbed by roots quickly before they
are dissolved and carried away by rain or by melting snow.

It is interesting that evergreenness and sclerophylly are
characteristics possessed by plants of both wet bogs and arid
regions, and that they possess survival value in these dis-
parate habitats for different reasons--mineral nutrition on
the one hand and water conservation on the other. This seems
to be an unusual instance in the history of the evolution of
plant life.

It can thus be seen that the concept of "physiological
drought" as the environmental condition giving sclerophylly
its adaptive value, as envisioned by Schimper, has fallen into
disfavor. As we shall see in Chapter 16, its value should not
be totally discounted. However, in general, the concept has
been replaced by one in which nutrient regimes in peat soils
are regarded as paramount in maintaining the populations of
evergreen bog plants in the moist peat soils of bogs and conifer swamps. Since the same morphological characteristics, as
well as the evergreen habit, are found in plant species of
arctic and alpine areas, and since the geographical range of
many of the common bog species extends far northward into
boreal and arctic regions as well as southward along mountain
ranges, it is perhaps reasonable to assert that these species
originated in environments other than bogs but are adapted,
almost by chance, to conditions therein. In postglacial time,
they have probably developed at least ecotypic (and perhaps

* Copyright 1972, the Ecological Society of America.

Table I. Nutrient Elements in Leaves and Twigs--Average Levels
on Upland Areas[a]

Species	Co	Mo	Zn
Populus tremuloides	0.29 (0.12)	0.09 (0.03)	67.9 (11.9)
Abies balsamea	0.17 (0.05)	0.18 (0.06)	31.8 (5.5)
Picea glauca	0.14 (0.05)	0.14 (0.06)	41.6 (6.8)
Picea mariana	0.20 (0.03)	0.20 (0.09)	38.0 (14.0)
Picea rubra	0.22 (0.06)	0.18 (0.10)	41.2 (14.7)
Chamaedaphne calyculata	0.11 (0.07)	0.23 (0.10)	20.7 (7.8)
Kalmia angustifolia	0.11 (0.04)	0.17 (0.13)	26.1 (6.0)
Ledum groenlandicum	0.14 (0.06)	0.18 (0.15)	24.7 (10.9)
Rhododendron canadense	0.15 (0.03)	0.25 (0.04)	25.0 (7.5)
Vaccinium spp.	0.16	0.15	34.5

[a]Data in ppp dry weight. Standard deviation in parentheses.

Table II. Average and Range of Elements in Different Seasons:
Twigs of Forest Species[a]

Element	Season	Coniferous
Co (ppm)	Summer	0.13 (0.11 0.16)
	Winter	0.21 (0.16 0.29)
Mo (ppm)	Summer	0.09 (0.02 0.14)
	Winter	0.23 (0.15 0.33)
Zn (ppm)	Summer	28.9 (17.0 43.3)
	Winter	42.2 (34.0 56.0)
Mn (ppm)	Summer	250 (198 317)
	Winter	288 (252 315)
Cu (ppm)	Summer	8.9 (8.8 9.0)
	Winter	3.4 (2.4 5.6)
Ca (%)	Summer	0.36 (0.31 0.40)
	Winter	0.46 (0.37 0.55)
P (%)	Summer	0.16 (0.14 0.18)
	Winter	0.28 (0.20 0.34)

[a]Data from Langille and Maclean (1976).

of Nutrient Elements in Leaves and Twigs of Plants Growing

Mn	Cu	Ca	P
83.7 (42.5)	13.1 (3.4)	0.57 (0.16)	0.16 (0.02)
286.0 (46.3)	7.5 (3.0)	0.47 (0.13)	0.14 (0.03)
228.4 (40.4)	6.9 (2.9)	0.41 (0.09)	0.15 (0.03)
255.4 (59.6)	5.9 (1.7)	0.41 (0.02)	0.13 (0.04)
305.0 (50.7)	11.7 (2.2)	0.36 (0.06)	0.15 (0.02)
376.9 (81.0)	9.2 (2.7)	0.54 (0.04)	0.09 (0.01)
305.3 (111.0)	7.9 (1.6)	0.54 (0.13)	0.10 (0.01)
373.2 (104.3)	19.0 (6.1)	0.65 (0.07)	0.09 (0.01)
584.0 (23.2)	10.5 (1.0)	0.40 (0.14)	0.09 (0.01)
231.4	---	0.84	0.06

Data from Langille and Maclean (1976).

Species	
Deciduous	Flora
0.21 (0.08 0.62)	0.10 (0.04 0.16)
0.16 (0.10 0.25)	0.16 (0.11 9.25)
0.09 (0.05 0.29)	0.12 (0.02 0.50)
0.14 (0.07 0.23)	0.20 (0.07 0.36)
48.0 (17.7 98.2)	28.3 (15.0 68.0)
40.7 (17.0 70.0)	34.8 (23.0 60.0)
290 (48 729)	286 (48 817)
218 (38 475)	217 (38 394)
13.1 (5.0 18.6)	15.8 (13.8 17.6)
8.8 (3.5 13.7)	8.0 (6.9 10.1)
0.62 (0.43 0.82)	0.66 (0.42 1.11)
0.62 (0.32 0.90)	0.69 (0.26 1.12)
0.16 (0.14 0.21)	0.12 (0.08 0.22)
0.12 (0.09 0.16)	0.10 (0.06 0.18)

varietal or subspecific) variations in morphology and physiological responses, as well as behavior patterns, that fit them marvelously for the bogs of the regions in which the plants grow. They are thus adequately fitted for survival there, as evidenced by their ability to persist until the present time. The lack of competition from species more commonly found on uplands serves to indicate their individualistic status in respect to the special environmental conditions that prevail in the bogs and swamp forests where they are found.

A comparison between plants of various species growing in bogs with plants of some of the same species growing on more upland sites can be made using data obtained by W. M. Langille and K. S. Maclean (1976), who analyzed leaves and one-year-old twigs of species in natural vegetational communities common in forested areas of Nova Scotia. A representative selection of data giving the mineral content of leaves and twigs from this study is presented in Table I. Samples of these species were taken in both summer and winter, and Langille and Maclean noted that most of the coniferous samples tended generally to contain more of the elements in winter than in summer, with the exception of copper. Deciduous samples showed the reverse, with samples containing more of the elements in summer than in winter, this time with the exception of molybdenum. Calcium appears to be present in about the same quantities in both seasons. Plants of the understory flora seem generally to show the greatest variation in element content between winter and summer. The data from Langille and Maclean showing these differences for the various elements are presented in Table II.

In summary, Langille and Maclean conclude that the different species accumulate varying levels of the elements, evidently due to the varying accumulation capacities of the species and probably to different geological conditions that affect the soil at different sites, and due also to differences among other environmental conditions.

Analyses of total biomass of leaves, stemwood, and the bark of plants in a leatherleaf-bog birch community has led to some question as to whether the leaves actually do serve as storage organs for the slow release to soil of nitrogen and phosphorus.

The total mass (kg/ha) of nitrogen and phosphorus in above-ground live plant material in a leatherleaf-bog birch community in central Michigan has been reported by Richardson *et al.* (1978) for May, when these elements were at a minimum, and for July, when at a maximum (see tabulation).

	May	*July*
Nitrogen	57.8 ± 19.2	78.8 ± 46.8
Phosphorus	4.3 ± 1.7	5.2 ± 3.3

Richardson *et al.* (1978) report that at the time of peak standing crop, half of the nitrogen and phosphorus was in stemwood and bark that had been produced the previous spring, with leaves holding 1% of the above-ground mass of these elements. To provide an advantage through storage, leaf content of these elements in the leatherleaf plants might be expected to be higher. On the other hand, the leatherleaf leaves stay on the plants, on the average, less than 2 years (see above), and mineral elements in the leaves may have been transported out the previous fall. The bog birch is deciduous, and hence by late summer may have already lost most of its nitrogen and phosphorus. Thus, analysis of total biomass in the community may conceal the fact that the leatherleaf foliage is actually serving as a storehouse for nitrogen and phosphorus, releasing these elements slowly and continuously. The issue is confused further by the report of Rich *et al.* (see Reader 1978b) that old leaves of leatherleaf contain relatively high quantities of nitrogen and phosphorus. Final resolution of the question obviously remains to be accomplished.

INTEGRATED FACTOR COMPLEX

The moist peat composed of *Sphagnum* and other mosses commonly inhabiting the northern bogs is highly acidic and, along with the highly acidic humus stratum of boreal forest soils, is certainly one of (perhaps the only) soil in the world possessing this characteristic to such an extreme degree and so consistently throughout the geographical range of the associated plant species. It is not unusual in boreal forest soils to find humus layers with a pH of 4.0 or lower; pH 3.3 has been recorded by the author in several soils in boreal regions and is probably not uncommon. This fact, along with others, renders the environment of the northern bogs and conifer swamps

unique. They possess, as additionally distinguishing features,
species of plants that are characterized by peculiar speciali-
zations that fit them for this unusual environment and evidently preclude their survival under more ordinary conditions,
where they encounter competition from more ordinary plants.

It is equally obvious, however, that none of the characteristics of the evergreen sclerophyllous species appear to
exist in what has been termed an obligate relationship with any
given feature of the climate or the soils. Evergreen plants
are found in wet bogs and also on such unusually xeric habitats
as rocky hilltops and sandy ridges in northern regions. Sclerophyllous leaves are found on the plants of wet bogs, but they
are also found on many plant species of very dry sites and in
such widely diverse regions as the African steppe and the limestone regions of Jamaica.

Since the evergreen sclerophyllous bog plants are inhabitants of regions where there is no deficiency of rainfall and
are found in the wettest sites that can still be reasonably
called terrestrial rather than aquatic, the evident resistance
of sclerophyllous leaves to desiccation does not seem relevant
in all instances, at all times, in all locations. That it does,
however, seem relevant in some regions and under some recurrent
conditions--notably early spring, winter, and late fall--is a
point that we now must consider.

TRANSPIRATION AND ENVIRONMENT

Studies of transpiration resistance and water loss by evapotranspiration in the woody evergreen bog plants have virtually
dispelled the notion, first popularized by Schimper in 1898,
that the xeromorphic features of bog plants are due to physiological drought created by limited availability of water despite its abundance. On the other hand, transpiration rates
and the physiological processes, as well as morphological
changes, that occur as a consequence of changes in water supply
to tissues, are complex and cannot be understood on the basis
of single-factor or simplistic explanations. There are many
physiological factors at work, and some may indeed be affected
in a pronounced way by xeromorphic structural features of
leaves, especially at times when unusual environmental events
occur. Thus, survival over the large part of the year may not
depend upon the sclerophyllous characteristic of leaves, but
the entire population could be wiped out during one spell of
inclement weather--hot or cold--and, thus, the adaptation
conferred by the characteristic is just as essential as though
the environmental conditions were encountered every day.

Small (1972a,b,c), like previous investigators, failed to find notable restrictions of transpiration in bog plants, leading to rejection of the relevance of the concept of physiological drought to bog species. Small, however, cites the work of Montfort, who much earlier (1921) had found that immersion of roots in bog water had little effect upon plants. Small, however, wrote that transpiration data alone "cannot definitely settle the question of whether bog plants are under drought stress, since adaptations could be present which maintain high rates of transpiration despite drought stress." He added that "water potential is probably the best single indicator of the internal water balance of plants and provides a more valid indication of possible drought stress than does transpiration."

Water potential is a term now widely employed (replacing a variety of synonyms) to designate the rather complex relationship existing between the water content of plants and the water status of soil and air. To attempt a brief definition of water potential is to oversimplify; there is now virtually a library of research literature on the topic. In essence, however, it can perhaps be described as the osmotic force existing in the tissues of a plant that has lost more water by transpiration than roots have been able to furnish. A fully turgid plant has a water potential of zero; a water deficit in the tissues, on the other hand, results in a water potential (which is always expressed as a negative) created by the osmotic pressure of solutes in the plant cell. Other factors are involved in water potential, but osmotic force is the major one; the osmotic force creates a water potential that exists until sufficient water has been imbibed by the plant to create a turgor pressure in the cells that equals the osmotic pressure, and water potential then becomes zero.

The unit in which water potential is measured is the bar or the atmosphere (1 bar = 0.987 atm.); thus, a cell with a water potential of -10 bars is exerting an osmotic force that can be equalized by a pressure of 10 bars across the cell membrane. Typical osmotic potentials of plant cells are -10 to -20 bars, although large differences exist among species and even in plants of the same species growing on different sites. Xerophytic plants have values of -30 to -40 bars, and halophytes are known to have values exceeding -100 bars. In most soils, the osmotic potential of the soil solution ranges between -1 and -2 bars, which is negligible in counteracting the osmotic pressure existing in the plants.

Small found water potential comparable between bog and non-bog plants, and similar to plants in habitats lacking drought stress. He found no evidence that xeromorphy in bog plants

was related to water loss in any way. Why then did xeromorphy
apparently contribute to the competitive advantage of bog
ericads in accustomed habitats? The answer to the question was
not (and still is not) clear. Small (1972c) summarized:

> If xeromorphy in bog plants does not reflect adaptation
> to conditions of actual drought stress within the plants,
> then another explanation should be sought. The following
> hypotheses may be suggested. (1) The xeromorphy of bog
> plants may be explained as simply reflecting a more general
> correlation of xeromorphic leaves with nutritionally de-
> ficient environments. (2) The xeromorphy of (boreal) bog
> plants may have been selected in response to low tempera-
> ture of the boreal bog environment, especially the coldness
> of the substrate (Williams, 1970). The short growing season
> of cold environments may make evergreenness advantageous,
> and sclerophyllous, evergreen leaves, as are present in many
> bog plants, appear resistant to winter desiccation (Gates,
> 1914). (3) It may be that the nature of bog species was
> selected for partly on the basis of adaptive value in other
> habitats. Many of the plants found in the bog investigated,
> including *Kalmia angustifolia, Gaylussacia baccata, Vaccin-
> ium marocarpon, Vaccinium myrtilloides, Aronia melanocarpa,*
> and *Betula populifolia,* frequently occur in such arid habit-
> ats as dunes, sand ridges, and dry fields, where water is
> physically in short supply, and where features retarding
> water loss may be expected to be adaptive.*

What, then, can be said of this rather wide variety of
possible reasons for the xeromorphy of the bog plants, and
particularly the sclerophyllous characteristics of the leaves?
The above-cited paragraph aptly summarized the discussions
on this point that have been presented in the previous pages.
Perhaps all of the reasons are valid, at one time or another
and under certain relatively rare or unusual circumstances.
Some recent observations are interesting and may bear importantly on this point.

It has often been shown, for example, that water uptake by
plant roots is primarily the result of a hydraulic pressure
difference acting across root membranes, a point reiterated
recently by Dalton and Gardner (1978). It has also been
shown--and this may be a most significant point--that the rate
of water flow through roots cannot invariably be explained on
the simple basis of hydraulic pressure and viscosity of water;
while absortion of water may usually be a passive process, at
times there is an active pumping of water into the plant by
some kind of biochemical mechanism. As Dalton and Gardner
point out, active uptake of water by plants is dependent upon
temperature, in the same kind of temperature relationship that

is seen in chemical reactions. It is thus apparent that cold temperatures, or temperatures that are not cold but only relatively cool, will have an influence upon the rate of water uptake by plant roots that is greater than might be expected if this principle involved in active uptake were not taken into account. The degree to which this chemical principle has an effect in bog plants is, as yet however, unknown, and undoubtedly represents an area of study that should be explored.

The consequence of this, however, is obvious--low temperatures in bog soils in fall, winter, and spring may, indeed, have a great influence upon the capacity of the plants to resist desiccation. At these times, sclerophyllous leaves may well have a role in water retention and conservation, since transpiration may be reduced more at such times by xeromorphic characteristics than is the case in midsummer, when most experimental work and observations of bog plants have been conducted. As Gates pointed out, and has been reviewed at length in an earlier section, both summer and winter conditions bear upon the unique survival capabilities of the evergreen ericads in their accustomed bog habitats (Fig. 3).

For some definitive observations upon the effect of winter conditions on evergreen sclerophyllous species it is pertinent to turn to the boreal forest of Alaska--where conditions are, in many respects, similar to those in the bogs of the northern United States and the adjacent areas of Canada. Cowling and Kedrowski (1980) found that the Alaskan evergreen trees have rather definite adaptations to prevailing conditions:

> In Interior Alaska, subfreezing temperatures prevent vascular plant roots from absorbing water for several months each winter and evergreen trees face the danger of desiccation. Under these conditions the two species of spruce which are native to interior Alaska appear to remain healthy, whereas introduced species of pine show browning of needle tips in the wintertime and appear to be less hardy...
> Spruce shows the characteristics of drought tolerant species, having high conductances and closing stomates at low relative water contents and xylem potentials, while yellow pine and lodgepole pine show the characteristics of drought avoiding species, having low conductances and maintaining high relative water contents and xylem water potentials. Wintertime damage to pine needles may be due to low rates of photosynthesis; however, carbohydrate reserves are not unduly low, and more data are necessary to test this hypothesis.

Fig. 3.   Snow on this small patch of open bog covers most of the species that make up the community, but here and there tufts of C. calyculata protrude above the snow.   The adaptations of the evergreen ericads that make it possible for them to survive such conditions are discussed in the text.

SUMMARY

We come to the end of this discussion of bog plant sclerophylly and xeromorphy, then, on a somewhat inconclusive note,
made necessary by the still hypothetical nature of much of the
available commentary on the adaptive relevance of these characteristics to the needs of the common plant species inhabiting
the northern bogs. Many questions remain to be clarified before they can even be asked, and there is undoubtedly much
additional knowledge to be acquired. There are times when the
morphological characteristics of plant species are almost self-
evident in their adaptive value in the prevailing environmental conditions. Such is not the case with the sclerophyllous
bog evergreens, and perhaps much of the fascination that the
xeromorphic ericads have for the botanist and ecologist is
that they are mysterious in their very physical appearance.
Why should they possess such a unique morphology? Why are
they able to survive where they do? For what reason do they
lack any real competition from other plants in the rather
special habitats they customarily inhabit? These are questions
that still lack satisfactory answers.

16 Evergreens: Nutrient Dynamics

Nitrogen is an important constituent of proteins, and for this reason it is one of the more significant elements in the nutrition of plants. In terms of the numbers of atoms of each present, nitrogen is the fourth most abundant element in plant tissues preceded by carbon, oxygen, and hydrogen. Without adequate supplies of nitrogen, growth is greatly slowed, and plants suffering nitrogen deficiency become chlorotic--the leaves turn pale and yellow--and take on a thin and spindly appearance.

The bog and swamp habitat is often deficient in nitrogen and other nutrient elements available to plants since much of what is present is tied up in undecayed dead plants. Peat is also exceptionally low in nutrients other than nitrogen, notably phosphorus, and it has long been suspected that there is a direct causal relationship between the lack of nutrients in bogs and the fact that so many of the bog species of plants are evergreen.

Why should there exist a relationship between low levels of soil nutrient elements and evergreenness? The reason seems to be that evergreen leaves make more efficient use of the nutrients available to them than other kinds of plants. They are adept at retaining for longer periods of time what limited quantities of nutrients they can obtain, giving leaves a longer time to translocate the valuable mineral nutrients from older leaves to the newer ones and thus keeping the materials in the plant.

Some nutrients are always lost in leaf fall, but an appreciable portion of the mobile nutrients are almost always transported to other parts of the evergreen perennials in the autumn. When leaves are evergreen there is thus a longer period of time available for the plant stem and root tissues to reabsorb nutrients from the foliage before leaf abscission takes place. There is absorption of carbohydrates and other products of photosynthetic and biochemical syntheses from leaves before they are lost, and it seems reasonable that nutrients can be

translocated just as well. The mineral nutrients are translocated probably as part of the other products of synthesis
to new leaves, roots, cambium, and so on, to be used again.

In a most interesting study of plants in and around a bog
near Ottawa, Small (1972a,b,c) found that bog evergreen species
evidently can manufacture about 235% more photosynthate per
unit of nitrogen before the latter is lost than can bog deciduous species. Moreover, even the deciduous bog species have
adopted conservation measures regarding nitrogen, manufacturing
about 60% more photosynthate per acquired unit of nitrogen
than do the nonbog deciduous species.

The bog plants subsist on lower levels of nitrogen in
foliage than do plants in at least most other kinds of habitats, but they make exceedingly thrifty use of the nitrogen
they do possess. The nutrient elements in leaves are found
principally in the enzymes and cofactors involved in photosynthesis and other synthetic activities, such as manufacture
of lipids and proteins. The recycling of these nutrient elements is obviously of direct significance to the maintenance
of high rates of metabolic processes in the evergreen bog plant
species. It may account in no small measure for the competitive success of the bog species in the unusual bog environment.

The fact that leaves linger on the plants at least until
well into their second summer, and for as long as up to four
or more growing seasons, contributes significantly to mineral
nutrition of the plants. They reabsorb the nutrients from old
leaves before leaf fall, they begin active photosynthesis as
soon as temperatures permit in the spring, and they conserve
the carbohydrates that otherwise would be needed to produce a
whole new suit of leaves every year. These must all contribute
to the competitive advantage that the evergreen bog plants have
in comparison to the deciduous species. That they do, indeed,
have competitive superiority over the deciduous species is
evidenced by their relatively much greater abundance in the
restricted range of conditions existing in bogs.

It is also apparent that even deciduous bog species make
more efficient use of nutrient elements than do deciduous non-
bog species. Whether this is a result of evolutionary adaptations conferring greater efficiency on the bog plants, or
whether all plants make better use of available nutrients when
the latter are in short supply, is not clearly brought out in
the studies of these plants that have been conducted to date.
It is clear, however, that some inborn and genetically trans-
mitted capacities are very apt to be involved.

It is interesting that the greater efficiency in use of
acquired nutrients in evergreen bog species is accomplished
despite generally lower rates of photosynthesis in these plants
compared to deciduous species. Evergreen leaves are forced to

carry on photosynthesis at lower rates than deciduous leaves
because of certain unavoidable handicaps. For one thing, evergreen leaves have a thick epidermis, and less light gets through
to the chloroplasts than is the case with thin deciduous leaves
possessing little cuticular material. Moreover, other morphological characteristics often found in evergreen leaves of bog
plants also restrict the rate at which photosynthesis can be
carried on. They have a higher proportion of structural tissue, which gives the leaves a toughness to withstand the rigors
of the bog environment, particularly in winter and spring, but
proportionately reduces the volume of photosynthetic tissue.
Their revolute margins, hairiness, and other characteristics
of xerophytic morphology all tend to reduce available space
for photosynthetic processes. The fact that stomata are often
closed or at least protected by pits and dense hairs also reduces the amount of carbon dioxide that can enter leaves, which
may also be a limiting factor in rates of photosynthesis in the
evergreen bog plants.

There are thus disadvantages to the xerophytic morphology
that enables the evergreen bog species to survive under harsh
environmental conditions, but the advantages must decidedly
outweigh the disadvantages since these plants are obviously
successful occupants of the bog habitat. Less competitive advantage is lost through the evergreen habit than is gained.
Deciduous species can compete with evergreen plants where it
costs more to retain leaves through the winter than it does to
grow them every spring. In short, evergreen species survive
best where it is cheaper in terms of energy expenditure to
maintain leaves throught the winter than it is to grow them
anew every year.

The leaves of the evergreen ericads continue to be capable
of carrying on photosynthesis as long as they remain attached,
and although the leaves decline in total photosynthetic activity as they get older this seems to be the result of a general
decline in nitrogen content. Relative to the amount of nitrogen in the leaves, old leaves are as efficient in fixing carbon through photosynthesis as young leaves. As Reader (1978a,
b) found in a 2-year study of the evergreen ericads in a peat
bog in southern Ontario, it seems as though the photosynthetic
material present in old leaves is as efficient as that in
young plants; and it is simply that the older leaves have less
chlorophyll, judging at least from the total amount of nitrogen present in leaf tissues.

Of the three plant species studied by Reader, *K. polifolia*
had the highest rate of photosynthesis in both new and old
leaves, *L. groenlandicum* was intermediate, and *C. calyculata*
had the lowest rate. *Ledum groenlandicum* retained its leaves
longest, *K. polifolia* was intermediate, and *C. calyculata* lost

its leaves more quickly than the others. Reader also found
that newly synthesized material was translocated rapidly out
of leaves and not stored in leaves, as has been believed by
some workers who have conducted research on the bog species.
The levels of nitrogen and phosphorus, however, decreased in
old leaves rather abruptly during the few months prior to leaf
fall, suggesting that the nutrient materials needed for photosynthesis were moved out of the leaves in time to save them
when the old leaves were about to be lost.

   This preabscission translocation of nitrogen and phosphorus
is not the case in all bog plants, however. Richardson and
co-workers (1978) found phosphorus concentration in the tissues
of sedges, willows, and bog birch did not decrease markedly in
late summer. These are deciduous species, and these plants
would be likely to conserve nutrient materials by translocating
them to stem and roots before leaves were lost in autumn. The
same was true even in the case of tamarack, a deciduous conifer
in which the needles did not lose significant amounts of phosphorus prior to needle fall. Richardson and colleagues also
questioned whether there is significant translocation of nitrogen and phosphorus from the leaves of bog ericads before they
are lost; since there is so much more nitrogen and phosphorus
in stems and bark than in the leaves of these species, as shown
by their analyses, there was some question as to the advantage
to the plant of translocating what little nitrogen and phosphorus exist in the leaves. Even though it is apparent that
some nitrogen and phosphorus is lost before abscission, Richardson and co-workers believe it may be lost by leaching of soluble
materials from the leaves by rain.

   This is obviously a topic on which some additional research
is needed before it will be possible to resolve these differences in opinion concerning the interpretation of the available
data.

NUTRIENTS RECYCLED--1

   Nitrogen and other nutrient elements present in the peat
soils of bogs and swamps are almost entirely incorporated into
organic compounds. Very little nitrogen is ever available at
one time in forms that plants can use--as, in chemical terms,
ammonium, nitrite, or nitrate ions. Nitrogen, as well as
other critical nutrients such as phosphorus, potassium, calcium, magnesium, manganese, boron, zinc, copper, molybdenum,
and chlorine, are bound up in organic compounds that form the
tissues of plants. In peat soils, these tissues have not decayed, at least totally, because of the low temperatures, high
acidity, and waterlogged anaerobic conditions, with the result

that water of bogs and conifer swamps are relatively low in
nutrient elements and compounds (Sjörs, 1950; Damman, 1978).

Decay is carried on by microorganisms, and the conditions
in bogs are inhibitory to activity of the microorganisms capable of breaking down proteins, nucleic acids, and other compounds that contain most of the nitrogen and other elements
essential to cell metabolism in living plants. The biochemical
reactions involved in the decay of dead plant tissues are complex and far from understood, but outlines of the processes
involved have emerged from a few studies conducted directly on
peat soils and from the more numerous studies of humus horizons
in farmland and forest soils, which can be considered to also
apply to peat soils.

One interesting aspect of the breakdown of proteins and
other complex compounds in peat soils is that microorganisms
responsible for decomposition will work on these compounds much
faster in laboratory test tubes than in actual soil. The
reason, at least as postulated by bacteriologists, is that under natural conditions in bogs some protection is afforded
these compounds by other materials in the peat. The theory,
at least, is that proteinaceous materials form complexes with
lignin or other common plant materials, and in this complexed
form they are somewhat immune to attack by microorganisms.

This is actually a rather important point, because it may
account in large measure for the failure of peat soils to furnish available mineral nutrients to plants even though there
are large amounts present. Nutrients are present, but they
are not in available form, the result of the fact that decay
processes have been so slow. The rate at which organic nitrogen is converted to ammonium and nitrate ions is called the
mineralization rate, and in peat soils the rate is very slow
compared to that in most farm and forest soils. The mineralization of nitrogen is related to the rate at which carbon
compounds, such as cellulose and lignin, are decomposed, since
the bacteria responsible for release of nitrogen as nitrate
and ammonium depend on carbohydrates for their energy supply.
Thus the slow rate of nitrogen release is also tied up with
the fact that there are few bacteria in peat soils capable
of breaking down complex carbohydrate compounds into forms
suitable for utilization by the bacteria that attack proteins
and nucleic acids.

There are other biochemical reasons for the slow release
of nitrogen in peat soils. A large number of different species
of microorganisms is involved in the breakdown of nitrogenous
compounds, but the first step in the process is always undertaken by microbial strains capable of producing exogenous en-
zymes--enzymes released from the body of the bacterium itself
and capable of working outside the living organism. This,

simply, is because the large protein molecules are too big to get through the cell wall of the bacteria and must first be broken down outside the microorganisms. Once the large molecules have been split into their component amino acids or other compounds of similar size, then they can be absorbed by other strains of bacteria and broken down further, finally to the point where nitrate and ammonia are produced.

Under aerobic conditions, in which oxygen from air is liberally dissolved in the water of peat soils, one group of bacteria is involved in protein decomposition. Under anaerobic conditions, in which the deeper layers of peat are deficient in free dissolved oxygen, another group of bacteria is involved. The result is quite different in terms of the biochemical mechanisms at play in the decay processes. Under aerobic conditions, usually at--or at least within a few inches of--the peat surface, the major products of protein breakdown are carbon dioxide, ammonium and nitrate ions, sulfate ions, and water. Under anaerobic conditions deeper beneath the surface of the peat, decomposition follows an entirely different series of pathways, and the familiar smells of putrefaction are common, produced by compounds that are final products of this kind of decay--organic acids, indole, mercaptans, skatole, and hydrogen sulfide, as well as carbon dioxide, ammonium ions, and amines.

In general, microbiology of the breakdown of complex organic compounds found in living tissue is not well understood. It is apparent, however, that anaerobic bacteria dominate the scene when sufficient oxygen is not available in free dissolved form. The bacteria probably dominate in neutral or alkaline environments, but fungi and actinomycetes also contribute to the decomposition process in acid aerobic environments. In the upper aerobic strata of bogs in northern regions, fungi are of more importance in decay than they are in neutral or alkaline aerobic soils. It is also of considerable significance that ammonium is produced only under anaerobic conditions, and this is then converted to nitrate only in well-aerated sites. There is always ample opportunity for anaerobic conditions to develop in very small areas--one might call them microsites-- anywhere in a peat soil, however, even in places near the surface where most of the material is well aerated. In peat soils there are probably rarely any sites where conditions are uniformly and completely aerobic; it is likely that anaerobic microorganisms are always active at spots near the surface but only in greatly reduced proportions compared with deeper levels in peat soil. The acid conditions also tend to depress but not to completely eliminate the decomposition of nitrogenous organic compounds and mineralization.

The simpler compounds released by extracellular enzymes that accomplish initial breakdown of complex materials include amino and nucleic acids, which in turn are the carbon and nitrogen source for a wide variety of microorganisms. It is believed that the nitrogen of most amino acids is extracted first, and the carbohydrate portion of the molecule broken down later by the microorganisms; the first reaction is termed *deamination* and the second *decarboxylation*. After the molecule is deaminated, it is attacked by other enzymes and broken down eventually to carbon dioxide and other products. Finally, there is another group of organisms capable of carrying on what is termed *denitrification,* which is simply the release of gaseous nitrogen from compounds containing ammonium and the nitrate ions. Thus, if denitrifying bacteria are numerous and active, nitrogen that might otherwise be utilized by growing plants is released directly to the atmosphere and is as unavailable--more so, actually--as it was as part of an undecomposed organic molecule. Only by the process of nitrogen fixation will nitrogen lost through denitrification be made up in the soil budget. Nitrogen fixation is carried on in nature both by biological and nonbiological processes; the latter is the result of atmospheric events such as lightning during rainstorms, which results in the production of nitrous oxide that is then carried to the soil in rainfall. In biological nitrogen fixation, microorganisms carry on the same process, taking nitrogen from the air and incorporating it into compounds that plants can utilize. The biochemistry of this process is most interesting, but so complex that it is still not fully understood. Biological nitrogen fixation, however, is one of the major sources of soil nitrogen in natural forest lands, and it must also be of considerable importance on bogs and swamps. It is a subject of such great importance that it will merit much research given over to exploring the process and its global ecological ramifications (Daly, 1966; Voigt and Stevcek, 1969; Granhall and Selander, 1973; Basilier *et al.,* 1978; Sprent *et al.,* 1978; Schwintzer, 1979b).

NUTRIENTS RECYCLED--2

One of the dangers of ecological research ought to be called the "hazard of the easy answer," and this is simply the temptation to ascribe an all-to-obvious cause to an ecological phenomenon. On further analysis, this presumed cause often is shown not to be involved in the event at all or to be important only to a lesser degree. Thus, for example, a superficial re-

connaissance of the conditions in bog soils might lead to an
erroneous conclusion that high acidity is the sole--or at least
the prime--cause of low rates of decomposition of cellulose,
hemicellulose, lignin, and protein in dead and decaying plant
materials in peat. This would be the consequence of the fact
that it is relatively easy to take pH readings. It is also
just as easy to acquire data on temperatures, and so both low
pH and low relative temperatures can easily be selected as the
causal factors involved in slow rates of decomposition. It is
more difficult, on the other hand, to make determinations of
the amount of free dissolved oxygen in soil moisture, and this
factor might easily be ignored altogether--yet it is probably
by far the most important one. The reasons for the slow decomposition of organic materials in peat soils are actually
very complex, involving at least all three of these factors--
oxygen, acidity, and temperature--in some degree.

Let us look at conditions in bog soils and see why this is
so. First of all, these soils are anaerobic beneath a rather
shallow aerobic surface layer. In this anaerobic environment,
fungi capable of decomposing cellulose are virtually eliminated
since they require free oxygen in dissolved form to live. Some
common fungi, however, are fully capable of decomposing cellulose in aerobic surface layers, and in these layers both fungi
and bacteria are very active in breaking down the organic matter in peat. The major groups of microorganisms active in the
protein breakdown in aerobic acid conditions are actually the
fungi, but anaerobic bacteria dominate in conditions where free
dissolved oxygen is absent. Thus, at depths in the peat, decomposition of cellulose, lignin, and protein is largely the
result of the activity of anaerobic, acid-tolerant bacteria.

The anaerobic bacteria, however, never break cellulose
down at very rapid rates in the lower depths of the peat soils,
and the rate of decomposition there is very slow. The most
common anaerobic bacteria that decompose cellulose are members
of the well-known genus *Clostridium,* and the products of cellulose decomposition are commonly carbon dioxide, hydrogen,
ethanol, and such organic acids as lactic, acetic, butyric,
succinic, and formic. A secondary group of bacteria utilize
these acids in metabolism, generating quantities of methane
as a product.

The major proportion of the initial breakdown that occurs
in peat is carried out by fungi in the aerobic surface layers
of the soil. When the initial proteolysis has been accomplished,
other organisms take over further degradation, secreting pro-
teinases and peptidases that lead to cleaving of linkages between amino acids. This latter population consists of aerobic
bacteria, fungi, and actinomycetes. At lower depths in peat,

the process is continued in the oxygen-deficient environment
by a number of microorganisms that are either strict or facultative anaerobes. The major end products of aerobic protein
breakdown are carbon dioxide, ammonium, sulfate, and water.
The anaerobic products include, in addition to carbon dioxide,
such strong-smelling compounds as ammonia, organic acids, hydrogen sulfide, mercaptans, indole, skatole, and various amines.

Mineralization is also influenced by pH of the soil, and
this--the production of ammonium and nitrate--is lower in acidic than in neutral or alkaline soils. Organic nitrogen can,
as a result, accumulate in partly decomposed products of proteolysis and remain in that form for long periods of time, until
conditions change so that further, more rapid decomposition
can occur.

Ammonium and nitrate compounds can also be attacked by
denitrifying bacteria, and these are broken down into their
elements, releasing the nitrogen directly to the atmosphere as
gaseous nitrogen, thus removing it from the soil altogether.
The denitrifying bacteria can function as denitrifiers only
when oxygen is in reduced supply, but enough oxygen must be
present, on the other hand, to accommodate the formation of
nitrate. It thus appears that denitrification can occur only
under conditions in which there are microsites such as inter-
stitial pores in peat where oxygen is lacking, but in which
oxygen is available at least to some extent elsewhere in the
soil. Denitrification must occur, then, only at places near
the surface of the soil where there is lowered oxygen tension
but where free dissolved oxygen is not absent altogether. The
most acid soils, however, have only a sparse denitrifying population, and the numbers of these bacteria are high only at a
pH of 5.5 or above.

It is thus apparent that there are no simple or easy single-
factor explanations for the lowered nitrogen content of the
peat soils; all of the factors mentioned are involved, and some
are more important than others at any given time and place.
All of these factors, along with the kind of vegetation present,
the presence or absence of nitrogen-fixing organisms, and the
soil animals--invertebrates--that churn and mix the soil materials, are so intimately interwoven in the ecosystem that it
is not easy to separate the effects of one from another.

There are, moreover, many aspects of weather that vary
greatly from year to year, and these contribute to creation of
different ecological regimes that individually occur only rarely. Yet one of these conditions may exist at the time of a
research study and may be taken as representative of conditions
that prevail most of the time. Thus, a relatively unusual and
dynamic state may be considered to be typical by researchers
who have only limited time and money to carry on a study of a
peatland area.

Thus recondite events result in invalid or inaccurate interpretations of data obtained in natural areas, peatland included, and there is always the danger of advocating the easy ecological answer to a very complex and involved question. Many results of research programs now accepted as accurate and useful may in the future be revealed as representing situations that in actuality are quite anomalous. It is possible that some studies now accepted as fundamental and classic may ultimately be found to seriously misrepresent what occurs in bogs and other natural vegetational communities. This is simply to be expected as a consequence of the growth of knowledge.

MINERAL UTILIZATION

Peat is formed by a unique combination of chemical, physical, and microbial processes, for the large part under anaerobic conditions on wet sites. Peat is a varied mixture of cellulose, hemicellulose, lignin, cutin, proteins, fats, sugars, starches, waxes, resins, alkaloids, and pectins, as well as these compounds in various stages of decomposition by microorganisms and various spontaneous chemical reactions such as oxidation and reduction.

The ultimate sources of nutrients in bogs and swamps are the mineral soil in surrounding land areas that form the watershed, the incoming groundwater, and the atmosphere. The groundwater is often limited in mineral content, and in such instances the nutrient supply is largely in the rain that falls, bringing with it dust particles and compounds formed in the atmosphere. Elements present in very low levels in rain, such as phosphorus, become seriously deficient in bog soils as a result.

It is not unusual for highly acid peat to develop on bogs that are located in regions with alkaline mineral soils; the processes at work to create acid conditions in bogs are sufficiently effective to neutralize the base-rich materials and convert the bog soils to a highly acid condition.

In very acidic peat soils, the availability of certain nutrients, particularly calcium, phosphorus, and nitrogen, is very low even though these elements may be present in considerable quantities in unavailable form.

These then, in summary, are the edaphic characteristics of the soil and the nutritional regime to which the bog plant species are adapted to a greater or lesser degree. The fundamental chemistry of the peat soils is not well understood compared to the soils of agricultural importance, and the analyses that have been carried on were almost invariably conducted using samples that had been exposed to air, which, as in the case particularly of these largely anaerobic soils, greatly modified

their chemical dynamics. The very low supplies of nitrogen,
phosphorus, calcium, magnesium, and sodium in the tissues of
bog plants have usually been considered to be the result of
low concentrations of these elements in the peat soil. Another
factor that contributes to the low concentrations in plants,
however, is the waterlogged condition of bogs, which results
in an inhibition in the ability of plants to absorb ions since
they do so with difficulty under anaerobic conditions. Roots
may also suffer retarded ability to carry on active metabolic
accumulation of mineral elements because of a lack of sufficient quantities of oxygen to carry on active transport of ions
across cell membranes.

The opinion was once widely held that bog plants are acido-
philic in soil preference, but this has been shown not to be
the case since many of them grow rapidly and well in the green-
house on alkaline soils. Rather, they are tolerant of conditions that put other species at a serious competitive disadvantage. As Heinselman (1970) has stated:

> The notion that bog plants are acidophilous is erroneous.
> It is more correct to say that the total ecological re-
> quirements of these plants in competition with other vege-
> tation often limit them to acid environments. There is
> evidence that most plants will grow over a wide pH range
> (at least pH 4 to 8) providing other factors are in balance
> .... While the control mechanism is not always clear, in
> nature certain plants are nevertheless characteristic of
> given pH ranges.... In Minnesota black spruce is said to
> be the most common in acid bogs, while northern white cedar
> occurs chiefly on circum-neutral peats.... pH may well in-
> fluence floristics, even though production depends chiefly
> on nutrients and other factors.*

The relationship between the pH values of organic soils
and the availability of nutrients has been studied to some extent, and the summarizing report of Lucas and Davis (1961)
gives a brief account of the nutrient status of peat soils in
regard to major nutrients. It does their work a disservice
to summarize it further, but some of the more salient points
are emphasized in Table I (Lucas and Davis, 1961).

Very acidic peat soils show low availability of many elements, chiefly potassium, calcium, nitrogen, boron, copper,
and molybdenum. It is of some interest, however, to note that
the maximum availability of these elements in peat soils is
often at pH values from one to two points below the value at
which they are at maximum availability in mineral agricultural
field or pasture soils. There is considerable variability in
the case of several of the nutrient elements, and an example
of this is furnished by the element copper; the status of

* Copyright 1970, the Ecological Society of America.

Table I. Effect of Soil Acidity upon Nutrient Availability[a]

Nutrient	pH Range of greatest availability	Value below which availability is restricted	Value at which availability is at maximum	Percentage of element in peat soil at pH below 4.0[b]	Percentage of element in well-supplied soil
Nitrogen	5.0–8.5	4.5	5.2	1.00	2.00
Phosphorus	5.0–7.0	4.5	5.5	0.01	0.05
Potassium	5.0–7.5	4.5	---[c]	<0.10	0.15
Sulfur	5.0–9.0	4.5	---	<0.10	0.40
Calcium	5.0–8.5	5.0	---	0.60	1.20
Magnesium	4.5–6.5	4.5	5.0–6.5	Ca:Mg; 5:1	Ca:Mg; 25:1
Iron	4.5–7.5	4.5	5.0–7.0		100 ppm[d,e]
Manganese	<4.0–5.5	<4.0	4.0–5.5	0.02	0.02
Boron	4.5–6.0	4.5	5.5		20 ppm[d,e]
Copper	5.0–6.5	4.5	5.2	2–15 ppm	6–20 ppm
Zinc	<4.5–6.0	<4.0	5.0		20 ppm[d,e]
Molybdenum	5.5–9.0	5.0	7.0		0.01[d,e]

[a] Soil acidity in pH values. Data from Lucas and Davis (1961).

[b] 1% is equal to 10,000 ppm dry weight basis. [c] No data available.

[d] Amount in soil or availability is not as critical as with other elements since the amount is generally high above the pH value noted in column 2.

[e] Data from Epstein (1972).

copper as an available nutrient is quite variable, due probably to great sensitivity to edaphic conditions that at present are either not ordinarily measured or not recognized. Copper is sensitive in its response to the presence of a number of other elements in the soil and to organic complexes, as well as to physical conditions, and its complex chemistry in regard to these responses probably accounts for the variable nature of its availability from one site to another.

Two of the nutrient elements--manganese and zinc--present unusual circumstances in that high amounts in the soil are significant to the response given by some plant species and not by others. Manganese and zinc are, in short, toxic to some species when they are present in high concentrations but other species are able to resist absorption of these elements even when they are present in concentrations that are quite toxic to more sensitive species. Thus, Gerloff et al. (1966) found in a study of plants in a northern Wisconsin bog of very low pH that the water had a manganese content of 1.86 ppm, seven times that of media commonly used for plant culture. The tissues of plants growing in the bog had manganese concentrations of 1061 ppm on the average, and one species, G. hispidula, had a maximum concentration of 3000 ppm. Crop species, on the other hand, show manganese toxicity symptoms when tissue contents are 1000 ppm or less.

There were, interestingly enough, several species with relatively low manganese concentrations, particularly Cornus canadensis. "This indicates," Gerloff et al. (1966) wrote, "selective exclusion of manganese as another mechanism associated with successful plant survival in the bog environment." The species of Cornus evidently possess different capacities for such exclusion, however, as the data in Table II (Gerloff et al., 1966) demonstrate.

Table II. Selective Exclusion of Manganese by Species of Cornus[a]

Species	Mn content (ppm)	Mn content of other species at same site (ppm)	Date sampled	pH of soil
C. canadensis	149	936	7-12-59	4.0
C. racemosa	71	905	6-18-59	5.1
C. racemosa	28	122	7-13-60	5.8
C. rugosa	64	210	6-29-59	5.6
C. stolonifera	37	52	7-14-60	7.4

[a]Data from Gerloff et al. (1966).

Table III. Selective Absorption of Zinc by Native Plants of Wisconsin[a]

Species	Zn content (ppm)	Other plants from same site
Ambrosia psilostachya	143	35
Baptisia leucantha	158	55
Betula nigra	212	--
Betula pumila	164	--
Monarda punctata	118	35
Nemopanthus mucronata	711	--
Picea glauca	117	--
Populus deltoides	177	--
Salix amygdaloides	154	25
Taxus canadensis	209	--
Trandescantia ohioensis	105	27
Viola pubescens	128	35

[a]Data from Gerloff et al. (1966).

Table IV. pH at Which Ions Are Precipitated as Hydroxides[a]

Ion	pH
Fe^{3+}	2.0[b]
Al^{3+}	4.1[b]
Cu^{2+}	5.3[b]
Fe^{2+}	5.5[b]
Zn^{2+}	$5.3{-}6.8$[c]
Mn^{2+}	$8.5{-}8.8$ [c]
Mg^{2+}	10.5[c]

[a]Data from Malyuga (1964)* as given by Brooks (1972).
[b]Precipitation occurs at these values or _lower_.
[c]Precipitation occurs at these values or _higher_.

In contrast, many other species possess the ability to accumulate certain mineral elements far in excess of what would be expected from the soil content of the elements. A list of such accumulator species is presented in Table III (Gerloff et al., 1966), all of which contain many more times the amount, for example, of zinc than non accumulators (not all are bog species). It is not unusual, as pointed out by Gerloff et al., for leaf samples of a plant showing selective exclusion to be low in an element, while an accumulator plant growing immediately next to it will be very high in content of the element. Three genera, Populus, Salix, and Betula, were generally consistently high in zinc content. Four others --Corylus, Carpinus, Ostrya, and Alnus--show absolutely no indication of an unusual capacity for zinc accumulation.

These species, and others showing the same capacities for either selective accumulation or selective exclusion, thus are able to influence uptake of elements from soil in one way or another. They differ from those species--which are perhaps in the majority--that simply reflect soil content of the elements, more or less passively absorbing elements that are present in large amounts and suffering deficiencies when they are absent. They are unable to store elements when a surplus is available for use later--when, for example, leaching by rainwater removes available elements from the rooting soil zone. They simply reflect an unusually high content of one or several elements or an unusually low content of these or other elements in the soil. One of the interesting possibilities is that accumulator species retain certain elements in a plant community that otherwise might be in short supply; the elements they accumulate may thus be kept in circulation and generally available to all plants of the community. On the other hand, a very marked accumulation of some elements, manganese for example, could result in a manganese content in leaf litter that is toxic to seedlings of other species--thus giving the accumulators a competitive advantage at early stages of the life cycle.

PRECIPITATION OF ELEMENTS

At extremely high ranges of acidity (low pH), ions of many of the metallic elements are precipitated as hydroxides, and since it is likely that there are microsites in peat in which the acidity is much higher than the pH reading indicates for a soil sample, there is probably some precipitation of these elements in peat at all times. The acidity at which precipitation occurs for some critical elements is shown in Table IV (as well as elements affected by alkalinity).

Interactions of elements are affected by solubility, and when any are precipitated by high acidity or, in the case of the five shown above, by alkalinity, they are no longer capable of interactions with other elements. These latter interactions are what, in many cases, render an element available to absorption by plant roots, and inability to interact results in the element remaining in unavailable form. Thus, for example, phosphorus in the form of phosphate is released at a more rapid rate in anaerobic soils low in phosphate than in aerobic soils low in phosphate, a difference attributed to conversion of the phosphate binder ferric oxyhydroxide to ferrous form as a result of reduction. Ferrous oxyhydroxides are gellike materials, and present greater surface area than ferric oxyhydroxide. Hence, they release phosphorus to the soil solution at a faster rate than does the ferric compound. The ferrous forms also absorb phosphate faster than the ferric form when phosphate is in high concentration in the soil solution (Patrick and Khalid, 1974). Thus, the amount of dissolved inorganic phosphate in bog soils depends on the presence of ferrous forms that release phosphate to solutions low in phosphorus and absorb it from solutions high in phosphorus. The reactions determine whether the phosphorus concentration in the soil water is adequate to meet the nutritional requirements of the plants.

It should be emphasized that this particular reaction is only one of many, all in a sense working synchronously, that have an effect upon availability of nutrient elements in the soil. Other chemical relationships, such as the concentrations of Ca^{2+} and Mg^{2+} for example, also influence exchange of phosphorus in soils, although their effect is probably less pronounced than that of the iron compounds. This is but one example of what must be an almost countless array of interrelationships among various elements and compounds in bog soils or, for that matter, humic soils of all kinds, particularly those of northern forests. The relationships are not understood in anything resembling a really detailed manner. Since the very process of removing peat from its natural environment and transporting it to the laboratory for analysis results in subtle and unidentified shifts in conditions, study of these soils is always difficult and the best that can be accomplished for some time to come will be a rather general assessment of the chemical nature and biochemical significance of the more common elements and compounds present in peat soils.

17 Nutrients and Plant Communities

Nutrient availability in the soils of bogs and conifer swamps has an apparently decisive influence upon the plant species that grow there. In these nutritionally depauperate habitats, there is a competitive advantage, for example, for plants with evergreen, sclerophyllous leaves, as well as other apparently xerophyllous morphological characteristics typical of bog ericads and species such as *Betula pumila* and *Betula glandulosa* commonly found in peatland habitats.

It at least appears that the nutritional status of the soil bears importantly upon the floristic composition of plant communities in such areas, as well as upon the successional relationships among plants making up the community. These are coincident with regional differences and probably at times are difficult to distinguish from them. Thus, far northern bogs have a somewhat different flora and differing successional relationships among species than do lowland communities at the southern fringe of the region where the bogs are commonly found. Community differences over distance, then, are the result of responses to regional climatic differences as well as variations in nutrient status among the bogs in any given local area (Fig. 1).

Certainly one of the most interesting and convincing demonstrations of the influence of nutrients upon composition of bog communities was described by Watt and Heinselman (1945), who studied the peatlands of northern Minnesota. They observed that areas downslope from exposures of mineral soil support a rich swamp forest that contrasts sharply with adjacent areas lacking such exposure.

They summarized the relationship as follows:

> There is circumstantial evidence that forests located downslope from margins and islands are productive and floristically rich because these sites are enriched by mineral-bearing ground water, while the adjacent muskegs are poorer because the accumulation of sphagnum peat has

Fig. 1. This peatland in the far north of Canada (west of Great Bear Lake) is visually not greatly different from the conifer bogs of the Great Lakes region, but the conifer forest in Canada is much more extensively distributed over the landscape, occupying both uplands and lowland areas. The dominant trees here are stunted Picea mariana and the shrubs are B. blandulosa and L. decumbens.

isolated them from mineral-bearing waters. Where a mineral
soil island occurs within a peatland, there is commonly a
linear band of rich swamp forest downslope from the island.
Such bands of floristically different vegetation have been
termed "water tracks" because they seem to mark the course
of mineral bearing ground water....*

Nitrogen and phosphorus levels in black spruce foliage
collected from good sites in the water tracks, and also from
very poor muskegs bearing stunted trees, were significantly
correlated with site quality. The higher levels of nitrogen
on the good sites were probably the result of nitrogen fixation by *Alnus*, abundant on good sites but absent from poor ones.
The roots of the alder have well-developed nodules, and nitrogen fixed by alders becomes available eventually to other plants
in the area.

Calcium and presumably other minerals are available in much
greater quantity in water tracks than in other areas of muskeg.
These minerals come from inorganic soil substrata, from litter
of plants such as *Alnus* and *Larix* that have a high mineral content, and from movement of water from nearby mineral islands.
Higher levels of minerals on better sites probably also result
from more rapid decay and mineralization of organic material.
One factor or a combination of the above factors accounts for
the more vigorous and diversified communities found in water
tracks, evidence that availability of nutrient minerals is an
important environmental influence upon plant communities in
peatland.

OTHER INFLUENCES: ALLELOPATHY

Nutrient supplies are but one factor influencing plant
growth in peatlands. Another of the more interesting but little
understood factors is allelopathy. Bioassays conducted by
Peterson (1965) in eastern Canada indicated that dry leaves of
K. angustifolia hinder root development in black spruce. The
germination percentage of black spruce seeds is evidently un-
affected by *Kalmia*-leaf extracts, but the presence of *Kalmia*
on upland sites appeared to be associated with abnormally poor
tree growth. Laboratory studies showed that a substance in
leaf extracts destroys epidermal and cortical cells in the
roots of seedlings and, presumably, of older trees as well.

It is well established that plants of some species produce
chemical compounds that inhibit the growth of other plants,
but the extent to which this phenomenon occurs in bogs and
marshes is still not known. That it is possibly of widespread
significance, however, is demonstrated by a study conducted on

* Copyright 1965, the Ecological Society of America.

extracts from 59 species of living and dried plants (Brown, 1962). Germination of jack pine seeds was inhibited by a variety of materials; one of the strongest inhibitors was an extract from a species of *Solidago*. Equally interesting was the fact that some of the extracts apparently increased germination percentage. The effect of such materials upon germination, growth, and development in the common bog species, as well as upon the relationships among the species in the communities, would probably be found to be of considerable significance if studies were undertaken.

NUTRIENTS AND SUCCESSION

On north slopes of hills in central Alaska, there is a progression of forest to bog; in the coniferous forests there is a relatively rapid accumulation of mosses on the soil surface, the permafrost rises, nitrogen becomes less and less available, and growth of trees declines. The process continues until the forest is converted to a *Sphagnum* bog with stunted spruce. At this latter stage, conditions are unfavorable for mineralization of nitrogen, available nitrogen is in short supply, and most of the nitrogen present is confined to the colder depths of the active layer. In one study, that of Heilman (1968), radiocarbon dating showed that 18-28 in. of *Sphagnum* peat had accumulated in less than 185 years.

That nitrogen and other nutrient minerals were in short supply was also indicated by foliar analysis, and Heilman found significant declines in phosphorus, potassium, and nitrogen in black spruce foliage as succession proceeded from forest to bog. The levels of magnesium, calcium, manganese, and zinc in black spruce foliage, however, appeared to be above deficiency levels in all stages of succession and showed no significant relationship to succession.

In the soil, perhaps the most significant development was the increase in depth of the moss and peat layer, which had an effect on the availability of nutrient mineral elements as well as on the acidity of the soil water. In general, the total nutrient concentrations were considerably higher in mineral than in organic soils and horizons. The various nutrient elements respond differently to the changing conditions as succession proceeds, due to differing chemical properties, and Heilman found that the proportion of exchangeable over unexchangeable forms of the various elements was modified by increasing acidity as succession progressed. It was of interest that there were higher concentrations of exchangeable manganese and zinc in the *Sphagnum* soils; this, too, was the result of lower pH and, for manganese, reducing conditions. Only a small proportion of the zinc and manganese was in exchangeable form in mineral soils.

Heilman concluded that declining availability of nutrients is a primary factor in reducing the rate of tree growth and the forest tree productivity, although total productivity in dry weight of organic matter in the *Sphagnum* bogs remained substantial, due to the relatively rapid growth of the invading mosses.

There have been few other studies of the correlation between nutrient status and plant community succession in bogs, but it must be inferred or assumed that correlative changes occur whenever successional changes take place. There is still a lack of detailed knowledge, however, on the response of the various nutrient elements to changes in soil and vegetation as succession occurs.

One pertinent study indicated, moreover, that nutrient conditions on a free-floating mat of the bog studied were essentially identical to those on a grounded mat in the same bog. This was the result of a study by Schwintzer (1978b), who measured amounts of 11 nutrients, as well as conductivity, temperature, color, and dissolved oxygen in a bog in northern lower Michigan.

This bog, however, was evidently not typical of the bogs in the region, since six other bogs studied to form a basis of comparison had much lower values for potassium, orthophosphate, soluble phosphate, and ammonium nitrate. The other bogs were also more acidic, but values for calcium, magnesium, sodium, chlorine, and iron seemed comparable. A comparison of the six ombrotrophic bogs with the one somewhat more minerotrophic bog gives a good idea of the range of values for the various nutrients to be expected in such communities (Table I).

In making the study, expectations were that there would be somewhat greater differences between the grounded mat and the free-floating mat in nutrient content, since it was believed that the vegetational community differences were such that a nutrient differential would be expected (Schwintzer, 1978a). Critically, one might say that the differences are not all that great and are generally insufficient to indicate either a difference in vegetation (in the case of nutrients) or in nutrients (in the case of the vegetation). The differences between Bryant's bog and the other six bogs are, moreover, attributable, as Schwintzer pointed out, to the presence of septic tank seepage, release from trees following a period of high mortality, and runoff from the watershed following logging and fire some 80-100 years previously. These might account for the somewhat anomalous values for nitrogen and phosphorus.

Schwintzer states in addition that the vegetational differences between the free-floating and the grounded mats might

Table I. Chemical and Physical Characteristics of Bryant's Bog and Six Other Bogs in Northern Lower Michigan[a]

| | mg/liter | | | | | | µg/liter | | | | | | |
	Ca	Mg	K	Na	Cl	Fe	Si	O-p[b]	S-p[c]	NO_3-N	NH_4-N	pH	Cond-[d]
Bryant's Bog[e]	1.9	0.5	1.8	1.4	1.4	0.8	500	730	765	0.0	1600	4.7	40
Bryant's Bog[f]	1.9	0.6	1.5	1.7	1.5	0.9	600	470	500	0.0	850	4.3	48
Six other bogs[g]	3.2	0.7	0-5	1.6	1.7	1.1	170	32	80	8.2	230	4.1	58

[a] Data from Schwintzer (1978).

[b] Orthophosphate.

[c] Soluble phosphate.

[d] µmho/cm at 25°C.

[e] Grounded mat, average of observations.

[f] Free mat, average of observations.

[g] Average of observations.

well be accounted for by a difference in depth of the aerobic
zone, a factor shown by other workers to be important in controlling the composition of wetland plant communities (Bannister, 1971; Moore and Bellamy, 1974; Jeglum, 1973; Jeglum *et
al.*, 1974; Vitt and Slack, 1975).

RARE EXTREME CONDITIONS

Cupriferous bogs, muskegs, and swamps occur where copper-
bearing springs enrich peat with unusually large amounts of
copper. The same enrichment may also take place in the case of
many other mineral elements, but available knowledge is restricted to the effect of high concentrations of copper in peatland areas. Copper content of peat can, in fact, be employed
as a geochemical indicator of copper deposits.

Boyle (1977), for example, describes a northern cupriferous
bog apparently first noticed around 1898 by a farmer who owned
the land. The vegetation of the area failed to regenerate after a fire, and when the farmer later used peat from the bog
as a fertilizer he succeeded only in killing his cucumbers.
Analysis revealed copper in high concentrations. The bog was
later visited by prospectors who attempted to find a way to
extract copper from the peat economically. Mining companies
interested in locating the copper deposit drilled in the area,
but none were successful in locating copper ore.

The aspect of the story that interests us here, however,
is that in parts of the bog where copper concentrations were
unusually high there was a virtual absence of plants. Some in
the area, *Stereocaulon* and *Cladonia* (*Cladina*) species were
found on patches of sand and gravel, but the dominant plant was
the moss *Pohlia nutans*. In such areas, this moss appears chlorotic, contrasting with its normally dark green color, and
seedlings of conifers, deciduous trees, and shrubs may germi-
nate and take root but they soon become chlorotic and die.

Cupriferous bogs are found in many parts of northern regions, and it has been shown that the copper is bound chemically to humus materials and on such sites is not necessarily
available in quantity to plants. Whenever there is a fire in
the area, however, copper humates are exposed to oxidation and
much of the copper becomes available to the plants, which then
become chlorotic and die relatively young. Apparently only
one plant is noteworthy for its capacity to tolerate the high
amounts of available copper, and this is the *P. nutans*. A
number of other so-called copper mosses have been suspected of
being indicators of copper, but it is not known whether these
are actually indicators of copper or whether they are capable
of lush growth where sulfur is readily available. Thus, some

might better be termed "sulfur mosses," growing where sulfides
are present, whether of copper or other metallic elements. It
seems certain, however, that *P. nutans* is a copper indicator,
capable of growing where copper is abundant, becoming chlorotic
when the metal attains very high quantities in available form.
Other moss species that have been designated copper mosses include *Coscinodon cribrosus, Grimmia atrata, Mielichhoferia
elongata,* and *Mielichhoferia mielichhoferi,* all of which are
relatively rare. Some or all, however, seem to select areas
rich in sulfide minerals of copper, iron, or other elements
upon which to grow. Another rare moss found on copper-bearing
rocks is *Scopelophila ligulata* (also known as *Merceya ligulata*),
which has been found once in the Upper Peninsula of Michigan,
according to Crum (1976), who briefly describes its affinity
for copper-bearing rocks. Shacklette (1967) cites a number of
papers reporting its presence, often on mineralized areas, in
Europe, through the Himalayas, Japan, North America, and South
America. Noguchi (1956) wrote: "It is a remarkable fact that
M. ligulata grows only on soil containing such metallic substances as copper, iron, silver, etc., or on soil moistened
with sulphuric water in hot springs areas." Persson (1956)
found an average copper content of 94.5 ppm in the substrates
of samples of this moss from Java, India, Turkey, USSR, France,
and Switzerland. The moss has also been found on a Civil War
mining site in Tennessee, as well as on sites in Japan containing, variously, limonite, pyrrhotite, copper, and antimony.
Whitehead and Brooks (1970) show that some aquatic mosses can
also accumulate uranium.

Studies of heavy metal concentrations in plants growing on
mine sites have been carried out to a limited extent, both in
higher plants (Bradshaw *et al.,* Bradshaw and Chadwick, 1980;
Brooks, 1972; Cairns, 1980; Wickland, 1981) and in bryophytes
(Groet, 1976), and reclamation of mine sites has become a
topic of considerable interest worldwide due to increasing environmental awareness. Additional studies along this line can
be anticipated.

SUMMARY

In summary, it is thus evident that a wide variety of environmental conditions affect growth of plants in the northern
bogs and conifer forests, not least of which are supplies of
nutrients and other substances in soils. These may be present
in both available and unavailable forms in relation to plant
nutrition, as well as in a wide variety of concentrations from
levels so low that nutritional deficiencies occur to levels
so high that the soil is toxic. The wide range of materials

present in peatland soils makes it evident that the chemical
milieu is a complex one, and that in the future it will be one
of the more interesting and significant subjects for research
in the field of wetland ecology.

18 Soil Conditions and Microbiology
of Bogs

That the physical conditions of *Sphagnum* bogs are unusually
severe for the growth of plants was known at least as long ago
as the turn of the century. Early ecologists recognized this
fact, and attributed the unusual morphology of the common bog
plants to these conditions. A U. S. Weather Bureau scientist,
(Cox, 1910) obtained temperatures in a bog and in surrounding
uplands at Mather, Wisconsin, from May through October 1907,
and found that the average temperatures for this six-month
period were quite low indeed (Table I). The vegetation of the
bog at Mather was a dense growth of saturated *Sphagnum,* and
the upland site was a garden at the border of the bog. The
latter had a sandy loam soil and was situated at an elevation
of about 10 ft above the surface of the bog.

Commenting on the study some years later, Rigg (1916) pointed out that the significance of these temperature differences
in explaining the "peculiar flora of sphagnum bogs" seemed to
have been overlooked. He drew attention to the Cox study as
having "an important bearing on the possible causes of the inhibition from sphagnum bogs of plants other than bog xerophytes
...." Rigg explained further that Cox had undertaken the study
with, in Rigg's words, "a view to protecting the cranberry
crop in cultivated marshes by predicting frost and thus enabling
the growers to avoid danger to the crop by flooding the marshes."

It is probably unnecessary to add that the effort initiated
by Cox has today progressed to the point where forecasts of
nighttime bog temperatures are a regular feature of the six
o'clock news in areas of Wisconsin and elsewhere in which cranberry marshes represent a major agricultural investment. As
Curtis (1959) has pointed out, we have thus a rather unusual
instance in which the microclimate of a rare and unusual plant
community is better known to millions of Americans than any
environmental factor in any other community.

Frost is possible in the bogs at any time during the growing season, but equally significant in terms of plant growth
are the maximum temperatures that occur in the bogs during the
middle of summer days. Before going into the maximum bog tem-

Table I.   Temperature Conditions[a] in a Cranberry Marsh of
Wisconsin Compared with Adjacent Upland[b]

	Bog	Upland
Surface	41.9°F	45.6
Inches above surface		
2.5	40.4	44.7
5	40.2	44.8
7.5	40.7	44.9
10	40.9	44.9
12	40.9	44.9
15	41.2	44.9
30°	43.3	45.1

[a] *Average for six month period, May to October.*

[b] *From Cox (1910).*

peratures, however, let us look at the temperatures in some of
the other communities found in the same region, so that comparisons can be made.

In soils of the Wisconsin prairie, Curtis reports that
average July temperatures at 2 p.m. at a depth of 1 in. was
82°F over a three year period. The corresponding temperature
in an oak forest was 71°F. At a depth of six inches, the
following average temperatures were recorded in July:

	Average maximum (°F)	Average minimum (°F)
Prairie	91.5	56.7
Oak forest	75.7	59.1

The extreme maximum temperature in prairie was more than 100°F
on more than half the days, compared to temperatures in the
oak forest that exceeded 85°F only on three days and never
reached 90°F.

These are not the maximum temperatures ever recorded in
Wisconsin vegetational communities, however, for Curtis cites
temperatures of 120-130°F in the leaf litter of southern mesic
forests during clear days in early spring before the trees had

leafed out. These temperatures, in fact, appear to be needed
to break dormancy of flowers and leaves of the ephemeral species in the ground layer of the forests. The temperatures in
the sand barrens grasslands of Wisconsin are even higher,
reaching 140-155°F at the surface in midsummer, with one reading of 162°F having been recorded.

How do these compare with the conditions in the bogs? As
Cox pointed out, frost remains in the soil of unflooded bogs
until late in the summer season. He records instances in
which frost has been found in the soil of marshes as late as
July 4. Curtis affirms the general opinion that surface frost
is possible in the bogs at any time during the growing season,
and differentials of 20°-30°F between the temperatures at the
bog surface and on nearby uplands are common. He adds, however, that the plants can withstand low night temperatures
since they are adapted to them, and the resistance they possess
to freezing injury is probably one of the important adaptations
that allow the bog plants to survive in this unusual environment. It may well be that high daytime temperatures are equally influential in creating conditions that only bog species
with highly specialized adaptations can endure. During the
hottest days, surface temperatures in a bog can reach 95 or
even 100°F or more at the same time that roots at depths of a
few inches may be 45-50°F or lower, with a differential of
40-50°F between leaves and roots. In spring, the temperatures
of roots can be below freezing, while at the same time the
temperatures of the leaves will be at 80-85°F or more. The
water-absorbing capacity of roots is much reduced at cold
temperatures and is virtually nil at freezing temperatures,
and so the upper parts of the plants are actually suffering
desertlike conditions. This, says Curtis, very likely ex-
plains the xeromorphy of the leaves of the bog shrubs, which
must be as adept as desert plants at conserving water supplies
in leaf tissues at such times. It seems likely that this explanation is true at least in part, but as we have discussed
above there are probably other factors also involved. One not
yet mentioned, however, is the time available for active
growth--the length of the warm season in which physiological
activity can occur at rapid rates.

Length of growing season very likely also has an important
effect upon the kinds of plants that can grow in the northern
marshlands and bogs. In central Wisconsin, marshlands have
an average growing season of about 100 days, based on the
length of time between the last day in spring with freezing
temperatures or frost and the first day in fall with temperatures below freezing. Nearby upland areas have about 130 days
without freezing temperatures or frost. In northern Wisconsin
bogs, there are roughly 70 days without freezing temperatures
or frost, stretching from around the last week in June to the

first week in September. This frost-free period, however, can be truncated at either end, or split in two in the middle, by the occurrence of frost which in marshy areas can occur at night any time in July and August, spring, and fall.

Upland weather stations in northern Wisconsin have an average of as many as three days with minimum temperatures below 40°F in July and August, and it is more than likely that these nights produce frost or freezing temperatures in the bogs and marshes. On as many as 15 nights during the months of July and August temperatures drop to 50°F, and on some of these nights, too, conditions are most likely conducive to frost in bogs and marshes.

The conditions making frost a possibility at any time during the summer are numerous, and all must be realized for frost actually to occur. First, the sky must be clear, for only on a cloudless night will heat radiating from a bog be lost and not be reflected to the ground by clouds. This may seem an esoteric explanation to persons unfamiliar with basic meteorology, but it is one of the most important factors involved in summer frosts. A great deal of heat is transferred away from the surface of a bog on clear nights, and this flux is the single most important factor accounting for cold bog temperatures.

If there is any wind, of course, the cold air from the bog is swept away, and the warmer air from adjacent uplands is brought into the bogs, preventing frost from occurring. Thus, the night must be clear and cloudless, as well as without wind, for temperatures to fall low enough to produce frost. Other factors are also involved in the lowering of bog temperatures. There can, for example, be cold air drainage from the surface of upland openings. Cold air is more dense than warm air, and moves slowly into the lower areas of marshlands and bogs. Cold air drainage does not occur where there are dense forest stands, however, since the canopy of foliage effectively insulates the surface of the ground in forests and the temperature of the air beneath the trees is not usually significantly different from that elsewhere. In openings, however, where the surface of the ground is exposed directly to the sky, the temperatures can be very cool indeed. The temperature at the bottom of small kettleholes in forest openings can reach freezing on any night in summer. The same is true of any area such as low meadows, marshes, or bogs located in depressions that are surrounded by unforested uplands. Cool air at the surface of the ground on clear windless nights moves slowly down any topographic gradient, settling in the lowest part of a hollow, cooling the ground so that radiation during the night can reduce temperatures to below freezing. Another factor tending to keep bogs cool is evaporation during daytime hours, and this augmented by transpiration of bog plants. Both evaporation and transpiration tend to cool the leaves of the plants, much as water evaporating from one's hand will cool it, and this also tends to keep marshes and bogs at relatively low temperatures during daytime hours. Peat soils are capable of storing only small quantities of heat, and this, too, accelerates cooling of peatlands during nights when other conditions are favorable for attainment of low temperatures.

Because of the temperature differential between bog surface and air, there is often a night fog over peatlands that lingers into windless mornings. From an aircraft, it is often possible to see the bogs of an area outlined perfectly by the gray morning fog.

The weather stations in northern Ontario, all of which are located on uplands, have records indicating that there are about 100 frost-free summer days inland along the northern shores of Lake Superior, westward across northern Minnesota, and eastward from Sault Ste. Marie to North Bay, Ontario, thence to Quebec City and inland for a distance all along the north shore of the St. Lawrence River to the Strait of Belle Isle. Southward of this belt the season lengthens, northward it shortens. It is of some interest that a small oval stretch of land northeast of Lake Superior, midway between Lake Nipigon and Lake Nipissing (North Bay), has an exceedingly short season, 40 days, equivalent to the frost-free season on the south end of Baffin Island and at Ft. Chimo in Ungava Bay, both of the latter decidedly arctic areas far north of the continental tree line. It is thus apparent that the conditions in the northern bogs have a definite similarity to those in the Arctic, and that there are environmental explanations for the similarity of species in the plant communities.

BOG WATERS

We have seen that the formation of bogs in the Great Lakes region is basically a consequence of the Pleistocene glaciation, or perhaps we should say the Pleistocene deglaciation since it is the latter event that left the typical topography of a formerly glaciated landscape, including the multitude of undrained kettleholes found in many areas throughout the Great Lakes region.

Kettleholes are large pits and hollows left where huge chunks of glacial ice were buried in deposits of sand and gravel remaining over the land after the continuous continental ice sheets had vanished. These chunks of ice melted and left depressions in the landscape that are now lakes or, when filled with the undecayed remains of vegetation, *Sphagnum* bogs. The bogs can be viewed as relicts of an era long past, when the recently deglaciated and barren land was filling with plants and animals that moved into the open space left in the wake of the retreating ice. Because the bogs had characteristics of colder and more arctic regions, plants adapted to cold conditions remained to grow and reproduce in bogs long after other members of the species had been forced from adjacent more temperate uplands by species better adapted to these warmer habitats. Thus we have such boreal species as *C. calyculata* and *L. groenlandicum* in bogs of Minnesota, Wisconsin, Michigan and other Great Lakes regions, species that are very abundant northward over the uplands as well as lowlands of Ontario, Manitoba, Quebec, and the other Canadian provinces and territories to the north. It is of some interest, too, that not only northern plants but also northern insects remain in the bogs as a testament to geological history; for example, 12 northern species of pselaphid beetle, called the mold beetles, are found today only in *Sphagnum* bogs south of their main range in the far northern Canadian tundra. These beetles have managed to survive in bogs as far south as the southern limit of glaciation in Minnesota, Wisconsin, Indiana, and New England, persisting in the bogs because they require a moist habitat and can withstand low temperatures. Like many plant species, these insects must have lived out the Pleistocene just south of the ice front, moving north when the ice wasted away, and for the most part following it north to what is now tundra. The greater proportion of the population moved north, but in doing so left small colonies in *Sphagnum* bogs across the continent where kettle lakes had been formed and later filled with peat to create bogs. Here, too, there were relict communities of northern plants, including the *Sphagnum* mosses, *Chamaedaphne, Ledum, Andromeda,* and *Kalmia.*

The water in these bogs possesses some unique characteristics, a result of the fact that the bogs are, in a sense, sealed off from the rest of the environment, having no outlet and obtaining water only from precipitation falling on the small surrounding watershed. The reason the bogs persist is that the amount of water received as rainfall and snowfall is at least equal to that lost in evapotranspiration. Any excess seeps slowly away through the sandy soil, or, in times of heavy rainfall, by flooding over the lowest part of the upland surrounding the bog.

There are thus environmental characteristics that are uniqu to bogs, among them a permanently--or at least usually--water-logged soil composed largely of peat, a vegetational cover of plant species with distinct adaptations to this special habitat, and a lack of nutrient minerals since much of what has been available is tied up in the undecomposed remains of dead plants. The bog waters have a very low level, or a virtual absence, of free dissolved oxygen. They possess a generally very high acidity and a reducing rather than an oxidizing chemical environment. There are, in the deeper levels of peat in the bogs, a distinctive aggregation of microorganisms capable of existing under cold, acid, anaerobic conditions, and they are accompanied by a select group of aerobic organisms in the upper surface strata of peat where oxygen is present. These latter organisms, along with some invertebrate animals, manage to accomplish most of the small amount of decomposition of organic matter that takes place in the bogs.

The basic chemistry of bog water has long been a subject of sporadic study. Table II is a comparison of chemical characteristics of the waters of bogs and swamps and of surface stream and forest soil moisture in northern Wisconsin, the data having been obtained by Wilde and Randall (1951).

As Wilde and Randall wrote: "Ground water of moss peat bogs, or 'muskegs,' presents an extreme condition of deoxidation and impoverishment; such water is characterized by a strongly acid reaction, an absence of oxygen and carbonates, a low specific conductivity, and a very low negative oxidation-reduction potential." They added that such an environment can support only poor growth of both coniferous and deciduous trees. Comparing growth conditions in bogs with those in sandy upland soils that allow rapid growth of pine and aspen, they showed that the latter soils possessed a higher concentration of minerals, a higher oxygen content, lower acidity, and a higher redox potential. Wood (rather than moss) peat soils, muck soils, and poorly drained sandy soils are each characterized by specific properties, but in general these are intermediate between bog soils and upland sandy soils supporting good tree growth.

The difference between moss peat and wood peat is actually quite striking, and this is brought out in data obtained in northern Ontario by Pierce (1953), who compared a number of sites on each substrate. A summary comparison of his data is presented in Table III.

The most noteworthy difference shown in the data is the decided increase in hardness, accompanied by an increase in specific conductance and pH, indicating the presence of higher amounts of bases in woody peat of the *Thuja/Abies* swamp than was present in the peat of the black spruce/*Sphagnum* bog *(P. mariana/Sphagnum* species).

An equally interesting comparison was made by Pierce (1953) among four wet soils, distinguished by chemical composition, vegetation, and rates of tree growth. This comparison is given in Table IV.

Table II. Comparison of the Chemistry of Bog Water, Surface Stream, and Forest Soil Water[a]

	Depth to ground water (in.)	pH	Hardness[b] (ppm)	Specific cond.[c]	Dissolved O_2 (ppm)	Redox[d]
Black spruce/tamarack bog	4	3.5	None	5.0	None	-364
Black spruce/tamarack bog	12	3.9	None	5.7	None	-335
Poor aspen stand	20	4.2	10	14.0	0.3	-305
White cedar/balsam fir bog	6	6.2	24	7.5	None	-42
White cedar/balsam fir bog	4	6.5	83	20.9	0.45	69
Lowland hardwoods	6	6.0	36	10.0	None	-81
Red pine/white pine upland	72	7.7	25	15.0	3.3	95
Creek draining cedar swamp	---	6.9	98	19.5	8.5	85
Creek from beaver dam	---	7.4	115	19.9	6.0	163
Lowland hardwoods (south)	24	8.2	107	28.0	0.4	161

[a]Data from Wilde and Randall (1951).

[b]Measures carbonates of calcium, magnesium, potassium, etc.

[c]Specific conductivity is a measure of dissolved minerals.

[d]Redox is a measure of reducing/oxidizing conditions present.

Table III. Chemistry of Moss Peat and Wood Peat[a,b]

	Moss peat (three sites)			Wood peat (three sites)		
pH	4.0	4.1	4.1	5.3	6.0	6.0
Redox	-213	-207	-208	-220	-203	-357
Free dissolved oxygen (ppm)	0.1	0.4	0.7	1.6	2.5	0.1
Specific conductance	4.7	5.1	4.4	7.2	5.4	6.8
Hardness (ppm)	9.6	10.0	7.2	28.2	28.0	22.1

[a] The moss peat sites supported P. mariana, Sphagnum, Ledum, and Chamaedaphne species. The woody peat swamp supported Thuja, Abies, Oxalis, and Coptis as major species in the plant communities.
[b] Data from Pierce (1953).

Pierce adds that his data and that obtained elsewhere in the Great Lakes region by other workers are generally comparable. Perhaps most interesting is the revelation of successional trends:

The results of the analysis also clearly indicate the general successional trend from a Hypnum peat swamp to the Sphagnum peat swamp, a trend enforced by the irreversible fixation of nutrient elements incorporated in the tissues of mosses, especially those of Sphagnum. The progressive retardation of ground water movement by the remains of Sphagnum undoubtedly contributes to the succession of plants and metamorphosis of organic soils, a process which eventually leads to a totally unproductive "leatherleaf" bog or Sphagnum fuscum "muskeg."

It is thus evident that peat soils of wetlands have many characteristics distinguishing them clearly from mineral forest soils; low pH, low free dissolved oxygen, low content of inorganic nutrient minerals, relatively high content of minerals tied up in undecayed organic compounds, and high water content in the waterlogged organic material. Different peats can be compared in terms of nutrient content and potential productivity. These are topics that can profitably bear closer inspection, and subsequent chapters will be given over to discussion of some of them in greater detail.

Table IV. Analysis of Ground Water in Black Spruce Stands in the Vicinity of Hearst, Ontario, Canada[a]

	Reaction (pH)	Redox potential (m.V.)	Dissolved oxygen (ppm)	Specific conductance mhos X 10^5	Hardness (ppm)
Black spruce of very slow rate of growth--about 3 cds/A. *Sphagnum Ledum-Chamaedaphne* site	5.9	-176	0.9	4.1	24
Black spruce with some swamp birch of slow rate of growth--5 to 10 cds/A. *Sphagnum-Kalmia-Ledum-Vaccinium* site with some *Calliergon schreberi* and *Rubus chamaemorus*	6.3	-145	1.8	7.1	74
Black spruce with some balsam fir of fair rate of growth--15 cds/A. *Calliergon-Vaccinium-Cornus* site	6.3	-131	2.2	5.8	43
Black spruce with some balsam fir and balsam poplar of rapid rate of growth--25 to 35 cds/A. *Hypnum-Dicranum-Lycopodium-Coptis-Maian-themum* site	7.0	-111	2.6	24.0	157

[a] Yields in standard cords per acre at an approximate age of 120 years. From Pierce (1953).

MICROBIOLOGY OF A BOG

A thin layer at the surface of peat soils is aerated and supports organisms with aerobic respiration; the subsurface strata are isolated from a source of atmospheric oxygen and support anaerobic respiration and fermentation. Aerobic activity is limited mostly to the upper inch or less of peat beneath the surface of waterlogged material.

Aerobic decomposition of organic material, in classical terms, results in release of carbon dioxide and other oxidation products. Anaerobic respiration and fermentation result in production of such gases as methane and hydrogen sulfide, in addition to a great variety of short-chain organic compounds including amines, alcohols, mercaptans, and organic acids. It is the gases and organic compounds that give fresh marsh peat its distinctive smell. These gases establish a basis for the idea that some are sufficiently combustible to ignite upon contact with oxygen of the air, resulting in the rare ghostly flame known as will-o'-the wisp, *ignis fatuus,* reportedly seen over some marshlands at night when organic gases bubble to the surface and ignite. Whether this kind of spontaneous combusion can ever occur is, however, open to question, but the phenomenon evidently has been observed and the cause is still something of a mystery.

It is presently not known how many different species of bacteria, actinomycetes, and fungi inhabit bog soils, but some indication of total numbers of organisms per gram of soil can be obtained from a study of soil microfungi (thus excluding mushrooms and the like) conducted by Christensen and Whittingham (1965) in 15 northern Wisconsin open bog and conifer swamp communities. The open bog communities were dominated by the ericaceous shrubs *A. glaucophylla, C. calyculata, K. polifolia,* and *L. groenlandicum.* The two other plant communities studied were dominated, respectively, by *L. laricina* and *P. mariana* and by *T. occidentalis* and *A. balsamea.* Moss species, mostly members of *Sphagnum,* were abundant in the ericaceous bogs and the *Picea-Larix* swamps but the *Sphagnum* species were replaced by other mosses in the *Thuja-Abies* stands.

The total numbers of the various categories of microorganisms in the soils of the various bogs and swamps were calculated as shown in the following tabulation:

Bacterial (all communities)	0.9-23.4 million/gm
Actinomycetes (all communities)	0.1-0.4 million/gm
Microfungi	
open bog	47.8 thousand/gm
Picea-Larix	285 thousand/gm
Thuja-Abies	403 thousand/gm

Microfungi populations in the open bogs were low in numbers, and this was attributed to the fact that bog peat is
more subject to waterlogging than the forested peat. The effect in terms of acidity can readily be seen from the following pH readings taken at the various study sites:

Site	pH
Open bog	3.0 - 3.7
Picea-Larix	3.3 - 3.6
Thuja-Abies	3.5 - 6.7

The number of different species of microfungi present and
the number of stands in which each was found are given in
Table V.

Thus, species numbers are high; many species occur only in
one stand. Species occurring in greatest abundance are few
in number, but these occur in all stands of a given community.
Species occurring in greatest abundance in the communities are
as follows:

Open bog--*Geotrichum candidum, Penicillium thomii*

Picea-Larix--*Cryptococcus laurentii, Mortierella vinacea,
   Oidiodendron flavum, Oidiodendron tenuissimum* (group), *Penicillium odoratum, Periconia* sp., and two species of yeast

Thuja-Abies--*Cryptococcus laurentii, Oidiodendron cerealis,
   Torulopsis aeria, Trichoderma* spp. (two), and a species of
   yeast

In each community a few species thus account for most of
the individual microfungi present, but there are nevertheless
a rather large number of species represented by only a relatively few individuals each. At least many of the species present
here in low numbers would most likely increase in number drama-
tically were conditions to change favorably for them; they are
species that more or less lie in wait for specific environmental events that may occur only infrequently, but when the proper
conditions do occur these microfungi will increase in number
and will continue to be abundant as long as the favorable conditions persist.

The species that are present in the bog and swamp communities in large numbers are those adapted to the conditions that
currently prevail. According to Christensen and Whittingham
(1965), these conditions are as follows: high acidity, low

Table V. Species of Microfungi Present in Different Soils[a]

Number of stands in which species was present[b]	Number of species		
	Open bogs	Picea-Larix	Thuja-Abies
5	2	8	6
4	3	7	12
3	7	9	17
2	13	11	32
1	83	69	114
Total	108	104	181

[a] Data from Christensen and Whittingham (1965).

[b] Five stands of each community type were sampled.

temperatures, seasonal inundation, undecomposed organic materials in abundance. As they summarize:

> Specific limiting factors probably could be demonstrated experimentally for individual species, but the soil micro-fungal community as a whole undoubtedly is influenced by a multiplicity of factors including microclimate, chemical characteristics of the substrate, and microfloral and micro-faunal associates.... In the populations as a whole, Asco-mycetes, yeasts, Dematiaceae, and Mortierella species were common, whereas Aspergillus, Fusarium, and Sphaeropsidales were rare. Approximately one-half of the identified species appear to be absent or rare in mineral soils, but several are well-known wood, wood-pulp, or litter forms. Species composition in the microfungal communities is correlated with species composition and maturity in the overlying higher plant community.

From the data it appeared that shifts in species composition correlated with maturity of the vegetation; the Thuja-Abies swamps were densely stocked with old trees; the Picea-Larix communities ranged from one stand with small trees to the old-est with trees 6 in. in diameter, and the bogs had been period-ically burned and possessed a relatively young community.

The adaptations of fungi that permitted growth in bogs and swamps, according to Christensen and Whittingham, were acid tolerance, cold tolerance, capacity to survive at least season-al inundation, and an ability to attack relatively undecomposed materials. About one-half of the species identified are rare

or largely absent from mineral soils, although several are
well-known wood, wood-pulp, or litter inhabitants.

A detailed study of the microbiology of peats in Alberta,
Canada, was carried out by Christensen and Cook (1970), who
compared the microflora of a fibrisol, a mesisol, and a humisol
in a muskeg, obtaining counts of up to two million psychro-
philic bacteria per gram oven-dry weight of peat in the shallow
upper horizons. Deeper and more humified layers had 3-10
million, with mesophilic bacteria about one-fifth more abundant
and thermophiles scarce with less than one million per gram of
dry peat. In the upper well-aerated levels there were abundant
fungi, from one to six million per gram in the upper 25 cm,
but numbers dropped sharply in lower levels probably due to
anaerobic conditions. Actinomycetes were virtually absent.

Tests on the peat showed that there was little or no nitrification or nitrogen fixation and only the first stage of
denitrification took place. Organisms converting nitrate to
nitrite were present in greatest numbers below the surface
layers. Bacteria capable of ammonification of protein were
present in significant numbers. Iron-reducing bacteria were
considerably more abundant here than in mineral soils. Christensen and Cook concluded that detailed study of the anaerobic
populations would be required to determine whether facultative
anaerobes are responsible for the increase in bacterial numbers at depth, but it was apparent that at least three-quarters
of the total soil population must be anaerobic.

The accumulation and distribution of nitrogen in bogs com-
prise one of the more significant aspects of bog soil chemistry.
A large proportion of nitrogen acquired by plants is eventually
tied up in undecomposed organic matter, thus becoming unavailable to growing plants. Additions of nitrogen to peat soils by
symbiotic fixation by nonleguminous plants or by algae may, at
least in places, occur in sufficient intensity to provide a
significant amount of nitrogen for plant growth. Among the
genera shown to fix nitrogen by this means are *Alnus, Ceanothus,
Myrica, Comptonia,* and *Shepherdia,* all of which may be found
growing at times around or near the edges of bogs. It seems
at least possible that significant additions to the nitrogen
capital of bog soils is accomplished by either free-living organisms or by nodule bacteria in symbiotic relationship with
species of the above genera. The addition of nitrogen to soils
could occur on sites adjacent to bogs and be carried into at
least the lagg zones by movement of ground water. As to the
importance of free-living bacteria in nitrogen fixation, little
is presently known, but it has been pointed out that anaerobic
Clostridium species might account for more nitrogen fixation
than has hitherto been suspected. Significant fixation by
these forms can occur under anaerobic conditions, according to

some studies, and it is evident that they may be of considerable importance in the largely anaerobic low strata of peat soils.

In summary, the peat soils of bogs are the result of rates of organic production greater than those of decomposition, the latter being inhibited by frequent or continual waterlogging, anaerobic subsurface conditions, and high acidity. Bog plants, as a consequence, must cope with these conditions as well as with low nutrient availability resulting from slow decay of organic matter and slow release of nitrogen, phosphorus, potassium, and other nutrients. As described in greater detail elsewhere, the prevalence of evergreen sclerophyllous species in bogs evidently is related to the ability of these plants to retain scarce nutrient elements by shedding leaves slowly, thus prolonging the period in which minerals can be used, as well as the length of time over which the nutrients are available in small amounts for uptake from the soil. These adaptations evidently make recycling of nutrients possible by avoiding a sudden release of nutrients in superfluous quantities, much of which would be lost since the plants probably would be unable to reabsorb such large amounts all at once. The latter concept must, however, presently be termed hypothetical, since little work has yet been conducted to show beyond a doubt that such is actually what occurs. The idea appears, at least at present, to be a reasonable explanation for the striking coincidence that these plant species are found so consistently in dominant positions in the bog communities.

19 The Mosses: Basic Ecology

Mosses are certainly among the most interesting and eco-
logically significant of the northern bog plants, yet there
are relatively few studies of the role they play in vegetational community dynamics (Fig. 1). That studies are so few is
probably due to the difficulty of identifying many of the species, especially those of the genus *Sphagnum,* as well as to the
fact that they are neither showy nor conspicuous since they
often lie hidden beneath the cover of shrubby and herbaceous
plants. The problems of identification are now becoming more
tractable, however, with the publication of regional species
lists and manuals that provide good illustrations and keys for
identification. It is perhaps of interest to note that lists
and manuals for the higher plants were being published in numbers by the turn of the century, but only recently have works
on mosses become available, even for such populated areas as
the Great Lakes region (Crum, 1976). As another example, while
the earliest collections of mosses in Labrador were probably
made by the Moravian missionaries in the eighteenth century,
these unfortunately lacked all data except the notation "Labrador," and only recently has an annotated listing of species
found in this remote region appeared (Brassard and Weber, 1978).
Interest in the mosses is due, surely at least in part, to
growing recognition that many moss species, especially those
of the genus *Sphagnum,* are exceedingly important in ecological
relationships of many native plant communities. As Busby *et
al.* (1978) pointed out:

> Mosses occupy a significant proportion of land and form
> a conspicuous component of the vegetation throughout boreal
> regions in North America and Europe. Little is known, how-
> ever, about the environmental factors which control their
> growth rates and habitat limits, or even what are the en-
> vironmental characteristics of these habitats.

Water is a fundamental factor controlling growth and
distribution of mosses. Moss water relations are different
from those of most higher plants; they lack root systems,

Fig. 1. Tufts of the moss genus Polytrichum are here covered with morning dew and shining in early sunlight. The dominant moss species in the bogs are Sphagnum species, but Polytrichum is at times found growing at the perimeter of the bogs.

conducting systems are generally not well developed, and they have no mechanisms for water storage or, as individuals, to reduce water loss.

Metabolic activity of most dry-habitat species is closely linked to the water regime. Activity increases rapidly when mosses are wetted, and decreases to a very low level, or ceases completely, when they dry out.... *

This latter characteristic is probably not limited to the
dry-habitat species, although the frequency of drying is surely greater in those mosses occupying the drier habitats.   The
rates of water loss and the frequency with which they are
moistened are critical in controlling moss growth and distribution according to Busby *et al.*, but other factors also must
play important roles: radiation (solar) intensity, temperature,
evaporation stress, wind, and source of water, whether precipitation or subsurface seepage.

Of the many moss species found in northern regions, both
in forest and bog habitats, those of the genus *Sphagnum* can be
said to be among the most important.   As Crum (1976) states:

> *Sphagnum* is exceedingly important in nature.   It con-
> trols and impedes drainage of the vast North.   Its effect
> on permafrost and maneuverability in the arctic is immense.
> It controls some kinds of hydrarch successions, not only by
> its remarkable ability to soak up water but also by creat-
> ing an acid habitat for itself and other plants active in
> the development of bogs.   This is done by the exchange of
> hydrogen ions for other cations (especially Ca^{++} and Mg^{++},
> less readily K^+ and Na^+) so that the species can flourish
> even in proximity to highly basic waters.   The first in-
> vaders are usually sedges, but the acidity which gives di-
> rection to bog succession is provided by *Sphagnum,* with
> different species in control at each stage of succession
> toward drier and more acid conditions.

As implied by these statements, some moss species attain
greatest abundance in wet habitats, others are intermediate,
and some are found in greatest abundance on dry sites.   In bogs,
Sphagnum mosses usually cover most of the area open to the sunlight as well as wet to moist in terms of water supply.   In
areas where shrubs and herbaceous species create shade and
where water is less abundant, other species are found in addition to *Sphagnum*.   Under very dense patches of trees and in
bog forests with a heavy canopy and relatively dry conditions,
Sphagnum may be reduced in abundance by the low light intensity, the covering of conifer needle litter, a deeper upper
level of the water table, and perhaps by the reduced water
supply from precipitation as a result of interception of rainfall by the tree canopy.   In such places the feather mosses
may be more abundant, with such dominants as *Pleurozium schreberi, Hylocomium splendens,* and *Ptilium crista-castrensis* making up the large proportion of the moss mat, along with *Dicranum* mosses and perhaps some liverworts.   The driest sites, often
exposed to winter winds, may have such species of mosses as
Tortula ruralis and *Ceratodon purpureus* (Anderson and Bourdeau,
1955; Clymo, 1963; Sparling, 1966; Bazzaz *et al.,* 1970; Peter-

son and Mayo, 1975; Stanek *et al.*, 1977; Lane, 1977; Pakarinen, 1978).

Mosses decrease in prevalence along topographic clines to more open upland forest, usually deciduous or of the kind known as the upland conifer-hardwood forest, where there is an increase in the herbs and shrubs. Here are found scattered representatives of the variety of moss genera that colonize fallen trees and the bases of tree trunks, rocks, recently burned areas, wherever a thick surface litter does not prevent growth, where moisture is available, and where the soil is otherwise favorable for moss growth.

Species of feather mosses, like species of *Sphagnum,* while often growing together on favorable sites over a large part of the region under consideration here, nevertheless have individual geographical distribution and ecological preferences, although they overlap through a broad range. *Hylocomium splendens,* for example, is found, according to Crum (1976), on humus, mineral soil, and rocks, and in moist and wet forests, deeply shaded ravines, rotten logs, and bases of trees; it is circumpolar, and found in North America south to Oregon, Colorado, Iowa, and North Carolina. It is alpine, subalpine, boreal, and arctic in distribution. *Pleurozium schreberi* is also circumpolar, boreal, and subarctic, and is found southward in North America to Arkansas and North Carolina; it is found on humus and soil, in dry open woods, as well as in bogs and wet coniferous woods. It is often the most abundant of the feather mosses in favorable habitats in the Great Lakes region. *Ptilium crista-castrensis* is circumpolar, Alaska to Newfoundland in North America, south to Oregon, Montana, Michigan, and North Carolina, often on humus and old mossy logs in moist and wet forests, but it is usually not as prominent as either *Hylocomium* or *Pleurozium* in the sites where feather mosses are found through their range.

The relationship of the feather mosses to the trees forming the canopy in conifer swamps can probably be said to conform closely to that described for *Hylocomium* in Scandinavia by Tamm (1964), who describes the growth rates of this moss as follows:

Among the first things observed was the dependence of the *Hylocomium* carpet upon the tree canopy. Outside the tree canopy the annual yield of the moss carpet decreases regularly with the distance from tree crown projections...until *Hylocomium* is replaced by other species. Shrubs or heather may under circumstances act as a substitute for trees. Exceptions from the dependence of the moss carpet on a living canopy are found on steep rocky slopes, where water often trickles through luxuriant *Hylocomium* tussocks.

Beneath the tree canopy *Hylocomium* yield varies inversely with light intensity. At the same time nutrient concentrations in the living moss increase with increasing shade, while the nutrient concentrations of mosses from outside the canopy were relatively constant, independent of exposure.

The reason for this variation in nutrient content is, according to Tamm, as follows: Tree crowns release plant nutrients in rainwater falling into the canopy, and the mosses possess an efficient absorbing system for these nutrients. Collecting funnels set up beneath tree crowns, as well as in the open, left little doubt that mosses such as *Hylocomium splendens* growing in a forest normally get most of their minerals from the tree canopy. As Tamm states:

> Even if it is dangerous to assume specific functions of certain morphological characters, it may be pointed out that such organs as the paraphyllia of *Hylocomium splendens* and the aerial rhizoids of *Dicranum* species are just such surface-enlarging structures that may be expected in plants getting their nutrient supply from intermittent showers of very dilute solutions.

A condensed version of Tamm's data on the amounts of soluble substances carried down by a year's precipitation at a point near Stockholm is given in Table I. It can be seen from the table that mosses such as *H. splendens* depend upon the leachate from tree crowns for at least a significant part of the mineral nutrients needed for nutrition. This nutrient source must also be of importance for other forest plants, including trees; it is conceivable also that leachate from forest trees in the surrounding watershed will contribute some nutrients to plants in open bogs without a tree canopy. Work cited by Tamm (1964), Lazrus *et al.* (1970), and others confirms that a large part of the potassium turnover in a forest occurs through rainfall leaching.

On the other hand, much of the nitrogen supply is not accounted for in this way, and the nitrogen in rainwater must be augmented by nitrogen from other sources such as biological fixation by algae and such plants as *Alnus* and *Myrica,* both of which are among the native plant species known to fix nitrogen in significant quantities. Analyses of the rain washings, however, indicate that the amounts of phosphorus, potassium, calcium, and presumably magnesium, manganese, and other minerals are of the same quantity as that required by the mosses. It is evident that the supplies received from the atmosphere and the canopy leachate, added to the input from waters flowing into the bog from adjacent uplands, can account for the nutrient minerals required by mosses as well as vascular

Table I.   Mineral Nutrients in Rainwater[a]

Canopy type	Minerals (ka/ha/year)					
	NH_4	K	Na	Ca	P	Total ash
Open field	n.d.[b]	3.9	5.0	5.1	0.2	46
Open field	1.8	1.4	2.8	4.6	0.1	28
Birch stand	6.7	19.5	14.4	13.2	1.9	128
Oak stand	3.2	15.8	9.5	13.1	1.1	108
Pine stand	5.5	10.0	19.4	17.0	0.8	157

[a]*Data from Tamm (1964).*

[b]*No data.*

plants (Lazrus *et al.*, 1970; Likens and Borman, 1971; Likens *et al.*, 1977).

THE SIGNIFICANT PARAMETERS

It is apparent that sources of nutrients other than rain-washings through a canopy are often sufficient for moss growth in the so-called ombrotrophic open bogs in which mosses are dominant species. One study, conducted by Busby *et al.* (1978), has wide significance.

The communities studied included one consisting entirely of *Tomenthypnum nitens* and another dominated by *H. spendens*, *P. schreberi*, and *P. crista-castrensis*. All four species are conspicuous components of northern bogs. The former is a very common and characteristic species in black spruce muskegs, open bogs, and fens, and in the Great Lakes area is found also in habitats such as cedar swamps where conditions are not as acid as in typical *Sphagnum* bogs. The other three species are, as pointed out previously, collectively known as the feather mosses.

It seems significant that *Tomenthypnum* possesses tightly compacted rhizoids that form a dense tomentum at the base of stem leaves. The species grows on sites with a sparse tree and shrub canopy, and were it not for this protection, water loss from evaporation would reduce its competitive capacity. Shoot densities of the feather mosses were only 30 percent those of *Tomenthypnum*, according to Busby *et al.*, and the study showed that growth rates of the moss were reduced by the removal of the shrub canopy even in mature forests because

evaporative stress in the open became very high. As a consequence, it can be inferred that lowered evaporative stress
is at least one reason why the feather mosses are restricted
to areas sheltered by trees and shrubs.

It is evident that both mineral nutrient and water supplies
are of primary significance in the rate of growth, habitat preference, and competitive status of *Tomenthypnum* and the feather
mosses. Another study, that of *Sphagnum*-dominated plant communities in Alberta, showed that water and mineral nutrient supplies are critical factors in the growth rates and habitat preferences of *Sphagnum* and that there are actually three environmental gradients of importance to *Sphagnum*. Horton *et al.*
(1979) show that the three gradients are

         ombrotrophic --------- minerotrophic

            wet   ---------   dry

        bog margin --------- bog expanse

and that in the ombrotrophic bogs the moisture supply is derived solely from precipitation. All species known to prefer habitats with a good supply of mineralized water are absent from the ombrotrophic bogs.

It is probably useful here to note the definitions of
terms presented by Horton *et al.* (1979) in order that precise
meanings be established. They write:

> The terms ombrotrophic and oligotrophic are often used
> interchangeably, but properly should be referred to two
> different gradients; ombrotrophic-minerotrophic as opposed
> to oligotrophic-eutrophic...When pH, cation concentrations,
> and conductivity readings indicate a contact with mineral
> soil water, the mire is termed a fen.... A fourth environ-
> mental gradient is chionophobus to chionophilous (i.e.,
> responses of the vegetation to snow cover and duration).
> This gradient has received less attention in studies of
> mires than the other three discussed above...it is probably
> of equivalent importance and should probably be considered
> when possible.

Horton *et al.* found that the driest habitat was the so-
called treed-tundra, in which small and scattered spruce trees
grew in a hummocky bog where *Sphagnum fuscum* and *Sphagnum nemo-
reum* were dominant mosses. The hummocks were covered with
herbs and shrubs, notably *Rubus chamaemorus, Betula glanduli-
fera, L. groenlandicum, L. decumbens (L. palustre),* along with
such lichens as *Cladina mitis, Cladina rangiferina,* and *Cladina
stellaris* (all formerly classified under the genus *Cladonia*).

In such communities, the substrate was highly acidic (pH 3.3-4.1), ombrotrophic (with Ca^{2+} concentrations of 0.4-5.5 ppm and Mg^{2+} concentrations of 0.01-0.3 ppm), and even depressions between the hummocks were firm and above the water level. Thaw-pockets are found in the treed-tundra, however, virtually lacking tree cover and with extensive floating carpets of *Sphagnum riparium, Sphagnum jensenii,* and *Sphagnum angustifolium.* These two communities represented the extremes along the moisture gradient; other changes in species composition occurred along a gradient from mineral poor to mineral rich. In summary, Horton *et al.* (1979) concluded that there are progressive changes in species of *Sphagnum* that dominate the communities along gradients from ombrotrophic treed-tundra, on the one hand, to thaw-pockets, on the other, and from dry minerotrophic habitats to wet minerotrophic habitats with conditions less acidic and richer in minerals. They conclude:

> In particular, the species of *Sphagnum* in the...study area are discriminating indicators of subtle changes in the environmental gradients of moisture, trophic status and exposure. Of these, the variations from rich to poor and from wet to dry are the more significant parameters. Moisture is the primary factor that controls the occurrence and distribution of the *Sphagnum* species. Their responsiveness to this gradient is most apparent in the transition from thaw-pocket to treed-tundra (particularly in places where the transition is gradual rather than abrupt). A more-or-less horizontal succession of species is related to an increasing vertical elevation above water level. In such a gradient, species of *Sphagnum* define at least five distinct niches relative to water level; in the same gradient, only two very broad responses are discernible in the vascular plants.

Other changes along the gradient from rich to poor in minerals were also apparent, and thus the gradient became two-dimensional, wet to dry along one axis, rich to poor along the other, with each species attaining greatest abundance at a given region in the two-dimensional field.

These responses to local conditions expressed in terms of site preference on the part of the various species must also have counterparts in the broad geographical performance of the species, although the latter is as yet little understood and difficult to study. The growth responses and competitive relationships of the mosses must be similar in important respects to those of the higher plants. As Horton *et al.* pointed out: "Further data are needed on the occurrence and relative abundance of species of *Sphagnum* in boreal and subarctic regions of North America and Asia in order to clarify the responses of species along the latitudinal gradient."

There must also be definable and significant differences in physiological response to habitat between the wide-ranging species and those that are more limited in range and confined to, for example eastern, western, or central North America, or to comparable areas in Asia. This marked regional difference in ability on the part of the different species to attain dominance in one or more plant communities is no better illustrated than in the studies of La Roi (1967; La Roi and Stringer, 1976); in the latter study, of the 32 most important moss species found in 26 black spruce stands distributed from Alaska to Newfoundland, only a very few retained dominant positions in all stands across the continent, and of these the feather mosses were most conspicuous for their ubiquity. Of the species noted for wide range and dominant positions in the vegetation across the continent, those most notable are listed in Table II.

Of the other species found in the stands studied by La Roi and Stringer, *Aulacomnium palustre* was of importance in some stands in the West but not in the East; *Sphagnum russowii* was of importance in some eastern stands but not in the far west.

As Horton *et al.* (1979) indicate, it is pertinent to state that:

> It is apparent from the literature...that the same species of *Sphagnum*...have similar tolerances in widely separated geographical localities, along these local environmental gradients of ombrotrophy to minerotrophy, mud-bottom or carpet to hummock, and mire margin to mire expanse. There are also regional gradients reflected in the distributions .... In general, regional gradients have not been given comparable emphasis to local gradients....

Studies of the significant factors that account in varying degrees for the abundance of the various moss species in favorable habitats over wide geographical ranges would be of considerable physiological and probably genecological significance. In such studies, however, the difficulties are as pronounced as in studies of the environmental tolerance limits and optima of species in local vegetational communities, and the difficulties are greatly compounded by the need to obtain experimental plant specimens from many widely separated places, as well as to make studies *in situ* of the plants growing in wetlands throughout a large geographical area. The studies would, of course, be of considerable scientific interest from the point of view of basic understanding of biogeographical ecology, but whether the costs of such a study could be justified on any practical economic grounds is at present probably somewhat uncertain.

Table II.   Dominance Status of Mosses   in Communities[a]

Species	% Presence in stands	% Cover (av. of all stands)
Hylocomium splendens	88	2.1-3.3
Pleurozium schreberi	96	5.1-20
Ptilium crista-castrensis	92	3.4-5.0
Dicranum fuscescens	65	less than 1.0
D. polysetum[b]	81	2.1-3.3
Pohlia nutans	42	less than 0.33
Polytrichum commune	38	less than 0.33

[a]Presence in stands and cover contributed by species noted for wide range and dominant positions in vegetational communities across the North American continent.   Data from La Roi and Stringer (1976).

[b]Not of great import in the far West.

MOSSES: PHYSIOLOGY AND HABITAT

We have seen that water is major determinant of the growth rate of mosses, but the evidence for this is, in a sense, circumstantial. The many different moss species are each found growing in a characteristic habitat, each somewhere along the scale from wet to dry, but why this preference? The answer undoubtedly must be formulated in biochemical, physiological, and genetic terms. It is, in any case, still not understood in anything resembling comprehensive detail.

There are, however, some known relationships between water supplies and physiological processes that may provide insights into the individual adaptations to the various habitats demonstrated by the various moss species. Net assimilation of carbon dioxide can be employed as a measure of the rate of photosynthesis, since a given amount of carbon dioxide must be absorbed to manufacture a given amount of carbohydrate photosynthate. This is the carbon dioxide taken up from the atmosphere by the leaf and does not include respired carbon dioxide reabsorbed directly within the leaf; presumably "gross" carbon dioxide assimilation would include both the atmospheric carbon dioxide and that released by respiration.

Various environmental conditions influence the rate of photosynthesis as measured by the carbon dioxide assimilation of a metabolically active plant in sunlight.

There is an optimal range for each of the various environmental factors involved--light intensity, temperature, water supply--and within this range the net carbon dioxide assimilation rate for each species attains its maximum. Thus, for each species there is an optimal range of temperature, light intensity, and water content of the leaf tissues, and when

all are within the optimal range then photosynthesis occurs at
a maximum rate.

The relationship between net carbon dioxide assimilation
rate and tissue water content is of particular interest because most mosses are usually subject to periodic changes in
the water supply; at some times they are soaking wet, at others
they are desiccated, and there are differences between the species in tolerance of dry conditions that have much to do with
habitat preference and geographical distribution. There is in
all species an optimal range of water content in tissues and
a decreasing rate with declining water content, until a point
is reached at which the dry moss no longer absorbs carbon dioxide in detectable amounts.

In higher plants, net photosynthesis occurs only in a
relatively narrow range of water content, and vascular plants
are able to control water content by opening or closing stomata
so that the limits of the plant are not exceeded. In such
species of mosses as *Hylocomium* and *Pleurozium,* however, the
range of water content is much greater than in the vascular
plant species, and while water is present the net assimilation
rates are high. Once the water has evaporated, however, net
photosynthesis also decreases. Mosses generally have a negligible resistance to water loss, and the ecological differences between the species lie in the relative tolerances of
the various species to desiccation and the rate of recovery
following rewetting. Mosses take up water as does a sponge,
by absorption, rather than in vascular tissues such as are
found in the higher plants, and much of the physiological activity of the mosses depends upon water available for absorption and rates of evaporation sufficiently low to prevent rapid drying out of the leaves of the mosses.

In the feather mosses, Busby and Whitfield (1978) found
an apparent inhibition of net assimilation at high tissue
water contents. This presumably is in marked contrast to the
response of the *Sphagnum* mosses, which prefer habitats where
saturation is continual or at least frequent. In these latter
species, desiccation is much less frequent than in the feather
mosses, and while data are still largely lacking on this point,
it is likely that the individual preferences in terms of water
availability, light intensity, and temperature conditions
account for the habitat selectivity of these moss species.

HABITAT PREFERENCE

Probably no other feature of the vegetational landscape
provides so clearly defined an example of the habitat preferences of both moss species and species of higher plants as do

the so-called patterned fens--otherwise also known as string
bogs--found in southern boreal regions. As Vitt *et al.* (1975a)
point out in their comprehensive study of the patterned fens
of the Swan Hills region, Alberta, much of the peatlands of
North America contain some patterning of the vegetation although it is most evident in a narrow band across North America.

In their studies of the vegetational patterning, Vitt *et
al.* (1975) found that the wetter stretches (flarks) between
the so-called strings are dominated by two plant communities,
one in which *Menyanthes trifoliata* is the most important vascular species and another in which *Carex limosa* is the dominant.
Both have *S. jensenii* as a dominant moss, as well as *Drepanocladus exannulatus.* The strings possess communities usually
dominated by either *B. glandulosa, Tomenthypnum falcifolium,*
and *Aulacomnium palustre* or by *P. mariana, Sphagnum magellanicum,* and *L. groenlandicum,* the latter obviously a community
dominated by trees and the former by shrub species, principally dwarf birch. The strings are somewhat more elevated above
the water table by accumulations of peat; the flarks often
have stretches of open water around which the mosses and *Carex*
and *Menyanthes* are emergent aquatic species.

The species found commonly in the flarks and strings of
the patterned fens in the Swan Hills region studied by Vitt
et al. (1975) are presented in Table III.

The species in the flarks were fewer and these species
were also found on the strings but not with the abundance or
density attained in the flarks. The more important species
on the strings were rarely if ever found in the flarks. A
large number of other *Sphagnum* species were also present in
the patterned bogs, but none of the others attained the abundance of those named above. They included the seven species
listed in Table IV. A number of vascular plants were also
present, but not in great numbers, and these included a number
of representatives of the genera *Carex* and *Equisetum.* Some of
the vascular species as well as the mosses are given in Table IV.

In another study, this one an analysis of the vegetation
of *Sphagnum*-dominated kettlehole bogs in relation to environmental gradients, Vitt and Slack (1975) found that there was
a segregation of community types along gradients of pH, light
intensity, and calcium and magnesium ion concentrations. The
communities could be distinguished according to whether they
were surrounding acid or alkaline lakes. Each possessed its
own continuum of community composition.

It seemed apparent that the successional patterns in the
communities were controlled by the *Sphagnum* mosses, and the
relationships appeared to be related to the water-holding
capacity of these mosses and their ability to absorb large
amounts of water and to create more acid habitats by exchange

Table III.   Species in Patterned Fens in Alberta[a]

Strings	Flarks
Vascular Plants	
Kalmia polifolia	*Eriophorum chamissonis*
Vaccinium oxycoccus	*Menyanthes trifoliata*
Smilacina trifolia	*Carex limosa*
Betula glandulosa	
Andromeda polifolia	
Ledum groenlandicum	
Picea mariana	
Vaccinium vitis-idaea	
Rubus chamaemorus	
Mosses	
Tomenthypnum falcifolium	*Sphagnum jensenii*
Sphagnum angustifolium	*Drepanocladus exannulatus*
Aulacomnium palustre	
Sphagnum magellanicum	
Pleurozium schreberi	

[a]*From Vitt et al (1975a).*

Table IV.   Species in Patterned Bogs in Alberta[a]

Mosses	Vascular species
Sphagnum compactum	*Viola palustris*
Sphagnum fuscum	*Coptis trifolia*
Sphagnum majus	*Empetrum nigrum*
Sphagnum riparium	*Equisetum fluviatile*
Sphagnum russowii	*Equisetum sylvaticum*
Sphagnum subsecundum	*Gaultheria hispidula*
Sphagnum teres	*Laris laricina*
	Rubus acaulis
	Carex pauciflora
	Carex aquatilis
	Carex chordorrhiza
	Carex rostrata

[a]*From Vitt et al. (1975a).*

of hydrogen ions for cations of Ca^{2+}, Mg^{2+}, Na^+, and K^+. The
Sphagnum species influence the direction of bog succession by
creating habitats for the vascular plants, mosses, and bryophytes adapted to the bog environment.

In the study, Vitt and Slack found one group of species
characteristic of wet habitats with a nearly neutral pH of
6.7 and concentrations of calcium and magnesium in soil water
of 8-11 ppm. Another group of species was characteristic of
habitats with a pH of 4.9 and calcium and magnesium concentrations of only 2-5 ppm. Dominant species in the former were
Sphagnum teres, Carex lasiocarpa, and *Callierogonella cuspidata.*
In the latter community, dominants included *Sphagnum capillaceum,
Carex exilis, V. oxycoccus,* and there were much greater densities of *K. polifolia* and *C. calyculata.* The association of
the species into groupings was a result of similar physiological tolerances of the species, resulting in similar distributions within the bogs. In instances where the species were
very sensitive to the conditions, the association was very
close. For example, *S. teres* and *C. lasiocarpa* were always
found together although the importance of the species varied.
In other instances, where several factors were of apparent
equal importance in determining species distribution, there was
not invariable association of one species with another; thus,
Sphagnum cuspidatum and *Rhynchospora alba* occurred together
in high densities in some areas but each occurred separately
elsewhere.

It should not be assumed without question that successional patterns follow the sequence indicated by hydrarch succession. There was evidence, however, that succession had occurred,
and Vitt and Slack found evidence that the *S. capillaceum* mat
had been preceded by the *C. lasiocarpa* community, high pH, and
greater concentrations of calcium and magnesium. Other species
found in alkaline but not acid bogs included *Potentilla palustris, Pogonia ophioglossoides, Hypericum virginicum,* and *Viola
nephrophylla,* and those in acid but not alkaline bogs included
*Carex paupercula, Eriophorum virginicum, Carex oligosperma,
P. mariana,* and *Larix laricina.*

In summary, both the mosses and the higher plants possess
an ecological diversity that makes them indicators of habitat
conditions; moreover, they evidently form a link by which comparisons can be made of the similar vegetational communities
of widely separated areas or even of different continents.
The three factors that appear to be most important in governing the species of plants that will be found in the community
are cation concentrations, pH of the soil water, and the water
table level or availability of soil moisture. These are undoubtedly important in themselves, but they are most likely
also indicative of other conditions that would be considered

of great significance in the distribution of the plants were
they more readily recognized; among these latter would be
microbial activity responsible for ammonification, nitrification, denitrification, nitrogen fixation, and a host of other
biochemical processes and reactions occurring selectively in
acid and alkaline conditions. Much remains to be done before
these relationships are understood.

20 Development of Communities I: Regional Relationships

There are regional variations in the plant communities that typically occupy peat bogs throughout the wide geographical range in which bogs are found. The variations, however, are less striking than the fact that the bog communities are readily identifiable and remarkably uniform in character (Fig. 1) throughout at least four major phytogeographic regions--or, to use various terms in common use, four biomes, formations, forest regions, or biotic provinces. These are the eastern deciduous forest, of which there are nine regional subtypes (Braun, 1950); the tall grass prairie; the boreal or spruce forests of the north; and the forest-tundra transition, otherwise known as the hudsonian lichen-woodland, found northward of the main boreal forest proper.

As Dansereau and Segadas-Vianna (1952) have pointed out, this extensive geographical range throughout such a wide variety of phytogeographic divisions poses some interesting questions concerning the relationships of this ubiquitous bog community with that of the much more diverse and variable upland communities. What are the relationships of the bog communities with these various and quite different and distinct regional upland communities? How were the bogs and the bog communities formed? What is their postglacial history? What influence has this distinct habitat had on the evolutionary development of the species that occupy them? What is the composition and structure (i.e., what species are present and in what abundance) of bog communities in each of these various phytogeographical regions? Do composition and structure differ from one province to another?

To discern these regional variations, the bog community (or communities) must be rather carefully defined so as not to compound the difficulties of identification and description by including communities that might more accurately be considered fens or swamps--communities often found adjacent to bog communities, intermingled with them, or into which they grade along topographical or hydrological clines. Other communities may develop into bogs by the natural process of succession and the

Fig. 1. Small open bogs are frequently surrounded by up-land deciduous forest. In this bog, the plant community is dominated by sedges and conifer tree species, although the latter are still small and widely spaced.

gradual accumulation of thicker and thicker layers of undecom-posed organic matter or peat. The distinctions are not always easy to make, since gradations of all kinds are commonly pre-sent in all regions, and the terms used for the communities are often considered virtually interchangeable--bog, swamp, marsh, muskeg, fen, wet meadow, heath, wetland, and so on (Rigg, 1940 a,b; Gorham, 1957).

For the purposes at hand, it is thus important to distinguish between the bog ecosystem and the marsh, swamp, and
fen ecosystem(s), even though there are readily demonstrable
examples in which the characteristics are intermediate, at
least in some respects. Dansereau and Segadas-Vianna (1952)
have delineated some of the contrasting characteristics and
the more obvious of these are as follows:

Bog	Marsh and swamp (fen)
1. Blocked drainage and slow decomposition causes an accumulation of organic matter; in the very late stage of development, trees invade and eventually may cover the area.	1. Drainage patterns allow a flow of water and conditions prevent a considerable accumulation of organic matter.
2. The water table reaches the surface during the spring, but is below the surface the rest of the year.	2. The water table is well above the surface in the spring and just at the surface or a little below the rest of the year.
3. The substratum is almost 100% organic; the mineral content is low.	3. The substratum has a variable percentage of organic materials, usually not peat, and the mineral content is high.
4. The pH of the peat is highly acid.	4. The pH is only slightly acid or nearly neutral.
5. Potassium and nitrogen are deficient in the soils.	5. Potassium and nitrogen are not deficient.
6. Vegetation is largely shrubs, herbs, and mosses, with *Sphagnum* species abundant.	6. The vegetation is composed largely of grasses, sedges, rushes, reeds. Mosses, at least *Sphagnum,* are generally absent.
7. Animal life is scarce, both in terms of species and of individuals.	7. Animal life is abundant, both species and individuals.

As Gates (1942) pointed out, bogs develop in depressions
and lowlands, especially in kettle holes in glacial moraines,
in low spots in uplands, in quiet bays of lakes, and in quiet
places in stream channels. Throughout the year, precipitation
supplies ample water. The original soil has little effect on
bog development. The definition proposed by Gates is perhaps
too restrictive to include all bogs, but it is of interest in
any case:

The term bog thus includes pre-eminently a type of vegetation which controls a habitat and changes the habitat,
in the course of its development, from an open area of water
to a mat and then to a grounded mat and finally to dry land.
One regularly associates lack of circulation of the water
with deficient oxygenation and slow decay....The plants in
bogs grow slowly. There is a dearth of minerals...These
conditions favor peat formation, in fact a bog may be defined as an area vegetated by a flora in which peat-forming
types of plants (including certain herbaceous, ericaceous
shrubs and coniferous trees) are particularly abundant.

The word swamp is often used to cover at least a part
of a bog, as defined above, but had best be kept to designate areas better drained, and without mats developing out
over the water. Muskeg is largely synonymous with bog,
but is used more to the north...

The development of a mat is one of the specific characteristics of a bog as opposed to a swamp.*

The initiation of a bog evidently requires that a sufficient
number of plants, predominantly sedges and often *Carex lasiocarpa,* become established around the edge of the depression in
which the mat is beginning to form. Rhizomes and roots of the
sedges and of *C. calyculata* then form a mat, floating on the
water, and from the lower surface of the mat pieces sink and
begin to build up the sediments on the lake bottom (Fig. 2).
The mat is independent of the lake bottom and proceeds to grow
out over the water of the central pool as far as it can develop vegetatively.

Eventually the mat becomes sufficiently established so that
C. calyculata, A. glaucophylla, and other species can become
established over water too deep for sedges. In time, bog
shrubs such as willows, dogwood, alders, and dwarf birches invade the bog surface and a dense thicket becomes established
that can support growth of *L. laricina* and *P. mariana.* According to the scheme of succession envisioned by Gates, the cedar
association then follows that dominated by black spruce.

It should, of course, be understood that the scheme de-
vised by Gates is neither rigid and undeviating, nor perhaps
ever followed anywhere with sufficient versimilitude to be
considered even the generalized pattern from which deviations
can be expected. The concept must be comprehended, however,
since it has profoundly influenced the thinking of ecologists
and it must be considered the hypothesis that stands to be
confirmed or refuted. It seems reasonable to assume that at
least some bog communities attained their present stage of
development through a continuum of developmental stages, and
whether or not a repeating pattern is to be discerned in these
individual samples of the bog communities remains to be de-

* Copyright 1942, the Ecological Society of America.

Fig. 2. A conifer bog surrounds this small lake. Spruce and some tamarack (P. mariana and L. laricina) have taken up occupancy near the lake edge where Carex and Chamaedaphne are pioneering species. The trees at the margin of the lake have created a closed-canopy forest, making it possible for shade-tolerant species to invade the area.

termined. The difficulties of obtaining data with which to demonstrate the existence, or nonexistence, of such a pattern are immense, and at the present time it can only be said that adequate data are not yet available. Perhaps it will be a very long time before ecologists can say with certainty that

succession follows a recognizable set of patterns, or, con-
versely, that it tends to occur in a kind of random sequential
replacement of species, a progression influenced more by chance
events than by the ability of species of one group to take over
the habitat from the species of another group characteristic
of an earlier successional stage.

The former possibility implies a kind of preordained capacity on the part of each species to play a given role in
succession, a role for which evolutionary processes of selection and adaptation have fitted it. Whether this is, indeed,
the case, we cannot yet say with certainty. The conclusion,
however, is one that can--and has been--supported by knowledge-
able and competent ecologists; but any inference that it describes what actually occurs in bog plant communities remains
just that--inference and not demonstrated fact.

BOG COMMUNITIES: STRUCTURE

Gates published the paper giving his successional scheme
for bog vegetation in 1942. By a decade later, newer techniques for plant community sampling and data analysis had been
developed by Curtis and associates at the University of Wisconsin, and these made it possible to shed more light on bog
communities and how they developed.

With these techniques, detailed data on the relative abundance of the various tree species, shrubs, herbs, grasses,
sedges, and so on, could be obtained in any plant community.
One adjunct to the method involved use of a similarity index,
a statistical device that constitutes the basis for what is
known as ordination--an arrangement of communities on a two-
dimensional chart so that communities most dissimilar to one
another are farthest apart and those most similar are closest
together. Data obtained in 90 conifer swamps in northern Wisconsin were used to group communities into eight segments of
an ordination, on the basis of herbaceous species in the
communities (Clausen, 1957).

The result was most interesting. The eight sections of
the array tend to follow Gates's successional sequence, from
communities dominated by *C. lasiocarpa,* at one end, through
those in which *L. laricina* and *P. mariana* were dominant, then
on to the other end of the array in which communities were
dominated by *A. balsamea* and *T. occidentalis.* The question
was obvious: Was this actually a successional sequence, or
were the species so arranged not as a consequence of succession but rather because of environmental differences among the
bogs sampled--temperature, availability of nutrients, and so
on? Clausen (1957) wrote:

Mineral content of the surface soil is strikingly correlated with the gradient. Calcium, magnesium, potassium,
and phosphorus contents of the surface soil increase sharply toward [the *Abies-Thuja* end of the array], calcium from
1000 pounds per acre to 8000 ppa, magnesium from 150 ppa to
700 ppa, potassium from 200 ppa to 500 ppa, and phosphorus
from 30 ppa to 70 ppa....Water holding capacity at the surface decreased from 850% at the left [the *Carex* end of the
array] to 500% at the right, a corollary of decreasing
Sphagnum peat....Those pH values lower than 4.0 occurred
near the left end of the gradient.

The amount of cover--influencing the intensity of shade at
ground level within the community--increased from about 20% on
the left to 65% on the right. In these northern bogs, nontree
species most abundant in the communities at the left end of
the array included *C. lasiocarpa, Eriophorum spissum,* and *C.
calyculata.* Species peaking at the left but extending somewhat
farther to the right include *Eriophorum virginicum, A. glaucophylla, K. polifolia, V. angustifolium, V. oxycoccus, L. groenlandicum, V. myrtilloides, G. hispidula,* and *G. procumbens.*
In the center of the scale, *R. pubescens* attains its greatest
abundance. Peaking to the right are *Coptis groenlandica,
Cornus canadensis, Trientalis borealis, Clintonia borealis,
Linnaea borealis, Pyrola secunda, Carex disperma,* and *Galium
triflorum.* Species limited to the right hand end of the gradient include *Viola pallens, Mitella nuda, Dryopteris disjuncta,
Aster macrophyllus,* and *Aralia nudicaulis.*
From Clausen's study it is evident that the bog communities
in northern Wisconsin tend in rather striking fashion to form
a continuum along the lines indicated by Gates--with *C. lasiocarpa* at one end and the *Abies-Thuja* stands at the other.
Commenting on this coincidence, Clausen (1957) states:

This ordering of stands is on the basis of community
resemblances at one point in time; it is not intended to
illustrate development of one community through a period
of time. Since the vegetation of a stand at a given time
closely resembles its immediately previous and immediately
following vegetation, if development is undisturbed, and
since the stands included were in various stages of development, the ordering unavoidably parallels the developmental
pattern in general.

The assumption here obviously is that the bog communities
follow a developmental pattern if they are not disturbed, at
least in the case of the herbaceous species. What about the
trees? Clausen (1957) continued:

The trees of the northern swamps show a high correlation
with the ordering of stands on the basis of herb layer.
This is to be expected since trees are influenced by many
of the factors which influence the herb layer, and because
the trees themselves influence the herb layer. Thus there
are two extreme types of conifer swamps in Wisconsin: the
spruce-tamarack type and the cedar-balsam type.

Certain curves of species amplitude taper across the
central area of the northern swamp gradient, and the curves
of two species peak there, indicating that the extreme types
are not distinct, but are related by intermediate types.
On the other hand, the number of intermediate-peaking species is small, and the number of intermediate stands is also small; segments 4 through 6 contain only 13 of the 90
stands. On the basis of these data alone, there is some
justification for drawing an arbitrary line between the two
community types.

The relative scarcity of intermediate communities is attributed by Clausen to "the apparent rapidity of the change
from one extreme to the other, and the relative stability of
stands of the extreme types." There is no doubt that the two
gradients--vegetational, on the one hand, and environmental
factors, on the other--are coincidental, and both occur together with great consistency, but is one the cause and the other
the effect or do both interact and influence one another, with
the result that development occurs along a relatively narrow
pathway of possible variations? Which differences in environmental factors are the result of the habitat being occupied by
different species? Which are the result of differences in
successional patterns? Which differences in species composition of communities are the consequence of differences in environmental characteristics? Does succession occur in these
communties with a rather rapid progression from spruce-tamarack
to cedar-balsam once the process has been initiated? These
are questions to which we do not as yet possess answers that
are unequivocal and clear.

The questions were, however, explored further to some
limited degree by Christensen et al. (1959), who, after considering the phytosociology of the northern lowland forests,
came to this conclusion:

The regional pattern is unusually uniform, with widespread agreement that *Larix laricina* is the first tree to
invade the ericaceous shrub stage of the open bog. This
is followed by *Picea mariana*. The two exist in varying
mixture in a quasi-stable forest community of potentially
great duration. At some later time, following changes

whose exact nature is in doubt, the *Larix-Picea* forest is
replaced by a more shade-tolerant forest dominated by *Thuja
occidentalis,* often with *Abies balsamea* and *Fraxinus nigra.*
Information is neither so plentiful nor so uniform regarding the terminal stages of these lowland forests, though
some type of hardwood forest, often with *Tsuga canadensis*
as a prominent member, seems to be indicated.

The last two sentences reveal the uncertainty associated
with the successional relationships of the lowland forests.
In the same year, Curtis (1959) wrote of the forest that:

> One of the difficult problems in the study of community
> dynamics of northern Wisconsin is the assessment of the
> relation between conifer swamps and [other communities]...
> the succession may go from white cedar-balsam fir-black
> ash swamp through yellow birch and hemlock, and finally to
> sugar maple or beech, if a sufficient improvement in soil
> drainage occurs. It appears equally probable that the coni-
> fer swamps may give rise to a terminal forest of white
> spruce and balsam fir if the climatic conditions are suit-
> able.

In this scheme, spruce forests undisturbed by fire are
eventually invaded slowly by cedar, and the latter, once established, rather quickly replaces the tamarack and black
spruce, shade-intolerant species that are unable to regenerate
in the deep shade of the cedar swamps. The forest is dominated
by white cedar in latter stages, but balsam fir, which is also
tolerant of shade as a sapling, is usually also present in
some abundance.

Curtis expresses the belief that most of the presettlement
forests of tamarack and black spruce were formed by classical
primary succession, set back periodically by windthrow, fire,
and changing water levels. Powell Marsh, in Iron and Vilas
counties, for example, has layers of charcoal fragments all
the way from surface peat to the underlying sand (Fig. 3).

From these studies, it is apparent that there are indications
of a certain regularity in the successional development of the
northern bogs and bog forests, and there are persistent in-
clinations on the part of ecologists to infer a direction to
community development (or succession as so defined). The data
are suggestive of such a linear trend in succession, but so
far the final definitive body of data to support such an
assumption unequivocally has not become available. It seems
rather clear that there is a somewhat persistent pattern of
succession in kettle holes and other small undrained depressions in which bogs form, leading eventually to the filling

Fig. 3. Powell Marsh in summer is now a vast wetland,
surrounded by channels of open water. Located in northern
Wisconsin, the area was once (perhaps many times) a dense
conifer bog, but repeated fires and other disturbances brought
about reversion to open peatland.

in of the low areas with peat and the subsequent growth of
trees to form a bog forest. The relationships of the trees,
shrubs, and herbaceous species in this process are not, however, clearly understood, and the conclusion, for example,
that a spruce-tamarack bog forest is capable of transition to
a cedar-balsam forest in a relatively rapid manner cannot be
said to have been fully substantiated.

ORGANIC PRODUCTION

Virtually by definition the soil of a northern lowland
forested bog is primarily peat, with the water table at or
near the surface, a paucity of available nutrients, and vegetation so characteristic that a listing of species is sufficient to identify the habitat in which they grow and differen-
tiate this lowland forest community from others (Reiners, 1972).
One of the first questions a student new to the ecology of bogs
is apt to ask, however, is one that even the most experienced
ecologist will have difficulty answering with assurance: "How
long did it take for the bog to form?"

The restriction imposed upon the answer is the result of
several circumstances. The rate of peat accumulation depends
both upon the productivity of the vegetation inhabiting the
bog and the proportion of dead material in annual litter fall
that remains in an undecayed state. For a peat bog to form,
more organic material must obviously be produced than is re-
moved by decomposition. The production potential of bogs
varies with the amount of nutrients available for plant growth,
nutrients that come into the bogs from dust and dissolved compounds in rainfall. They may also come into the bog from water seeping into the peat from subsurface mineral soils, as
well as from adjacent uplands, and as a consequence of bio-
genic nitrogen fixation, nitrification, and ammonification on
the enclosing watershed. The available information upon the
influence of atmospheric and substrate conditions on bog plant
growth rates and productivity is scant, but it seems intuitively apparent that growth varies greatly from one bog to another
and from one latitude to another, from year to year, as well
as from one part of a given bog to another part, so that gen-
eralizations will always be imprecise.

It is equally apparent, however, that the natural bogs in
the northern United States and lower Canada have utilized all
of postglacial time--probably some 10,000-12,000 years in
duration--to attain their present state of development. Even
a very severe fire in an extremely dry year will rarely if
ever set peat communities back to the stage in which raw
mineral soil or open water must be recolonized by aquatic or
emergent vegetation as a prelude to bog formation. The events
of the past can be reconstructed to some extent by the modern
techniques of palynology, but much remains conjectural when
attempts are made to reveal the history of any given bog.

Leisman (1953) reviews estimates in the literature of the
rate of peat formation, stating that they vary from 2 yr/ft
in certain parts of Germany to 1650 yr/ft in parts of the Great
Lakes region. Leisman adds that, as shown in other research,
the kind of vegetation is very important in determining the

rate of accumulation of peat in a bog. He noted, for example, that *C. lasiocarpa* is evidently the most abundant species forming peat in a bog studied near Itasca State Park in Minnesota, a site where the bog water has a high mineral content and where accumulation of organic matter in the sedge mat is slightly more than 0.5 in/yr or about 25 yr/ft.

In a peat bog in northern Wisconsin, Kratz (1981) estimated that reasonable values for annual peat accumulation were in the neighborhood of 75-150 $gm/m^2/yr$. The average rate of horizontal growth at the edge of the mat where it projects over the surface of the lake is 0.93 cm/yr. This rate can be compared to the estimate of Swan and Gill (1970) that the horizontal spread of *Chamaedaphne* over an artificial lake in Massachusetts was about 5 cm/yr and that of Schwintzer and Williams (1974) of 2.1 cm/yr for a bog in central Michigan. On the other hand, Buell *et al.* (1968) found that no horizontal encroachment had occurred in a bog lake in east-central Minnesota during the previous 30 yr. The slow growth of a bog mat over a lake in northern Wisconsin is recorded by Curtis (1959), who demonstrated that very little extension of the mat occurred over water of the lake during the period 1940-1957, and a photograph taken in 1980 of the same site reveals very little additional progress although nearby trees have grown to maturity in the interval (see Chapter 21, Fig. 6).

Studies of bog productivity reviewed by Reader (1978a,b) indicate that root production ranges from 140 to more than 500 $gm/m^2/yr$, and the production values for aboveground material range from 100 to more than 1000 $gm/m^2/yr$. In the bog marshes included in the study, no single species or even genus was consistently the most productive throughout. The vascular plants usually contributed more to the organic capital of the bogs than did the nonvascular plants, but there were exceptions, and it was apparent that no rules could be laid down in expectation that they would apply everywhere and at all times.

A sampling of the variation that can be expected in any wide-ranging study of bog ecosystems can be seen from the data in Table I. By way of comparison, a subarctic bog located in northcentral Manitoba held an aboveground biomass, including trees, shrubs, herbs, grasses, sedges, lichens, and mosses of 7939 kg/ha. Seven years after the area had been stripped of vegetation, plants recolonizing the surface had restored 2098 kg/ha, or 26.4%, of the original biomass (Sims and Stewart, 1981).

There is lower productivity at higher latitudes, but the diversity of the flora over large regions, as well as local variation in nutrient availability and so on, seem to preclude any meaningful correlations between temperature, latitude, or

Table I.   Biomass and Productivity Comparisons

Community	Above ground (A) or below ground (B) plant organs	Biomass (gm/m^2)	Annual production (gm/m^2/year)
Black spruce/ Cladonia[a,b]	A + B	4629 g/m^2	---
Alder swamp[c]	A only	5300	640
Alder swamp[c]	A only	3100	570
Fen forest[d]	A only	9808	651
Swamp forest[d]	A only	15941	1014
Peatland bog[e]	A + B	---	1943
Northern bogs[f]	A only	---	101–1026
Northern bogs[g]	B only	---	141–513

[a] Rencz and Auclair (1978). Woodland in Schefferville area, Quebec.

[b] Percentages by species: spruce, 61; Cladonia alpestris, 14%; B. glandulosa, 12; Stereocaulon, 5; L. groenlandicum, 4; other, 4. Of the total, 1292 g/m^2 was in belowground plant parts.

[c] Parker and Schneider (1975). Stands in Michigan.

[d] Reiners (1972). Stands in Minnesota.

[e] Reader and Stewart (1971). Of the total, the vascular species made up 1777 gm/m^2 of the plant material. Of this, 82% was below the surface of the ground (plant roots).

[f] Data from nine sites, range of values (Reader, 1978a,b).

[g] Data from nine sites, range of values (Reader, 1978a,b; from other sources). Low value is from blanket bog in Ireland.

other factors, and the primary productivity of any given species, of any of the genera, or even of the entire community.

21 Development of Communities II: Broad Ecological Relationships

The studies reviewed in the previous chapter were all carried out on a large number of small bogs. Another study, however, shows that there are also a wide variety of community types and environmental complexes on one single very large area of peatland--the Lake Agassiz Peatlands Natural Area in northern Minnesota. Located in the bed of former glacial Lake Agassiz, this vast and nearly continuous peatland is described by Heinselman (1963) as follows:

> This region is a distinct physiographic province, sharply delimited from the Laurentian Shield to the east and from the Drift Region to the south....These peatlands possess a remarkable variety of swamp, bog, and fen types which include floristically rich forested swamps, bogs supporting productive black spruce-feathermoss forests,poor black spruce muskegs, string bogs, patterned fens, and fields of regularly spaced forest "islands."
>
> A great range of forest sites exists. On the best sites black spruce *(Picea mariana),* the most abundant tree, attains diameters up to 15 in. and heights of 80 ft. But on the poorest muskegs it is reduced almost to a shrub, sometimes resembling the candelabra trees of the tundra transition. *

The species that are abundant in these bogs and peatlands have a wide range in North America, from Alaska and the Yukon to Quebec, the Maritime Provinces, and Newfoundland. Throughout this range, the density of the spruce overstory has an obvious correlation with the abundance of the various mosses and the species of ericaceous shrubs. As Heinselman (1963) points out:

> Feather mosses and *Dicranum* are most abundant under dense canopies and tend to drop out in favor of *Sphagnum*, sedges, the heath shrubs, alder, etc., in open stands....it has been repeatedly observed that *Calliergonella schreberi, Hypnum*

* Copyright 1963, the Ecological Society of America.

crista-castrensis, Hylocomium splendens, and the *Dicranums*
tend to dry up and die within a year after removal of the
spruce overstory.*

In the open, more upland black spruce-alder-herb forest,
speckled alder *(Alnus rugosa)* is the most conspicuous species
in the peatlands of northern Minnesota. As Heinselman continues:

> A comparatively rich herbaceous flora is the other dis-
> tinguishing feature. *Cornus canadensis, Rubus pubescens,*
> *Linnaea borealis, Coptis groenlandica, Trientalis borealis,*
> species of *Viola* and *Galium,* and several grasses, sedges,
> and ferns are typical. The Ericaceae are present, but
> usually not prominent except in transitions to other com-
> munities. *Ledum, Gaultheria hispidula,* and the *Vacciniums*
> are the normal species. *Chamaedaphne, Kalmia,* and *Andro-*
> *meda* are lacking....Mosses are less conspicuous than in
> other communities, but may still occupy 50 to 80% of the
> ground. *Sphagna* of the *palustre* group create loose hummocks,
> especially around alder clumps. *Calliergonella schreberi*
> and species of *Dicranum* carpet the hummocks around the bases
> of trees.*

At the other extreme are the wetter lowland muskegs, with
stunted spruce in relatively low densities and with the *Sphag-*
num mosses and ericaceous shrubs dominating the understory
community. As Heinselman points out:

> A distinctive aspect is lent to this community by the
> *Sphagnum* hummocks upon which occurs a dense cover of
> *Chamaedaphne, Ledum, Kalmia, Andromeda,* and *Vaccinium oxy-*
> *coccos.* The highest hummocks are built of *Sphagnum capilla-*
> *ceum* or related species....*Eriophorum* and *Sarracenia* are
> also typical members of the community, although *Sarracenia*
> is sparsely distributed. *Smilacina trifolia* is one of the
> few other herbs....Intergrades between muskeg and feather
> moss forest were common, but those with the black spruce-
> alder-herb community were rare.*

To summarize, the ombrotrophic peatland communities can be
broadly categorized into black spruce-alder-herb forests,
black spruce-feather moss forests, and open muskegs or bogs.
At one extreme are the black spruce-alder-herb forests in more
open areas with a deeper water table; at the other extreme
are the muskeg communities. The black spruce-feather moss
forests occur in habitats intermediate between the alder-herb
and muskeg communities. All three communities occur on peats
* Copyright 1963, the Ecological Society of America.

that are relatively shallow, but the alder-herb forest tends
to occur on the shallowest peats. The muskeg communities seem
to be consistently associated with the thickest accumulation
of raw undecayed *Sphagnum* moss, but not necessarily with the
greatest total depth of peat. The black spruce-alder-herb
forest typically has peat with pH values above 4.5; the feather
moss and muskeg communities have peat below 4.0. The acidi-
fying species of *Sphagnum* are closely associated with the lower pH values.

Discussing the theoretical implications of the range of
communities present in the Lake Agassiz peatlands, Heinselman
(1963) states:

> Neither the processes of bog expansion nor the patterned
> bogs and fens of the Lake Agassiz region fit the classical
> picture of succession in the Lake States. Conclusions are
> that: (1) Few bogs in this region are the result of a single
> successional sequence. (2) The bog types cannot be regarded
> as stages in an orderly development toward mesophytism.
> (3) Raising of bog surfaces by peat accumulation does not
> necessarily mean progression toward mesophytism. Such rises
> often cause concurrent rises of the water table and promote
> site deterioriation. (4) The climax concept does not con-
> tribute to understanding bog history in this region.*

Thus, the development of the succession concept in bog
vegetation begins with the classical scheme of Gates and comes
to a virtual dead end with that of Heinselman--who states that
the climax concept has little meaning when applied to vegetation of the peatlands. As a consequence, the present-day picture of the peatlands is that variation in the vegetational
communities can be relatively broad even on similar topographic
sites such as the kettleholes and wide expanses of flat lowlands characteristic of the glacial Lake Agassiz region and
elsewhere bogs are found (Janssen, 1967; Jeglum, 1971, 1972,
1973; Jeglum *et al.*, 1974; Schwintzer and Williams, 1974;
Schwintzer and Williams, 1974; Schwintzer, 1978a,b, 1981; Hemond, 1980; Boelter and Verry, 1977). The differences are
evidently the consequence of events that have given each individual community its own distinctive history--some conifer
swamp forests have, for example, been burned repeatedly, while
others nearby have escaped the fires. Some parts of a bog may
have been burned by a fire that left other parts untouched.
In such instances, the destructive events account for otherwise inexplicable variations in the species of plants present
in abundance in different bogs or parts of a single bog.

* Copyright 1963, the Ecological Society of America.

THE ROLE OF PIONEER

The view that *C. calyculata* is a pioneer in the hydrach invasion of kettlehole lakes by vegetation is supported by the observations of Rigg (1940a,b), who wrote that *Chamaedaphne, Kalmia,* and *Ledum* are the common shrubs growing out into the water, with stems submerged and tips and leafy portions in air. In these margins of the bog mat, *Sphagnum* is itself not a pioneer but invades after the shrubs have formed a matrix upon which it can rest. Rigg pointed out that *Sphagnum* is commonly preceded or accompanied in mat formation by *Carex, Drosera, Menyanthes, Potentilla,* and other bog species. The bogs may begin as a circle of *Sphagnum* around a pond, but as soon as the mat progresses into deeper water the *Chamaedaphne* and other shrubs take over the task of pioneering into deeper open water.

Swan and Gill (1970) concluded that development of a floating bog in Massachusetts could be largely understood in terms of growth of *Chamaedaphne.* They state, however, that other species are evidently of more importance in other areas, including *Menyanthes, Carex* species, *Myrica gale,* and a few other shrubs that also spread by means of adventitious root systems that make growth over open water possible, including *V. macrocarpon, Alnus rugosa, Aronia (Pyrus) melanocarpa,* and *Vaccinium corymbosum.*

On the basis of observations of plant species occupying concentric zones of a bog around a central pool of open water, Schwintzer and Williams (1974) envisioned that development of a typical bog begins with formation of a floating mat of sedges, which subsequently is invaded by *Sphagnum* mosses and ericaceous shrubs, including *C. calyculata.* The shrubs are eventually replaced by *L. laricina, P. mariana,* and *T. occidentalis,* forming a bog or swamp forest. Most of what is known about bog succession, Schwintzer pointed out, has been deduced from indirect studies such as the zonation of bog vegetation around open water, comparison of bogs in various stages of succession, or the plant remains in peat profiles from the bogs.

Schwintzer and Williams (1974), using a series of data obtained by Gates, showed that the vegetation of a bog in northern Lower Michigan changed from *Chamaedaphne*-dominated in 1917, through a high bog-shrub association during the dry years of the 1920s, to a bog forest that was well established by the late 1960s. The association then regressed to a *Chamaedaphne* association in the early 1970s, evidently the result of exceptionally high water levels.

As Schwintzer and Williams pointed out:

  Thus in a period of less than 100 years the vegetation
of Bryant's bog has progressed in a successional series
from the *Chamaedaphne* association to the high bog-shrub
association to a well-established bog forest, and regressed
again to a *Chamaedaphne* association. The presence of numerous logs in the peat (Gates, 1942) indicates that Bryant's
Bog underwent at least one similar cycle in the past. These
findings agree with Curtis' (1959) observations that Wisconsin bogs seldom pass through the stages of the primary
hydrosere successions from open water to conifer swamp un-
interrupted. Instead, many regress to an open-bog stage
due to disturbances such as fire related to fluctuations
in the water level.

  The changes in water level can occur as the result of many
natural events, including weather cycles and the damming of
streams by beavers, as well as to construction of drainage
ditches, roads, and other structures that accelerate or impede
water movement.
  In a study of bogs in the northern lower peninsula of Michigan, Schwintzer (1978a), found that *C. calyculata* was a dominant in the bogs of the region, with other ericaceous shrubs
and *Sphagnum* mosses abundant. There was a relatively slight
but readily apparent difference in community composition between the inner free-floating mat surrounding the pool of open
water and the grounded mat extending from the free-floating
mat to the outer edge of the bog. The frequency and cover
contributed by the plant species found in greatest abundance
in these two zones are given in Table I.
  Schwintzer pointed out that the free and grounded mats had
18 species in common. Five species were found only on the
free mat, including *K. polifolia* and *D. rotundifolia*. Six
species, including *Scirpus cyperinus,* were restricted to the
grounded mat. The abundance of *Pinus strobus,* which otherwise
might appear anomalous, is accounted for by the presence of a
massive nearby seed source; the individuals are small, chlorotic, and it was apparent that they would never reach maturity.
  By comparison, Schwintzer (1978b) found in a study of fens
--strongly minerotrophic bogs--in the same region that the
dominants in the plant community, in order of declining importance, were *Carex lasiocarpa, C. aquatilis, Myrica gale,*
Hypericum virginicum, Muhlenbergia glomerata, A. glaucophylla,
Campanula aparinoides, Potentilla palustris, Lycopus uniflorus,
Menyanthes trifoliata, Rosa palustris, Thelypteris palustris,
Typha latifolia, C. calyculata, Cladium mariscoides, V. oxy-
coccus, Aster spp., *Sarracenia purpurea, Galium tinctorium,*

Table I.   Bog Community in Michigan: Vegetation of the Free-Floating and Grounded Mats in a bog in Northern Lower Michigan[a]

	Free mat		Grounded mat	
	Freq.(%)	Cover (%)	Freq.(%)	Cover(%)
Ground layer				
Carex trisperma	80	8	40	1
Chamaedaphne calyculata	73	14	47	1
Gaylussacia baccata	40	5	7	1
Kalmia polifolia	33	1	--	--
Lycopus uniflorus	33	5	60	6
Mosses (except *Sphagnum*)	80	2	53	5
Scirpus cyperinus	--	--	33	1
Sphagnum spp.	100	69	87	20
Smilacina trifolia	40	3	13	2
Vaccinium angustifolium	60	1	27	1
Vaccinium myrtilloides	33	1	20	1
Tall Shrubs				
Gaylussacia baccata	--	--	27	1
Ilex verticillata	--	--	20	2
Nemopanthus mucronata	27	1	80	2
Pyrus floribunda	7	1	20	1
Viburnum cassinoides	--	--	40	1
Trees (frequency data only)				
Acer rubrum	7		27	
Betula papyrifera	13		7	
Larix laricina	73		7	
Picea mariana	100		73	
Pinus strobus	87		60	

[a]*From Schwintzer, 1978a.*

Dulichium arundinaceum, Carex limosa, Potentilla fruticosa, Lysimachia terrestris, Asclepias incarnata, Eupatorium maculatum, Salix pedicellaris, Utricularia intermedia, Galium trifidum, Lycopus americanus, Osmunda regalis.

Much of the general appearance of the fen community is due to *C. lasiocarpa*, *C. aquatilis*, and *M. gale*, in contrast to that of the bogs, in which *Chamaedaphne* and *Picea* are dominants. The species in the fens are those that have been identified as indicators of minerotrophy in such regions as northern Ontario (Sjörs, 1963) and northern Minnesota (Heinselman, 1970), including *A. glaucophylla, C. lasiocarpa, M. gale, M. trifoliata, P. palustris, P. fruticosa, U. intermedia,* and *T. latifolia,* among others (Schwintzer, 1978b).

Observations by Kratz (1981) of the peat found at various depths indicated that *Chamaedaphne* was an important species in initial formation and growth of the mat and that it continues to be the principal species in floating mat formation and growth in northern Wisconsin. The same is true in Michigan (Davis, 1906), in Nova Scotia (Nichols, 1918), and in Massachusetts (Swan and Gill, 1970; Hemond, 1980). All of the kettlehole bogs studied by Kratz in northern Wisconsin had *Chamaedaphne* growing around the perimeters of their central lakes. *Chamaedaphne* here is undoubtedly the principal mat-forming species, providing the substrate upon which species of *Sphagnum, Carex,* and other bog species can cling. These observations seem to confound some classical descriptions of *Chamaedaphne* as a species that invades bog communities only in later stages of bog formation and after the peat mat has become grounded. In at least one other way the classical descriptions do not fit actual observation: the open bogs in northern Wisconsin often have *Picea* and *Larix* trees growing in clumps around the central lake (Fig. 1) in contrast to the classical picture in which the trees are to be found around the far outer perimeter of the bog where succession is presumed to have been initiated and where it has been under way for the longest period of time. What circumstances account for this apparently anomalous reversal of expectations is not entirely clear, but some hints exist in recent work conducted in Wisconsin.

The bog in northern Wisconsin studied by Kratz (1981) had as dominants *C. calyculata, Sphagnum* mosses, *C. oligosperma,* and *Rynchospora alba (Rhynchospora alba).* Other species present were *A. glaucophylla, D. rotundifolia, E. virginicum, K. polifolia, L. laricina, L. groenlandicum, P. mariana, S. purpurea, V. angustifolium,* and *V. macrocarpon. Picea* and *Larix* were generally in low density throughout the bog, but there was a dense clump near the west edge of the lake. Kratz remarks that open bogs with trees present only near the lake margin--as contrasted to the classical picture in which trees

*Fig. 1. This bog with a growth of P. mariana on the
floating portion of the mat around the central pool of open
water demonstrates the capability of Picea to survive on the
particular habitat of the floating mat, which is not inundated
during periods of high water and does not dry out during
droughts.*

are confined to the outer edge of the bog--are common in
northern Wisconsin (see Fig. 1).

These bog characteristics are important in achieving accurate interpretations of the successional status of plant
communities occupying the bogs. Kratz (1981) pointed out that
Conway (1949), Dansereau and Segadas-Vianna (1952), and Gates
(1942), for example, describe *Chamaedaphne* as important in bog
communities only in later stages of succession and after the
mat has been grounded, and they state that the pioneer species
in floating mat formation are the sedges. This may indeed be
the case on occasion, but it seems likely that on many bogs,
as others have pointed out, *Chamaedaphne* is often the pioneer
over deeper open water. Other species that also perform this
function in some areas are *M. gale, A. glaucophylla,* and perhaps other shrubs such as *Betula* species. It seems likely
that, once established, the *Chamaedaphne* retains dominance in
the bog community until *Picea* and *Larix* invade and close the
canopy (Fig. 2). *Carex* is a pioneer around the edge of the
bogs and on peat surfaces exposed when drought or fire occurs;
the impression created by the composition of many bog communities is that small clumps of *Chamaedaphne* are invading only in
late successional stages, which have been preceded by *Carex*
dominance, but it seems more likely that *Chamaedaphne* pioneers
hydrarch succession and that *Carex* is pioneer in secondary
succession on peat following disturbance of one kind or another.
Stages of both successional sequences are often present in the
same bog, and recurrences of fire and flooding throughout postglacial millenia have resulted in a mosaic of vegetational
communities that is difficult to interpret in successional
terms. Even examination of the sequence of deposition in peat
strata is often inconclusive since some of the peat will have
been destroyed by fire or aerobic decomposition and gaps will
have been created in the stratiform record of peat accumulation.

A SUCCESSIONAL SCHEME

In his study confirming the importance of *C. calyculata*
as a pioneer at least in some areas, Kratz (1981) concluded
that in northern Wisconsin *Chamaedaphne* is a pioneering species
throughout the long succession of vegetation filling an ice-
block depression lake and its ultimate conversion to an open
Sphagnum-Chamaedaphne bog. Kratz discusses the classical concept of ecological succession in bogs, as presented by Clements
(1916), Davis (1906), Ganong (1902), Nichols (1918), Transeau
(1905), and the summary of the process as given by Whittaker
(1975), concluding that the latter description is a "mixture
of community and ecosystem level phenomena" that could--or
should--best be kept conceptually distinct and separate from
one another. Kratz points out:

*Fig. 2. Invasion of open bogs by coniferous tree species
is slow. Here it is confined to the edge, where the bog grades
sharply into upland deciduous forest as a result of the topographic gradient. Carex and Eriophorum species, combined with
Ledum and Chamaedaphne, as well as moss species, dominate the
plant community.*

The manner in which the mat encroaches centripetally into the lake, thickens, and deposits organic matter on the
bottom of the lake constitutes an ecosystem level process.
Description of species assemblages important to each stage
of development constitutes the community level portion of
the description. The distinction is important because

ecosystem level structure and function provides the context for and often constrains community level structure and
function.

   Studies of peat stratigraphy led him to conclude that
Chamaedaphne had been dominant throughout the lake-filling
process.
   Carex lasiocarpa was found to be an indicator of minerotrophic conditions in bogs and fens by Heinselman (1970), Vitt
and Slack (1975), Schwintzer (1978a,b), and others, and it
seems reasonable to accept the interpretation of Schwintzer
and Williams (1974) that this species may be among those establishing pioneering plant communities along shallow shorelines of minerotrophic waters but that the mat formed by this
species in shallow water is soon invaded by *Chamaedaphne,*
Sphagnum, and other characteristic species, which then function as pioneers in mat formation over water too deep for
sedges. The shrubs grow with stems often extending into open
water but curved upward so leafy tips are in air, as described
by Rigg (1940a,b) and others.
   In lakes on neutral or mildly acidic and nutrient-poor
glacial till, *C. oligosperma* or other sedges may perform as
pioneering species around the edges of lakes, and these likewise are invaded by *Chamaedaphne* and *Sphagnum* as soon as conditions are favorable, the latter then growing out over open
water too deep for sedges. The result ultimately will be a
compressed peat mat with *Chamaedaphne, Sphagnum,* bog shrubs,
as well as herbaceous species dominant until *Larix* and *Picea*
invade (Fig. 3). The latter are sooner or later destroyed by
fire during a period of drought, and succession on the surface of the mat is then returned to the *Carex* stage since the
entire bog will present a shallow substrate at or near the
level of the lake water surface when the drought ends and
water levels return to normal.
   During the course of postglacial development of the bogs,
succession and the accumulation of peat inevitably has been
interrupted many times by drought and fire (Curtis, 1959), a
history that will be recorded in composition of peat strata
in the bog. Difficulties encountered in interpreting successional history or inexplicably irregular patterns in bog vegetational communities are apt to be the result of episodes in
development of the bog of which there is no residual evidence.
Thus, for example, groves of *Picea* often observed around the
perimeter of a central bog lake, rather than the perimeter of
the entire bog as would be expected according to classical
succession (see Fig. 1) can be the remnants--or descendants--
of trees that survived a fire because of their proximity to
the lake margin where wet conditions permitted survival of

Fig. 3. This bog of moderate size has undergone complete invasion by C. calyculata, which is now the dominant in density throughout the bog. Conifer tree species, notably P. mariana, are invading around the perimeter of the bog and an occasional individual can be seen.

seedlings, saplings, or seeds released from serotinous cones of *P. mariana*. These lakeside clumps of spruce often are present when no spruce can be seen around the peripheral margin of the bog and the vegetation of the bog itself is dominated by *C. oligosperma, Sphagnum* species, *K. polifolia, A. glaucophylla, Eriophorum* species, and scattered individuals or clumps of *Chamaedaphne*. The latter can be expected to increase in density and dominance through the years until, finally, *Picea* and perhaps *Larix* again invade throughout the bog from the seeds released from the trees surviving around the small central lake. Some bogs in which the central lake has become extinct and filled with peat will have burned in a fire so severe that all trees have been destroyed; such bogs might now have a dense growth of *Chamaedaphne* but totally lack any *Picea* or *Larix* because seed sources are so distant that ecesis has not yet taken place. These bogs with pure stands of

Fig. 4. If maintained free of fire for a long period of time, the coniferous tree species, mostly black spruce (Picea mariana), begin to establish dominance, eventually converting a bog to a northern lowland conifer forest.

Chamaedaphne are rare, but they are to be found on occasion and it seems apparent that they will persist until seeds of *Picea* find their way into the area or they again revert to pioneer status following fire (Fig. 4).

It is apparent, as Kratz (1981) pointed out, that the floating portions of a bog around the margin of open water remain wet even during a period of drought when the level of the lake sinks. The remainder of the bog becomes dry, however, and if fire sweeps the bog at such times all vegetation excepting that on the wet floating portion of the bog would be destroyed.

Trees ringing the open water, however, might well survive, as
well as seedlings, saplings, and seeds from serotinous cones
of Picea, and the shrubs, herbs, sedges, and grasses occupying
the margin of the floating portions of the bog.

REGIONAL DIFFERENCES

     Other events, in addition to fire, can have a profound ef-
fect upon the composition and structure of the vegetation of
a bog. Inundation and changes in the drainage pattern caused
by beavers or any of a number of causes will all have an effect. Absence of a source of seed at a critical time may account for the absence of conifer tress on some small bogs
surrounded by deciduous forest. There may be differences or
variations in the pH of the water flowing into a bog, the result of periodic flooding of exposed mineral soils in the surrounding watershed. The one thing certain is that there are
always reasons for the vegetation differences, however obscure
they may be.
     These local dissimilarities in plant communities tend to
mask broad regional variation over greater distances. Thus,
in theory, if bog plant communities in northern regions had
been uniformly protected from disturbances of any kind throughout the entire period of postglacial time, it would now be
possible to detect differences in species composition in these
communities that would be due entirely to climatic and substrate variations from one place to another. We could then
conclude, for example, that the decreasing importance of such
species as C. calyculata and A. glaucophylla northward into
boreal regions is purely a consequence of their being adapted
to the northern boreal climate more poorly than to the climate
of the northern United States and southern Canada. The local
variation that does exist, however, tends to obscure this theo-
retically possible comparison. When, in fact, we see that
Chamaedaphne and Andromeda do indeed vary in density greatly
from one bog to another in the same northern Wisconsin county,
it is difficult to establish that variations in density from
Wisconsin to central Manitoba, for example, are determined by
differences in climate, substrate composition, and so on. However, it is inescapable that broad regional differences must
result from regional differences in the various environmental
factors, and it becomes of considerable ecological importance
to identify the community differences that exist from one region to another as a consequence of the environmental variations. Thus, the wet lowland communities of northern Minnesota
described by Heinselman (1963, 1970) differ from those of the
Hudson Bay lowlands described by Sjörs (1959), or, at the

other extreme, from communities in the lowlands of southern
Wisconsin such as those studied by Clausen (1957) and by Klop-
tek and Stearns (1978).

One of the most significant changes that occurs in the
bog plant communities over long distances latitudinally is a
result of the fact that many species of the bogs in northern
Minnesota, Wisconsin, and Michigan are obviously well adapted
to uplands northward; thus, *P. mariana,* for example, the only
major tree species (along with *L. laricina,* in lesser densities)
inhabiting the conifer swamps of the upper midwest in the
United States, becomes in northern Manitoba a dominant species
of the upland forests. The shrub *L. groenlandicum* inhabits
southern bogs in abundance and moves to uplands along with
spruce to the north. The same is true of other species that
possess a range extending from the Great Lakes region far northward into the boreal forest of Canada; among them, for example,
are such species as *V. vitis-idaea, V. uliginosum, B. glandulosa, E. nigrum,* and *R. chamaemorus.* Many of these species,
in contrast to *L. groenlandicum,* however, are relatively rare
or absent in many of the bog communities in the upper midwest.
They do, however, become abundant in bogs and conifer swamps
of far northern Minnesota and southern Canada, from there extending northward at least to the limit of trees and often far
beyond that, coming increasingly to dominate the upland forests
and tundra northward; at Ennadai Lake, at the edge of the barrens, they become dominant species over the entire landscape,
from lower slopes to rocky ridges where no trees are found,
as shown by the author in studies of the vegetation of the
Ennadai Lake area in southern Keewatin (Larsen, 1965).

Thus, on the tundra of the northern end of Ennadai Lake,
the following frequencies of these species were found in six
representative communities of the lower slopes of gently rolling hills in the area (Table II).

In a study of vegetational communities in the Ennadai Lake
area, it was apparent that the densities and habitat preferences of many of the species correlated with macroclimatic
factors. Perhaps most interesting are the few ubiquitous species that range widely through forest and tundra. They increase in frequency northward through the forest and then decrease beyond the forest border northward in the arctic tundra
communities. The species of this group, including *E. nigrum,
L. decumbens, R. chamaemorus, V. uliginosum,* for example,
attain their highest frequencies in the communities of the
forest-tundra ecotone, where they are the dominants in a floristically depauperate vegetation (Larsen 1967, 1971a, b, 1980).
Whether uniquely adapted or simply widely tolerant of harsh and
variable conditions, they are an interesting group for further
study.

Table II. Species Frequencies in a Northern Tundra Community[a]

	Stands					
Betula glandulosa	60	65	85	40	5	
Rubus chamaemorus	55	55	45	85	80	95
Vaccinium uliginosum	55	70	80	70	45	20
Vaccinium vitis-idaea	55	75	65	85	100	95
Empetrum nigrum	25	25			65	5
Ledum groenlandicum				15		
Eriophorum spissum	40	20	25	20	10	15

[a]*Frequencies of selected species in six representative plant communities on the lower slopes of gently rolling hills in the vicinity of Ennadai Lake, Keewatin, Northwest Territories, Canada. Data from Larsen (1980).*

IMPORTANCE OF TREES

     The trees perhaps not too arbitrarily can probably be considered the most important components in any forest community, since they modify both soil and microclimate and, as a result, greatly affect conditions important to their own ability to perpetuate the species as dominants in the community (Fig. 5). Trees also control almost completely the conditions under which shrubs and herbaceous species grow and reproduce (Stearns, 1951). It can be said that the trees dominating lowland conifer forests of northern Wisconsin and adjacent regions are the most important species in these communities and their role in perpetuating a community is of paramount ecological significance. Curtis (1959) pointed out one of the more puzzling aspects of spruce ecology in northern Wisconsin when he wrote:

     One of the difficult problems in the study of community
     dynamics of northern Wisconsin is the assessment of the
     relation between conifer swamps and terminal mesic forests
     ....The conifer swamp may give rise to a terminal forest of
     white spruce and balsam fir if the climatic conditions are
     suitable. This is shown by the high index of similarity
     of the swamp community and the boreal forests of wet or
     wet-mesic sites....Actually, the tamarack swamps south of
     the tension zone, which eventually evolve into wet-mesic
     southern hardwoods, showed much higher similarities with
     the boreal forest than they did with the southern forest in
     which they were present. It is possible to consider all of
     the conifer swamps of Wisconsin as wet-ground stages of the
     boreal forest, with the central and southern swamps isolated

Fig. 5. Invasion of this bog is in a relatively advanced stage; both *Picea mariana* and *Laris laricina* are present in considerable density and eventually will convert what was once open bog into a northern lowland conifer forest if no major disturbance occurs.

by postglacial climatic changes and only those in the extreme north in a position to develop into spruce-fir forest
by successional processes. Such a view is useful in certain
respects, but should not be held too rigorously, because the
supporting evidence available is inadequate for firm judg-
ments.

Whether this is the case or not is now open to some question, and the work of Carleton and Maycock (1978) leads to the
following conclusion:

In the absence of external catastrophe, some upland primary boreal forests seem to develop into secondary fir and
(or) spruce forests. Also apparent, however, are old deca-
dent forest stands typified by the complete absence of subsequent development or considerably delayed regeneration.

Whatever the successional relationships of the tree species
dominant in the conifer swamps, fire or other disturbance
probably occurs with sufficient frequency to return the plant
communities to pioneer stages of development long before steps
toward further succession can occur. Perhaps, on the other
hand, development of techniques for total fire suppression will
eventually permit ecologists to answer what is at the present
time a puzzling question.

In the affirmations of Carlton and Maycock we have the
culmination of a modern trend toward what we might call recognition of a neoclassical concept of succession. Whether the
concept will continue to evolve beyond even this stage, we do
not know, particularly as it is applied to the boreal forest
and, concomitantly, to the bog communities with which we are
concerned here. By the late 1950s and early 1960s, concepts
of succession held by ecologists began to diverge markedly from
the classical idea that succession is a quite predictable linear
progression of species, with one set of species following another
in dominance according to a regular pattern. In place of this
idea came the concept that, instead of a linear successional
sequence--at least in bogs and in the boreal forest generally--
there is a successional trend toward increasingly diverse communities, not toward a single uniform climatic climax community.
The new concept states that bog and boreal forest communities
are often stable for long periods of time, maintaining a kind
of status quo and becoming increasingly diversified in terms
of the species composition of individual stands. This progression continues until fire or insect infestation or some other

natural disturbance to the area brings about reversion of the
communities to a more pioneer stage, depending upon the sever-
ity of the disturbance. Following the disturbance, pioneer
communities then again begin to undergo change and progression,
in response to random events in the community and the environment, following one of many possible avenues of progression--
or "succession" if one continues to use the term--toward one
of many possible communities in which a degree of stability is
attained, but not toward a grand regional climatic "climax"
as envisioned by Clements and the members of the old ecological
schools. This trend in development is what might be called
the neoclassical concept of succession; relationship to the
water table and to soil conditions is discussed in detail by
Heinselman in his reports (1963, 1970) on the Lake Agassiz
peatlands, particularly the Myrtle Lake area.

VARIATIONS IN STRUCTURE

     The Lake Agassiz Peatlands Natural Area in Minnesota con-
tains much of what is known as the Myrtle Lake peatland, a
70-square mile area that is virtually undisturbed by man and
contains most of the vegetation types of the postglacial Lake
Agassiz region. These peatlands were studied intensively by
Heinselman (1963, 1970), who described the area as follows:

> The vegetation and peatland types of the Lake Agassiz
> Peatlands Natural Area are related to topography, waterflow
> patterns, water chemistry, and the evolution of the land-
> scape as recorded by peat stratigraphy. Eight peatland
> types are distinguished: (1) minerotrophic swamp, (2) weakly
> minerotrophic swamp, (3) string bog and patterned fen, (4)
> forest island and fen complex, (5) transitional forested
> bog, (6) semi-ombrotrophic bog, (7) ombrotrophic bog (raised
> bog), and (8) raised bog drain. Consistent differences in
> pH, Ca, and Mg were found between waters of contrasting
> peatland types....A general topographic alignment of vege-
> tation and peatland types agrees with the hypothesis of
> chemical controls....
> Landscape evolution included...recession of Lake Agassiz
> about 11,700 years ago....Development of fens, marshes, and
> carr during the post-glacial warm-dry interval....Paludifi-
> cation caused water tables to rise, and most water basins
> were overgrown....Invasion of minerotrophic swamp forests
> ...built the basal forest peats that now cover 48% of the
> substratum....Myrtle Lake rose steadily with paludification
> and now stands 11.8 ft (3.6 m) above the ridge 1 mile (1.6
> km) north of the lake. Water tables rose 10-20 ft (3.0-6.1

m) over much of a 70-square mile (181 km^2) area. This
history does not agree with early concepts of succession,
which postulate a trend toward mesophytism with peat accumulation. The only "direction" here is a possible trend toward landscape diversity.

On the basis of floristic and physiognomic criteria, Heinselman classified the peatland vegetational communities into
eight types. The physical land types delineated in Heinselman's study were based primarily on abiotic features, but they
were found to correspond in general to the vegetational communities. The evidence indicated that the vegetational communities were influenced primarily by nutrients and water sources,
since at least part of the water in the minerotrophic peatlands
had percolated through mineral soil, and such sites supported
a rich vegetation. Ombrotrophic peatlands were dependent upon
precipitation for water and minerals because their convex surface prevented inflow from mineral soil. Typical ombrotrophic
bog vegetation occupied such areas. Heinselman stated that
raised bogs with elevated *Sphagnum* domes are classic examples
of this kind of peatland, but other types of relief may also
prevent inflow of mineral soil water. It was Heinselman's
conclusion that the mineral content of the water strongly influenced floristics and vegetation types. The species that
were more or less consistently indicative of the various ranges
of water properties are shown in Table III.
These lists are not complete, Heinselman points out, but
are limited to plants having reasonable fidelity and some
measure of general abundance in areas with the indicated conditions.
Heinselman's studies revealed such a diversity of communities and such a range of environmental combinations that he
was led to the conclusion that no readily apparent successional
patterns could be discerned. He expressed the belief that the
literature concerned with the basin-filling sequence (hydrarch
succession), combined with phytosociological evidence for a
progression toward mesophytism with accumulations of peat,
created an infortunate bias in the observations of peatlands
by ecologists. He points out that the record of vegetational
changes in the peatlands he studied reveals "no consistent
trend toward mesophytism, terrestrialization, or even uniformity." Rather he adds:

there has been a general swamping of the landscape, rise
of water tables, deterioration of tree growth, and a
diversification of landscape types....One is tempted to
claim a "muskeg climax," asserting a general trend toward
paludification, the very opposite of the Clementsian view.

TABLE III. Chemical Characteristics of Soil Water in Relationship to Vegetational Community Composition[a]

---

pH 5.8–7.0; Ca, 10–25 ppm; Ca + Mg, 13–30 ppm

Thuja occidentalis	Rubus pubescens
Fraxinus nigra	Impatiens biflora
Betula papyrifera	Coptis trifolia
Abies balsamea	Mitella nuda
Alnus rugosa	Galium aparine, G. triflorum
Rubus strigosus	Caltha palustris
Cornus canadensis	Clintonia borealis
Dryopteris cristata	Linnaea borealis
Maianthemum canadense	Calamagrostis canadensis
Trientalis borealis	

pH 4.3–5.8; Ca, 3–10 ppm; Ca + Mg, 5–13 ppm

Larix laricina	Iris versicolor
Betula pumila	Utricularia spp.
Andromeda glaucophylla	Typha latifolia
Menyanthes trifoliata	Phragmites communis
Carex lasiocarpa	

pH 3.1–4.2; Ca, 0.8–2.8 ppm; Ca + Mg, 1.0–3.0 ppm

Picea mariana	Eriophorum spp.
Kalmia polifolia	Pleurozium schreberi
Chamaedaphne calyculata	Sphagnum fuscum

---

[a] Comparison of floristic composition of communities in relation to chemistry of the soil water in northern Minnesota. Data from Heinselman (1970).

But even this trend cannot persist indefinitely, because climate and physiography set limits on peat accumulation. The controls are the permeability of peats and steepness of water-table slopes in relation to water supply.

The factors of importance in determining the course of community development and rates of peat accumulation and decay are chemical and microbial, climatic, topographic, and mineralogical. To summarize Heinselman's views, the critical factors controlling the development of the vegetational communities in the Lake Agassiz peatlands are these:

1. Acidity and base status, nutrient content, and oxygen-carbon dioxide status of the soil water.
2. Topography of the peat surface, reflecting past rates of accumulation and decay.
3. The vegetation of ombrotrophic sites is depauperate, with a predominance of Sphagnaceae, Ericaeae, and of Larix and Picea. The vegetation of rich sites is varied and diverse, with many grasses, sedges, herbs, and tall shrubs.

The frequent recurrence of fire in the stands of conifers
in the peatlands under natural conditions probably makes consideration of succession largely theoretical in any case. As
in the upland boreal forest stands to the north, fire occurs
with sufficient frequency to make a continuing cyclic reestab-
lishment of the forest more likely than any succession beyond
this stage.

In summary, the question thus essentially remains unanswered:
Are the smaller bogs studied by Christensen *et al.* (1959) but
local, isolated representatives of segments in Heinselman's
continuous array of types? Are they thus generally static? Or
if they are indeed changing, are they changing in a directional
manner, or are they changing in directions that lead to ever
greater diversity, and not, as Christensen *et al.* suggest, toward the cedar-balsam community, or beyond?

The questions, it seems, remain unanswered. More recently,
the work of others has tended to confirm Heinselman's views,
although the ultimate developmental fate of the small bogs,
it is generally conceded, remains uncertain. The evidence is,
in a sense, fragmentary and circumstantial rather than definitive. There are, however, some other interesting studies that
tend to confirm Heinselman's views. First, perhaps we should
summarize Heinselman's conclusions regarding the differences
between the large peat areas and the smaller peat bogs. Heinselman (1975) concludes that it is only the basins without a
flow of water that exhibit the classic hydrarch basin-filling
succession, and he points out further that:

> In sheer numbers there may be millions of bog lakes in
> various stages of filling on the Canadian Shield, in the
> lake states of the United States, in Fennoscandia, and
> in the northern Soviet Union. Here deeper waters are filled
> by the gradual sedimentation of pollen, phytoplankton, zoo-
> plankton, aquatic macrophytes, calcium carbonate (marl),
> and other sediments, collectively called gyttja, copropel,
> or sapropel. Simultaneously, a floating mat vegetation may
> encroach centripetally across the water from the lakeshore.
> Later bog forests may invade....

On most of the other initial landforms, standing water
basins covered only a minor fraction of the landscape
prior to paludification; so other landforms account for
most of the *area* of the boreal peatlands. Most peat formation, therefore, occurred directly on mineral soils.
Water basins may have been the initial loci of peatland
vegetation, as in the Lake Agassiz Peatlands Natural Area,
but sedge fens, swamp forests, and even sphagnum bogs
occupied most of the mineral soils directly. Peat stratigraphy attests to these initial plant communities in most

lake plain, outwash plain, and coastal plain peatlands, as
well as on the more sloping terrains of morainic or bedrock
landscapes....

Eventually erosion would dissect lacustrine and marine
plains such as the Lake Agassiz plain or the Hudson Bay
lowlands....When slopes are steepened beyond the climatic
limit for peat formation, paludification will cease and
peat decomposition will ensue....The plant communities and
peatland types do change predictably if the full sequence
is known, but what occurs in any given area depends on an
extraordinarily complex series of interactions. This can
hardly be viewed as a fixed succession. And so it may be
for peatlands throughout the circumpolar boreal regions of
the earth. Ecologists have sought that elusive "climax"
for almost a century now. But perhaps there really is no
"direction" to peatland evolution--only ceaseless change!

Other ecologists who have studied the North American bogs
and fens appear generally to agree. Vitt and Slack (1975)
greatly amplified existing knowledge of the interrelationships
between vegetation and environment in their studies in eastern
North America. Up to the time of this work, most vegetational
analyses included the vascular plants but not *Sphagnum* and
other bryophyte species. In studying eight bogs in northern
Michigan, Vitt and Slack found that successional patterns in
many peatland types are often controlled by *Sphagnum*. The
latter absorbs water, impedes drainage, creates a more acid
habitat, and traps such cations as those of calcium, magnesium,
potassium, and sodium. They found that a number of vascular
plants and species of *Sphagnum* would often be found growing
together in a given community, a result of their possessing
similar physiological tolerances. For example, *S. teres* and
C. lasiocarpa were always found together although their relative importance varied from place to place. On the other hand,
some species of vascular plants, as well as *Sphagnum,* possess
broad tolerances, are in all community types, and are not
associated consistently with any other given species; an example of a vascular plant of this kind is *C. calyculata*. *Sphagnum magellanicum* is an example of a moss with wide ecological
tolerance.

Vitt and Slack found that pH and cation content greatly
influence the vegetation, and they summarized by writing that
the most significant conclusion to be drawn from their work is
that "the principle of hydrarch succession in kettlehole bogs
is an over simplification of the situation. Bog succession is
dependent on several interrelated features, of which pH and
cation content are important." But how acidity varies from
one site to another only a few meters distant is also significant:

These data suggest that when lake water is alkaline, the plant communities formed at the water's edge include plants which are found in alkaline conditions. These plants act as a buffer zone to the acidophilous communities farther from the water's edge. In this situation the acidophilous species of *Sphagnum* have been excluded....In contrast, in the acidophilous bog lakes, the edge zone is occupied by a relatively acidic plant community....

It is dangerous to assume that successional patterns in bogs as one sees them in a spacial sequence indicate succession in time (sensu hydrarch sere of Clements). Although we do not believe hydrarch succession can explain all types of bog and fen vegetation in northern Michigan, there is direct evidence...that succession through time has occurred.

The segregated community types studied by Vitt and Slack are shown to follow the gradients of pH, light intensity, and calcium and magnesium ion concentrations. The two types of kettlehole bogs that could be easily distinguished, those surrounding acid and alkaline bog lakes respectively, had each their own continuum of community types and, by inference, individual successional sequences.

Elsewhere, specifically in the peatlands of western boreal Canada, Vitt *et al.* (1975a) found that the vegetational communities in the so-called patterned mires could not be easily interpreted as undergoing a regular succession:

Whether or not the flarks which are deep and dominated by *Menyanthes trifoliata* are youngest and, with a gradual accumulation of peat, are filled in and dominated by *Carex limosa* is an interesting question. Likewise, are strings with *Picea mariana* on them older than those dominated by *Betula glandulosa?* The answer to this developmental question can only be answered by a complex study of peat cores and stratigraphy. At present there is no evidence to indicate a simple hydrarch succession.

It is interesting that the study of Vitt *et al.* shows that the surrounding upland soil plays an important part in determining which species will invade a lowland peat-covered area. A *Sphagnum*-dominated community develops in a region where the surrounding soil is acidic, and the sedge-moss community develops where the watershed is underlain by calcareous soils. In this, there is an obvious parallel with the tendency for different communities to develop in the bogs around acidic or alkaline lakes.

It is, from these works, evident that peat formation and accumulation depends on the complex interrelationships that

exists between climate, hydrology, soils, and probably a number of biological factors, and that these, in turn, have a
great influence upon the composition and structure of the plant
community; that there are complex interactions is apparent, and
consequently there is no definite "successional scheme or
pattern" in either the large peatlands or the small kettlehole
bogs. About all that one can say is that great variability is
the watchword of biology, and particularly ecology, and that
only detailed analysis will reveal the vegetational structure
in the vascular plant and bryophyte communities that might be
influential in determining succession. One must also take into
account a wide variety of environmental factors that will have
an influence--to a degree and intensity that, in the case of
individual species, is as yet largely unknown. We know that
the influences must exist, but what they are, how they act,
what species are affected, and what the consequences are in
terms of developmental schemes in the bogs and marshlands--of
these things, little is as yet known.

PLANT COMMUNITY VARIATION

    On the other hand, ample data are now available to indicate
without question that while bog communities in every region are
composed of a unique set of species, to some degree these differ from one region to another. Even if a species is circumpolar or otherwise widely distributed, it will vary regionally
in its ability to attain dominance since other species are more
vigorously competitive at one place or another, the result of
conditions more nearly approaching the optimum for them. Thus,
for example, C. calyculata is found in Eurasia and across North
America; it is a dominant species in the bogs of the Great Lakes
region, in Minnesota, Wisconsin, Michigan, Ontario, and Manitoba, but it declines markedly in importance to the north and
to the west.
    Regional differences in plant communities of bogs have been
discussed in some detail elsewhere and it is not necessary to
repeat them here. There are, however, local variations in the
communities that are the consequences of local differences in
characteristics of peat soils, and these latter may often also
account for differences in vegetation from one bog to another
that might otherwise appear inexplicable. These correlations
between plant community variations and soil characteristics
have not been studied in detail, however, and it is possible
here only to describe some of the circumstances supporting the
idea that such is the case. Many of the studies cited were
carried out in regions other than North America, but in many
instances the species involved are circumpolar in distribution

and it seems reasonable to infer that the same effects are to
be seen in the bogs of North America. Thus, Reader (1978a)
writes:

> Phosphorus, K, and N were the 3 elements most often found
> to be limiting bog marsh plant growth, although the relative
> importance of these elements as limiting factors changed
> from site to site. For example, the productivity of cotton
> grass *(Eriophorum vaginatum)* was most limited by K availabil-
> ity at bog marshes in Breconshire and Cardiganshire, UK, and
> by P at Smaland, Sweden...while neither K nor P was found to
> be limiting at Moor House, UK....The outcome of nutrient en-
> richment experiments conducted in the field is often in-
> fluenced by other site factors, such as substrate pH and
> water level. The solubility, and hence availability, of
> mineral nutrients is pH dependent....Waterlogging and the
> accompanying effects of poor aeration influence nutrient
> availability both directly, by impairing the ability of
> roots to absorb nutrients, and indirectly by restricting
> root growth to upper portions of the peat substrate.

There was no appreciable change in the growth rate of *C.
calyculata* and *B. pumila* in a Michigan bog as a result of fer-
tilization; but, as Reader adds, more experiments are needed
to establish firmly whether substrate conditions and climatic
regime have an influence on the primary productivity of the
northern bog marshes. "The only facts apparent at the present
time are that individual bog marshes vary considerably both in
their productivity and in their response to nutrient enrichment
and that the northern climate restricts the production potential
of bog marshes."

Among other species that appear largely indifferent to substrate characteristics are *V. vitis-idaea* and *A. uva-ursi,* both
of which are found in the more northern regions of both North
America and Eurasia, occupying upland pine and spruce woodlands,
conifer swamps, open bogs, alpine meadows, and arctic tundra,
and thus occurring on soils formed over a wide range of chemical
and climatic conditions. Such species may be shown to possess
somewhat narrow tolerance ranges locally, and many possess ecotypes showing definite habitat preferences, growing in smaller
numbers or absent entirely from unfavorable sites, but they
nevertheless possess much wider tolerance limits than do other
species with which they mingle in various communities over
their entire geographical range.

Species differences in adjacent communities are a consequence of the different response of each species to the various environmental factors and can be illustrated by means of
the data of many studies; one such study is that of Reader and
Stewart (1972), which is perhaps as illustrative of the prin-

ciple as any. In this study, they recorded the important species in four different communities, all found in a single lowland area bog in southeastern Manitoba. The communities included a bog forest, a muskeg with scattered trees, an open
bog, and a so-called lagg community--by definition a wetter
area subject to inflow of ground water and located usually
around the edge of a basin in which a bog or a bog forest is
found. Of the characteristics of bog forest, muskeg, and lagg,
the more pertinent are given in Table IV.

Species differences between the four vegetational zones
are as follows (only the more important species are listed and
they are given in order of importance, according to their relative frequency):

Bog forest: *Ledum groenlandicum, Picea mariana, Pleurozium
schreberi.*
Muskeg: *Ledum groenlandicum, Picea mariana, Sphagnum fuscum,
Chamaedaphne calyculata, Vaccinium vitis-idaea, Kalmia polifolia.*
Bog: *Chamaedaphne calyculata, Polytrichum juniperinum, Sphagnum
fuscum, Ledum groenlandicum, Oxycoccus quadripetalus, Vaccinium
vitis-idaea, Kalmia polifolia, Aulacomnium palustre.*
Lagg: *Chamaedaphne calyculata, Carex rostrata, Aulacomnium
palustre, Hypnum pratense, Calamagrostis canadensis, Salix
bebbiana, Salix serissima.*

A comparable change in composition of the plant community
along a transect from upland to lowland has been revealed in
an area of Alaska by Dyrness and Grigal, (1979). As they
write: "The vegetation associated with these sites is open
black spruce/feathermoss-*Cladonia* on ridge and upper slope,
a mosaic area at midslope where this community intergrades
with an open black spruce/*Sphagnum* community, a lower slope
dominated by *Sphagnum,* and in some cases a woodland/*Eriophorum*
community."

WATER, MINERALS, AND SPECIES

To elucidate the interactions between plants, water, and
nutrients in bogs, Jeglum (1971, 1972, 1973) undertook a study
of 119 wetland--predominantly peatland--communities in the
southern boreal forest of Saskatchewan. The area included in
the study encompassed a broad range of wetland and peatland
types, bogs, fens, swamps, muskegs, and moist coniferous
forests. By means of ordinations and principal components
analysis he found that vegetational community patterns correlated with physical factors, with moisture and nutrients
exerting the greatest influence upon the vegetation.

TABLE IV.   Age and Growth Rates of Representative Peat Samples[a]

Zone	Peat depth (cm)	Age (radio-carbon dated) (B. P.)		Annual weight increment $(gm/m^2/yr)$
Bog forest	185-190	4524	126	36.3
Muskeg	200-205	7939	103	26.8
Lagg	80-85	2960	73	51.7

[a]Radiocarbon dates of peat samples from a lowland bog in
southeastern Manitoba with calculated annual weight increment
of the peat in the bog. Data from Reader and Stewart (1972).
Copyright 1972, the Ecological Society of America.

In some communities, zonation of vegetation seemed to be
associated more with fertility status than with water supply.
Thus, in undrained minerotrophic depressions, there were sedge
mats of C. lasiocarpa at the edge of open water, S. pedicellaris
in wetter areas, C. canadensis at the upland margin. Abrupt
transitions from ombrotrophic open bog and black spruce muskeg to fens occurred where there was periodic inundation of
the fen by minerotrophic water. Muskegs were seen commonly to
grade into upland communities in places and abut fen or swamp
on lower borders. The position of each community could be
plotted in relationship to the nutrient status and drainage
pattern, and Jeglum concludes that there was a definite and
predictable relationship between the vegetational communities
and such factors as water and nutrient availability.
    On a regional basis, the critical factors permitting the
existence of bogs and other peatlands are climatic in the sense
that only a certain range of climatic conditions favor the
formation and persistence of these communities; these conditions
are essentially temperature and precipitation regimes. Locally,
however, the controlling factors are nutrient availability as
well as position and movement of subsurface water, which in
turn is influential in determining nutrient availability. Other
factors involving disturbance--windthrow, disease, fire, beaver
flooding, drainage, logging--also affect nutrient availability
and water levels.
    It is possible to make a general comparison of vegetational
composition and physical factors in the bogs of two different
regions, in this case northern Minnesota and central Saskatchewan, by simply listing the data for water and nutrient para-
meters and the species of plants found dominant in communities
in the two regions (Table V).
    In the case of the conifer swamps, there appears to be
little tendency for succession to occur through any regular
pattern although, as pointed out, there may be progression to
a white cedar and balsam fir community. In general, the perma-

TABLE V. Chemical and Physical Characteristics of Bogs in Relation to Vegetational Community Composition: Dominant Species in Bogs of Various Physical Characteristics in Northern Minnesota and Central Saskatchewan[a]

	Minerotrophic	Weakly minerotrophic	Ombrotrophic
Environmental conditions[b]			
Northern Minnesota			
pH	5.8–6.7	4.3–5.8	3.2–4.2
Ca (ppm)	10–30	4–12	0.6–2.3
Mg (ppm)	1.1–2.8	1.2	0.2
Peat depth (cm)	30–180	300–760	90–900
Water movement	Strong	Sluggish	Blocked
Water table	High	Below surface	Below surface
Central Saskatchewan			
pH	5.6–6.7	5.0–6.6	3.1–4.6
Peat depth (cm)	50–150	60–220	75–115
Tress/acre	0–2.8	20–190	8–197
Shrub cover	0–72	30–80	65–100
Depth to water below (+) or above			
(−) ground	−25 to +1	+22 to +42	+60 to +69
Dominant species			
Northern Minnesota			
	Thuja occidentalis	*Larix laricina*	*Picea mariana*
	Abies balsamea	*Picea mariana*	*Kalmia polifolia*
	Betula papyrifera	*Betula pumila*	*Chamaedaphne calyculata*

Brasenia schreberi Gmel.	Water shield
Calla palustris L.	Wild calla
Calopogon pulchellus (Salisb.) R. Br.	Grass pink, swamp pink
Carex canescens L.	
Carex comosa Boott.	
Carex diandra Schrank	
Carex disperma Dew.	
Carex interior Bailey	
Carex lasiocarpa Ehrh.	*C. lasiocarpa* var. *americana*
Carex leptalea Wahlenb.	
Carex limosa L.	
Carex livida (Wahlenb.) Willd.	
Carex oligosperma Michx.	
Carex pauciflora Lightf.	
Carex tenella	
Carex tenuiflora Wahlenb.	
Carex trisperma Dew.	
Chamaecyparis nootkatensis (Lamb.) Spach	Alaska yellow cedar
Chamaedaphne calyculata (L.) Moench	Leatherleaf, cassandra
Chiogenes hispidula	see *Gaultheria hispidula*
Cinna arundinacea L.	
Cinna latifolia (Trev.) Griseb.	
Cladium mariscoides (Muhl.) Torr.	Twig rush
Clintonia borealis (Ait.) Raf.	Bluebead lily
Coptis groenlandica (Oeder) Fern.	Goldthread (See Hulten, 1968)
Coptis trifolia (L.) Salisb. var. *groenlandica*	see *C. Groenlandica*
Cornus canadensis	
Cornus stolonifera	
Cypripedium acaule Ait.	Moccasin flower, Lady's slipper
Darlingtonia californica Torr.	California pitcher plant
Decodon verticillatus (L.) Ell.	Water willow
Drosera intermedia Hayne	
Drosera rotundifolia L.	Round-leaved sundew
Dryopteris bootii	see Gleason and Cronquist (1963)
Dryopteris austriaca (Jacq.)	see *Dryopteris cristata*
Dryopteris cristata (L.) Gray	see Gleason and Cronquist (1963)
Dryopteris thelypteris (L.) Gray	Marsh fern

Dulichium arundinaceum (L.) Britt.	Three-way sedge
Empetrum nigrum L.	Black crowberry
Equisetum fluviatile L.	Water horsetail
Equisetum scirpoides Michx.	Dwarf scouring-rush
Eriophorum angustifolium Honckeny	
Eriophorum callitrix Cham.	
Eriophorum chamissonis C. A. Mey	
Eriophorum gracile W.D.J. Koch	
Eriophorum spissum Fern.	
Eriophorum tenellum Nutt.	
Eriophorum viridi-carinatum (Engelm.) Fern	
Eriophorum virginicum L.	
Fraxinus nigra Marsh.	Black ash
Gaultheria hispidula (L.) Bigel	Creeping snowberry
Gaultheria procumbens	Wintergreen
Gaultheria shallon Pursh	W
Gaylussacia baccata (Wang.) K. Koch	Black huckleberry
Gentiana douglasiana	W
Gentiana sceptrum	W
Habenaria clavellata (Michx.) Spreng.	Green woodland orchis
Habenaria dilatata (Pursh) Hook.	Leafy white orchis
Habenaria obtusata (Pursh) Richards.	Blunt leaf orchis
Hypericum virginicum L.	Marsh St. John's wort
Ilex verticillata (L.) Gray	Black alder
Iris versicolor L.	Blue flag
Kalmia angustifolia L.	Lambkill, Sheep laurel E
Kalmia polifolia Wang.	Bog, pale laurel
Larix laricina (Du Roi) Koch	Tamarack
Ledum columbianum Nutt.	see *L. glandulosum* W
Ledum glandulosum Nutt.	Trapper's tea W
Ledum glandulosum Nutt. var. *columbianum*	(Piper) Hitchc., see Hitchcock and Cronquist (1973)
Ledum groenlandicum Oeder	Labrador tea
Linnaea borealis L. (var. *americana* (Forbes) Rehd.	Twinflower
Lonicera canadensis Bartr.	Fly honeysuckle
Lonicera villosa (Michx.) R.& S.	Mountain fly honeysuckle

Lycopus uniflorus Michx.
Lysichitum americanum Hult. Yellow skunk cabbage
  & St. John
Maianthemum canadense
Menyanthes trifoliata
Mitella nuda L. Naked miterwort
Myrica californicum Cham. California sweet gale W
Myrica gale L. Sweet gale
Nemopanthus mucronata (L.) Mountain holly
  Trel.
Nuphar variegatum Engelm. Bullhead lily
Nymphaea odorata Ait. Fragrant water lily
Osmunda cinnamomea L. Cinnamon fern
Oxycoccus see *Vaccinium*

Parthenocissus inserta
  (Kerner) K. Fritsch
Parthenocissus vitacea see *Parthenocissus inserta*
  inserta

Phragmites communis Trin. Reed
Picea glauca (Moench) Voss White spruce
Picea mariana (Mill.) BSP. Black spruce
Picea rubens Sarg. Red spruce E
Picea sitchensis (Bong.) Carr. Sitka spruce W
Pinus banksiana Lamb. Jack pine
Pinus contorta Dougl. *ex* Lodgepole pine PC
  Loud. var. *contorta*
Pinus monticola Dougl. Western white pine PC
Pinus resinosa Ait. Red, Norway pine
Pinus rigida Mill. Pitch pine E
Pinus strobus L. White pine
Pogonia ophioglossoides Pogonia
  (L.) Ker.
Potamogeton species Pondweeds
Potentilla palustris (L.) Scop. Marsh cinquefoil
Pseudotsuga taxifolia (Poir) Douglas-fir
  Britton
Pyrola secunda L. One sided pyrola
Pyrus floribunda Lindl. Purple chokeberry E
Pyrus melanocarpa (Michx.) Black chokeberry E
  Willd.
Rhamnus alnifolia L'Her. Buckthorn
Rhododendron californicum see *R. macrophyllum*
Rhododendron canadense (L.) Rhodora
  Torr.
Rhododendron macrophyllum Rhododendron PC
  G. Don.
Rhus vernix L. Poison sumac
Rhynchospora alba (L.) Vahl White beak-rush

Ribes triste Pall.	Red current
Rubus chamaemorus L.	Baked apple berry
Rubus pubescens Raf.	Dwarf raspberry
Rynchospora	see *Rhynchospora*
Salix bebbiana Sarg.	Long-beaked willow
Salix candida Flugge	Hoary willow
Salix planifolia Pursh	
Sarracenia purpurea L.	Pitcher plant
Scirpus cespitosus L.	
Scirpus cyperinus (L). Kunth	
Scirpus rubrotinctus Fern.	
Smilacina trifolia (L.) Desf.	
Spiranthes romanzoffiana C.&.S.	
Symplocarpus foetidus (L.) Nutt.	Skunk cabbage
Thelypteris palustris	see *Dryopteris thelypteris*
Thuja occidentalis L.	Arbor vitae, white cedar
Thuja plicata D. Don.	Western red cedar W
Triadenum virginicum	*Hypericum virginicum* W
Trientalis arctica Fisch.	
Trientalis borealis Raf.	Star flower
Triglochin maritima L.	
Tsuga canadensis (L.) Carr.	Hemlock
Tsuga heterophylla (Raf.) Sarg.	Western hemlock W
Tsuga mertensiana (Bong) Sarg.	W
Typha latifolia L.	Common cattail
Utricularia minor L.	Bladderwort
Vaccinium angustifolium Ait.	Late sweet blueberry
Vaccinium corymbosum	Highbush blueberry E
Vaccinium macrocarpon	Cranberry
Vaccinium myrtilloides Michx.	Velvet-leaf blueberry
Vaccinium oxycoccus L.	Small cranberry;
Vaccinium vitis-idaea L. [var. *minus* (Lodd.)].	Mountain cranberry
Viburnum cassinoides L.	E
Viola pallens (Banks) Brainerd	

B. COMMON MOSS SPECIES INHABITING NORTHERN LOWLAND BOGS AND
    CONIFER FORESTS

Aulacomnium palustre (Hedw.) Schwaegr.
Calliergon giganteum (Schimp.) Kindb.
Calliergon stramineum (Brid.) Kindb.
Callierogonella cuspidata (Hedw.) Loeske
Camptothecium nitens (see Tomenthypnum nitens)
Ceratodon purpureus (Hewd.) Brid.
Dicranum fuscescens Turn.

Dicranium polysetum Sw.
Drepanocladus aduncus (Hedw.) Warnst.
Drepanocladus exannulatus (BSG) Warnst.
Drepanocladus revolvens (Sw.) Warnst.
Drepanocladus uncinatus (Hedw.) Warnst.
Hylocomium splendens (Hedw.) BSG.
Hypnum lindbergii Mitt.
Pleurozium schreberi (Brid.) Mitt.
Pohlia nutans (Hedw.) Lindb.
Polytrichum commune Hedw.
Polytrichum juniperinum Hedw.
Ptilium crista-castrensis (Hedw.) De Not
Sphagnum angustifolium (see *Sphagnum recurvum* P.-Beauv. *sensu lato* var. *angustifolium* (Russ.) C. Jens.
Sphagnum capillaceum [see *Sphagnum capillifolium* (Weiss) Schrank]
Sphagnum capillifolium (Weiss) Schrank
Sphagnum cuspidatum Ehrh. ex. Hoffm.
Sphagnum fimbriatum Wils. ex. J. Hook.
Sphagnum fuscum (Schimp.) Klinggr.
Sphagnum girgensohnii Russ.
Sphagnum imbricatum Hornsch. ex. Russ [see *Sphagnum papillosum* Lindb. in Crum (1976)]
Sphagnum magellanicum Brid.
Sphagnum majus (Russ.) C. Jens
Sphagnum palustre L.
Sphagnum papillosum Lindb. (see also Crum, 1976)
Sphagnum recurvum P.-Beauv. *sensu lato* var. *angustifolium* (Russ.) C. Jens.
Sphagnum riparium Ångstr.
Sphagnum russowii Warnst.
Sphagnum squarrosum Crome
Sphagnum subsecundum Nees ex. Sturm sensu lato
Sphagnum teres (Schimp.) Ångstr. ex. Hartm.
Sphagnum warnstorfii Russ.
Tomenthypnum falcifolium (also *Tomenthypnum nitens*)(Hedw.) Loeske var. *falcifolium* (Ren. ex. Nich.)
Tomenthypnum nitens (Hedw.) Loeske
Tortula ruralis (Hedw.) Gärten., Meyer, & Scherb.

Bibliography*

Aaby, B., and H. Tauber (1974). Rates of peat formation in relation to degree of humification and local environment, as shown by studies of a raised bog in Denmark. *Boreas* *4:* 1-17.

Adams, C. C. (1906). "An Ecological Survey in Northern Michigan." Report of the State Geological Survey for 1905, Ann Arbor, Michigan.

Agassiz, L. (1850). "Lake Superior" (facsimile ed., 1974). Robt. E. Kreiger Publ. Co., Huntington, New York.

Anderson, L. E. (1974). Bryology 1947-1972. *Ann. Missouri Bot. Garden 61:* 56-85.

Anderson, L. E., and P. E. Bourdeau (1955). Water relations in two species of terrestrial mosses. *Ecology 36:* 206-212.

Argus, G. W. (1966). Botanical investigations in northern Saskatchewan: the subarctic Patterson-Hasbala lakes region. *Can. Field Nat. 80:* 119-143.

Armentano, T. V. (1980). Drainage of organic soils as a factor in the world carbon cycle. *Bioscience 30:* 825-830.

Baldwin, W. K. W. (1958). "Plants of the Clay Belt of Northern Ontario and Quebec." National Museum of Canada, Bulletin, 156, Ottawa.

Bannatyne, B. B. (1964). "Preliminary Survey of Bogs for Peat Moss in Southeastern Manitoba. Manitoba Department of Mines and Natural Resources, Publ. No. 63-5, Winnipeg.

Bannister, P. (1971). The water relations of heath plants from open and shaded habitats. *J. Ecol. 59:* 51-63.

Bannister, P. (1976). "Introduction to Physiological Plant Ecology." Wiley, New York.

Barclay-Estrup, P., and D. V. Nuttall (1974). Some aspects of the distribution and ecology of crowberry *(Empetrum nigrum L.)* on the north shore of Lake Superior. *Can. Field Nat. 88:* 171-181.

Not given are references to very early works of historical interest since these are unavailable in most libraries.

Barrs, H. D. (1968). Determination of water deficits in plant tissues. *In* "Water Deficits and Plant Growth," Vol. 1 (T. T. Kozlowski, ed.), pp. 235-368. Academic Press, New York.

Basilier, K., U. Granhall, and T. A. Stenström (1978). Nitrogen fixation in wet minerotrophic moss communities of a subarctic mire. *Oikos 31:* 236-246.

Bazzaz, F. A., D. J. Paolillo, and R. H. Jagels (1970). Photosynthesis and respiration of forest and alpine populations of *Polytrichum juniperinum*. *Bryologist 73:* 579-585.

Beals, E. W., G. Cottam, and R. J. Vogl (1960). Influence of deer on vegetation of the Apostle Islands, Wisconsin. *J. Wildl. Manage. 24:* 68-75.

Bell, P. R. (1959). The ability of *Sphagnum* to absorb cations preferentially from dilute solutions resembling natural waters. *J. Ecol. 47:* 351-355.

✓ Berglund, E. R., and A. C. Mace (1972). Seasonal albedo variation of black spruce and sphagnum-sedge bog cover types. *J. Appl. Meteorol. 11:* 806-812.

Biberg, I. J. (1749). Oeconomia naturae. *Amoen. Acad.* 2: 1-52.

Billings, W. D., and H. A. Mooney (1968). The ecology of arctic and alpine plants. *Biol. Rev. 43:* 481-529.

Black, R. A., and L. C. Bliss (1978). Recovery sequence of *Picea mariana-Vaccinium uliginosum* forests after burning near Inuvik, Northwest Territories, Canada. *Can. J. Bot. 56:* 2020-2030.

✓ Bliss, L. C. (1971). Arctic and alpine plant life cycles. *Annu. Rev. Ecol. Systematics 2:* 405-438.

Boelter, D. H., and E. S. Verry (1977). "Peatland and Water in the Northern Lake States." General Technical Rep. NC-31, U. S. Forest Service, St. Paul, Minnesota.

Bourdeau, P. F. (1959). Seasonal variation of the photosynthetic efficiency of evergreen conifers. *Ecology 40:* 63-67.

Botts, L. (1981). Visit a wetland--it's not just for snakes. *Great Lakes Communicator 11*(9): 7.

Boyle, R. W. (1977). Cupriferous bogs in the Sackville area, New Brunswick. *J. Geochem. Explor. 8:* 495-527.

Bradshaw, A. D., and M. J. Chadwick (1980). "The Restoration of Land. The Ecology and Reclamation of Derelict and Degraded Land." Univ. of California Press, Berkeley.

Bradshaw, A. D., T. S. McNeilly, and R. P. G. Gregory (1965). Industrialization, evolution, and the development of heavy metal tolerance in plants. *In* "Ecology and the Industrial

Brassard, G. R., and D. P. Weber (1978). The mosses of Labrador, Canada. *Can. J. Bot. 56:* 441-466.

Braun, E. L. (1950). "Deciduous Forests of Eastern North America." Blakiston, Philadelphia.

Brill, W. J. (1980). Biochemical genetics of nitrogen fixation. *Microbiol. Rev. 44:* 449-467.

Society" (G. T. Goodman, R. W. Edwards, and J. M. Lambert, eds.), pp. 327-344. Wiley, New York.

Broecker, W. S., T. Takahashi, H. J. Simpson, and T.-H. Peng (1979). Fate of fossil fuel carbon dioxide and the global carbon budget. *Science 206:* 409-418.

Brooks, R. R. (1972). "Geobotany and Biogeochemistry in Mineral Exploration." Harper & Row, New York.

Brown, R. T. (1962). Germination influencing substances in living and dried plants. *Bull. Ecol. Soc. 43:* 117-118.

Brown, R. T. (1967). Influence of naturally occurring compounds on germination and growth of jack pine. *Ecology 48:* 542-546.

Brown, R. T., and J. T. Curtis (1952). The upland conifer-hardwood forests of northern Wisconsin. *Ecol. Monogr. 22:* 217-234.

√ Buell, M. F., H. F. Buell, and W. A. Reiners (1968). Radial mat growth on Cedar Creek bog, Minnesota. *Ecology 49:* 1198-1199.

Buffon, G. L. L. (1742). Memoire sur la culture des forets. *Hist. Acad. Roy. Soc. Paris* 1742: 233-246.

Burt, W. H. (1948). "The Mammals of Michigan." Univ. of Michigan Press, Ann Arbor.

Burt, W. H. (1952). "A Field Guide to the Mammals." Houghton Mifflin, Boston.

Busby, J. R., and D. W. A. Whitfield (1978). Water potential, water content, and net accumulation of some boreal forest mosses. *Can. J. Bot. 56:* 1551-1558.

Busby, J. R., L. C. Bliss, and C. D. Hamilton (1978). Microclimate control of growth rates and habitats of the boreal forest mosses, *Tomenthypnum nitens* and *Hylocomium splendens*. *Ecol. Monogr. 48:* 95-110.

Cairns, J., Jr. (ed.) (1980). "The Recovery Process in Damaged Ecosystems." Ann Arbor Science Publ., Ann Arbor, Michigan.

Canadian Press (1981). There's profit in peat says agrologist. *Thunder Bay Times-News,* Thunder Bay, Ontario, p. 16.

Carlton, T. J., and P. F. Maycock (1978). Dynamics of boreal forest south of James Bay. *Can. J. Bot. 56:* 1157-1173.

Catenhusen, A. J. (1944). Some aquatic and sub-aquatic plants from the region of Glacial Lake Wisconsin. *Trans. Wis. Acad. Sci., Arts and Lett.* 36: 163-169.

√ Catenhusen, J. (1950). Secondary successions on the peat lands of glacial lake Wisconsin. *Trans. Wisconsin Acad. Sci. Arts Lett. 40:* 29-48.

Caughey, M. C. (1945). Water relations of pocosin or bog shrubs. *Plant Physiol. 20:* 671-689.

Chamie, J. P. M., and C. J. Richardson (1978). Decomposition in northern wetlands. *In* "Freshwater Wetlands" (R. E. Good, D. F. Whigham, R. L. Simpson, and C. G. Jackson, eds.), pp. 115-194. Academic Press, New York.

Chang, P.-C., and R. Knowles (1965). Non-symbiotic nitrogen fixation in some Quebec soils. *Can. J. Microbiol. 11:* 29-38.

Cheney, L. S. (1893). A contribution to the flora of the Lake Superior region. *Trans. Wisconsin Acad. Sci. Arts Lett. 9:* 233-254.

Christensen, E. M., J. J. Clausen, and J. T. Curtis (1959). Phytosociology of the lowland forests of northern Wisconsin. *Am. Midl. Nat. 62:* 232-246.

Christensen, M., and W. F. Whittinghom (1965). The soil micro-fungi of open bogs and conifer swamps in Wisconsin. *Mycologia 57:* 882-896.

Christensen, P. J., and F. D. Cook (1970). The microbiology of Alberta muskeg. *Can. J. Soil Sci. 50:* 171-178.

Clausen, J. J. (1957). A phytosociological ordination of the conifer swamps of Wisconsin. *Ecology 38:* 638-646.

Clements, F. E. (1916). "Plant Succession: An Analysis of the Development of Vegetation." Publ. No. 242, Carnegie Institution of Washington, Washington, D. C.

Clements, F. E. (1920). Plant Indicators. Carnegie Institution of Washington, Washington, D. C.

Clements, F. E. (1928). Plant Succession and Indicators. Hafner Press, New York. (Reprint of 1916 and 1920 publications.)

Clymo, R. S. (1963). Ion exchange in *Sphagnum* and its relation to bog ecology. *Ann. Bot. 27:* 309-324.

Clymo, R. S. (1964). The origin of acidity in *Sphagnum* bogs. *Bryologist 67:* 427-423.

Clymo, R. S. (1970). The growth of *Sphagnum:* Methods of measurement. *J. Ecol. 58:* 13-49.

Clymo, R. S. (1973). The growth of *Sphagnum:* some effects of environment. *J. Ecol. 61:* 849-869.

Clymo, R. S. (1978). A model of peat bog growth. *In* "Production Ecology of British Moors and Alpine Grasslands" (O. W. Heal and D. F. Perkins, eds.). Springer-Verlag, New York.

Cody, W. J., and A. E. Porsild (1980). "Vascular Plants of Continental Northwest Territories." National Museum of Natural Sciences, Ottawa, Canada.

Colinvaux, P. A. (1967). Quaternary vegetational history of arctic Alaska. *In* "The Bering Land Bridge" (D. M. Hopkins, ed.), pp. 207-231. Stanford Univ. Press, Stanford, California.

Conard, H. S. (1979). "Mosses and Liverworts" (rev. ed., P. F. Redfearn, Jr.,), Wm. C. Brown Co., Dubuque, Iowa.

Conway, V. M. (1949). The bogs of central Minnesota. *Ecol. Monogr. 19:* 173-205.

Cooper, W. S. (1913). The climax forest of Isle Royale, Lake Superior, and its development. *Bot. Gaz. (Chicago) 55:*1-44.

Costello, D. F. (1936). Tussock meadows in southeastern Wisconsin. *Bot. Gaz. 97:* 610-649.

Cottrille, B. D. (1965). Northern spruce bogs. *In* "The Bird Watcher's America" (O. S. Pettingill, Jr., ed.), pp. 192-205. McGraw-Hill, New York.

Cowles, H. C. (1899). The ecological relations of the vegetation on the sand dunes of Lake Michigan. *Bot. Gaz. (Chicago) 27:* 95-117, 167-202, 281-308, 361-369.

Cowles, H. C. (1901). The physiographic ecology of Chicago and vicinity: a study of the origin, development, and classification of the plant societies. *Bot. Gaz. (Chicago) 31:* 73-108, 145-181.

Cowles, H. C. (1911). The causes of vegetative cycles. *Bot. Gaz. (Chicago) 51:* 161-183.

Cowling, J. E., and R. A. Kedrowski (1980). Winter water relations of native and introduced evergreens in interior Alaska. *Can. J. Bot. 58:* 94-99.

Cox, H. J. (1910). "Frost and Temperature Conditions in the Cranberry Marshes of Wisconsin." Bull. T, Weather Bureau, U. S. Dept. of Agriculture, Washington, D. C.

Cox, H. T. (1949). Studies in the comparative anatomy of the Ericales. II. Ericaceae-subfamily Arbutoideae. *Am. Midl. Nat. 40:* 493-516.

Crafts, A. S. (1968). Water deficits and physiological processes. *In* "Water Deficits and Plant Growth," (T. T. Kozlowski, ed.), pp. 85-133. Academic Press, New York.

Cronquist, A. (1968). "The Evolution and Classification of the Flowering Plants." Houghton Mifflin, New York.

Crum, H. (1976). "Mosses of the Great Lakes Forest," rev. ed. University Herbarium, Univ. of Michigan, Ann Arbor.

Curtis, J. T. (1959). "The Vegetation of Wisconsin." Univ. of Wisconsin Press, Madison.

Dalton, F. N., and W. R. Gardner (1978). Temperature dependence of water uptake by plant roots. *Agronomy J. 70:* 404-406.

Daly, G. T. (1966). Nitrogen fixation by nodulated *Alnus rugosa. Can. J. Bot. 44:* 1607-1621.

Damman, A. W. H. (1964). "Some Forest Types of Central Newfoundland and Their Relation to Environmental Factors." Contrib. No. 596, Forest Research Branch, Canada Dept. of Forestry, Ottawa.

✓Damman, A. W. H. (1965). The distribution patterns of northern and southern elements in the flora of Newfoundland. *Rhodora 67:* 363-392.

Damman, A. W. H. (1971). Effect of vegetation changes on the fertility of a Newfoundland forest site. *Ecol. Monogr. 41:* 253-270.

Damman, A. W. H. (1977). Geographical changes in the vegetation pattern of raised bogs in the Bay of Fundy region of Maine and New Brunswick. *Vegetatio 35:* 137-151.

Damman, A. W. H. (1978). Distribution and movement of elements in ombrotrophic peat bogs. *Oikos 30:* 480-495.

√ Dansereau, P., and F. Sagadas-Vianna (1952). Ecological study of the peat bogs of eastern North America. I. Structure and evolution of the vegetation. *Can. J. Bot. 30:* 490-520.

Davis, C. A. (1906). Peat: essays on its origin, uses, and distribution in Michigan. *Geol. Survey Michigan Annu. Rept. 1906,* 93-395.

de la Cruz, A. A. (1978). Primary production processes. *In* "Freshwater Wetlands" (R. E. Good, D. F. Whigham, R. C. Simpson, and C. G. Jackson, eds.,), pp. 79-86. Academic Press, New York.

De Luc, J. A. (1779). *Letters physiques et morales sur 1' histoire de la terre et l'homme.* La Haye. (Cited in Clements 1916, reprinted 1928).

Dhowian, A. W., and T. B. Edil (1981). Consolidation behavior of peats. *Geotechnical Testing J. 3:* 105-114.

Diggs, G. M., and G. J. Breckon (1981). Generic circumscription in the Arbuteae (Ericaceae). *Bot. Soc. Am. Misc. Ser. Publ. 160.*

Drury, W. H. Jr. (1956). "Bog Flats and Physiographic Processes in the Upper Kuskokwim River Region, Alaska." Contrib. Gray Herbarium No. 178, Harvard Univ., Cambridge, Massachusetts.

Durno, S. E. (1961). Evidence regarding the rate of peat growth. *J. Ecol. 49:* 347-351.

Dyrness, C. T., and D. F. Grigal (1979). Vegetation-soil relationships along a spruce forest transect in interior Alaska. *Can. J. Bot. 57:* 2644-2656.

Edil, T. B., and A. W. Dhowian (1979). Analysis of long-term compression of peats. *Geotechnical Eng. 10:* 159-177.

Egler, F. E. (1951). A commentary on American plant ecology, based on the textbooks of 1947-1949. *Ecology 32:* 673-695.

Eichenlaub, V. L. (1979). "Weather and Climate in the Great Lakes Region." Univ. of Notre Dame Press, South Bend, Indiana.

Epstein, E. (1972). "Mineral Nutrition of Plants: Principles and Perspectives." Wiley, New York.

Esau, K. (1977). "Anatomy of Seed Plants." 2nd. Wiley, New York.

Fassett, N. C. (1929). Preliminary reports on the flora of Wisconsin. II. Ericaceae. *Trans. Wisconsin Acad. Sci., Arts Lett. 24:* 257-268.

Fernald, M. L. (1950). "Gray's Manual of Botany." American Book Co., New York.

Fernald, M. L., and A. C. Kinsey (1958). "Edible Wild Plants of Eastern North America" (rev. ed. R. C. Rollins). Harper, New York.

Flower-Ellis, J. G. K. (1973). Growth and morphology of the
    evergreen dwarf shrubs *Empetrum hermaphroditum* and *Andro-
    meda polifolia* at Stordalen. *In* "Primary Production and
    Production Processes" (L. C. Bliss and F. E. Wielgolaski,
    eds.), pp. 123-136. IBP Tundra Biome Steering Committee,
    Edmonton-Oslo.
Forrest, G. I. (1971). Structure and production of North
    Pennine blanket bog vegetation. *J. Ecol. 59*:453-479.
Fowler, D. P., and R. E. Millin (1977). Upland-lowland eco-
    types not well developed in black spruce in northern On-
    tario. *Can. J. Forest Res. 7:* 35-40.
Frenzel, B. (1968). The Pleistocene vegetation of northern
    Eurasia. *Science 161:* 637-649.
Fryxell, P. A. (1957). Mode of reproduction of higher plants.
    Bot. Rev. 23: 135-226.
Ganong, W. F. (1902). The vegetation of the Bay of Fundy salt
    and diked marshes: an ecological study. *Bot. Gaz.
    (Chicago) 36:* 429-455.
Gates, F. C. (1914). Winter as a factor in the xerophylly of
    certain evergreen ericads. *Bot. Gaz. (Chicago) 57:* 445-
    489.
Gates, F. C. (1942). The bogs of northern lower Michigan.
    Ecol. Monogr. 12: 216-254.
Gerloff, G. C., D. G. Moore, and J. T. Curtis (1964). "Min-
    eral Content of Native Plants of Wisconsin." Research
    Rep. No. 14, Experiment Station, College of Agriculture,
    Univ. of Wisconsin, Madison.
Gerloff, G. C., D. G. Moore, and J. T. Curtis (1966). Selec-
    tive absorption of mineral elements by native plants of
    Wisconsin. *Plant Soil 25:* 393-405.
Gleason, H. A. (1917). The structure and development of the
    plant association. *Bull. Torrey Bot. Club 44:* 463-481.
Gleason, H. A. (1926). The individualistic concept of the
    plant association. *Bull. Torrey Bot. Club 53:* 7-26.
Gleason, H. A. (1939). The individualistic concept of the
    plant association. *Am. Midl. Nat. 21:* 92-110.
Gleason, H. A. (1958). "The New Britton and Brown Illustrated
    Flora of the Northeastern United States and Adjacent
    Canada," Vols. 1-3. Hafner Publ. Co., New York, for the
    New York Botanical Garden, New York.
Gleason, H. A., and A. Cronquist (1963). "Manual of Vascular
    Plants of Northeastern United States and Adjacent Canada."
    Van Nostrand, Princeton, New Jersey.
Godwin, H. (1978). "Fenland: Its Ancient Past and Uncertain
    Future." Cambridge Univ. Press, Cambridge, England.
Good, R. (1964). "The Geography of the Flowering Plants."
    Wiley, New York.
Goode, D. (1981). The threat to wildlife habitats. *New Sci.
    89:* 219-223.

Gorham, E. (1957). The development of peatland. *Quart. Rev.* ✓
    Biol. 32: 145-166.
Granhall, U., and U. Selander (1973). Nitrogen fixation in
    a subarctic mire. *Oikos 24:* 8-15.
Gray, A. (1950). "Manual of Botany," 8th ed. (rev. and en-
    larged, M. L. Fernald). American Book Co., New York.
    (1970 corrected printing: Van Nostrand, New York.)
Gregerman, S. (1981). They improve water, they reduce floods--
    and all for free. *Great Lakes Communicator 11:* 4.
Greulach, V. A. (1973). "Plant Function and Structure." Mac-
    millan, New York.
Griggs, R. F. (1936). The vegetation of the Katmai District.
    Ecology 17: 381-417.
Groet, S. S. (1976). Regional and local variations in heavy
    metal concentrations of bryophytes in the northeastern
    United States. *Oikos 27:* 445-456.
Habeck, J. R. (1958). White cedar ecotypes in Wisconsin.
    Ecology 39: 457-463.
Habeck, J. R., and J. T. Curtis (1959). Forest cover and deer
    population densities in early northern Wisconsin. *Trans.*
    Wisconsin Acad. Sci. Arts Lett. 48: 49-63.
Hadley, E. B., and L. C. Bliss (1964). Energy relationships
    of alpine plants on Mt. Washington, New Hampshire. *Ecol.*
    Monogr. 34: 331-357.
Hagerup, O. (1953). The morphology and systematics of the
    leaves in Ericales. *Phytomorphology 3:* 459-464.
Hamerstrom, F. N., and J. Blake (1939). Winter movements and
    winter foods of white-tailed deer in central Wisconsin.
    J. Mammalogy 20: 206-215.
Hamerstrom, F. N., and F. Hamerstrom (1951). Mobility of the
    sharp-tailed grouse in relation to its ecology and dis-
    tribution. *Am. Midl. Nat. 46:* 174-226.
Harper, F. (1964). "Plant and Animal Associations in the In-
    terior of the Ungava Peninsula." Misc. Publ. No. 38,
    Univ. of Kansas Museum of Natural History, Lawrence,
    Kansas.
Havranek, W. M., and U. Benecke (1978). The influence of soil
    moisture on water potential, transpiration, and photo-
    synthesis of conifer seedlings. *Plant Soil 49:* 91-103.
Heal, O. W., and D. F. Perkins (eds.) (1978). "Production
    Ecology of British Moors and Montane Grasslands."
    Springer-Verlag, New York.
Heilman, P. E. (1966). Change in distribution and availability
    of nitrogen with forest succession on north slopes in
    interior Alaska. *Ecology 47:* 825-831.
Heilman, P. E. (1968). Relationship of availability of phos-
    phorus and cations to forest succession and bog formation
    in interior Alaska. *Ecology 49:* 331-336.

Heinselman, M. L. (1963). Forest sites, bog processes, and
    peatland types in the glacial lake Agassiz region, Minne-
    sota. *Ecol. Mongr. 33:* 327-374.
Heinselman, M. L. (1970). Landscape evolution and peatland
    types, and the environment in the Lake Agassiz Peatlands
    Natural Area, Minnesota. *Ecol. Monogr. 40:* 235-261.
Heinselman, M. L. (1975). Boreal peatlands in relation to
    environment. *In* "Coupling of Land and Water Systems"
    (A. D. Hasler, ed.). Springer-Verlag, New York.
Hemond, H. F. (1980). Biogeochemistry of Thoreau's bog, Con-
    cord, Massachusetts. *Ecol. Monogr. 50:* 507-526.
Hernandez, H. (1972). Surficial disturbance and natural plant
    recolonization in the Mackenzie Delta region. *In* "Botani-
    cal Studies of Natural and Man-Modified Habitats in East-
    ern Mackenzie Delta Region and the Arctic Islands" (L. C.
    Bliss and R. W. Wein, eds.). Dept. of Indian Affairs and
    Northern Development, Arctic Land Use Research Program,
    Yellowknife, Northwest Territories, Canada.
Hernandez, H. (1974). Possible effects on vegetation of the
    proposed gas pipeline from Prudhoe Bay, Alaska and the
    Mackenzie Delta, to Alberta. *In* "Research Reports: En-
    vironmental Impact Assessment of the Portion of Mackenzie
    Gas Pipeline from Alaska to Alberta," Vol. IV, pp. 37-68.
    Environmental Protection Board, Winnipeg, Canada.
Heslop-Harrison, Y. (1976). Carnivorous plants a century after
    Darwin. *Endeavour 35:* 114-122.
Heslop-Harrison, Y. (1980). Digestive glands of the carni-
    vorous plants. *Bot. Soc. Am. Misc. Ser. Publ. 158:* 51.
Heslop-Harrison, Y., and J. Heslop-Harrison. (1981). The di-
    gestive glands of Pinguicula: structure and cytochemistry.
    Ann. Bot. 47: 293-319.
Hicklenton, P. R., and W. C. Oechel (1976). Physiological
    aspects of the ecology of *Dicranum fuscescens* in the Sub-
    arctic. I. Acclimation and acclimation potential of CO_2
    exchange in relation to habitat, light, and temperature.
    Can. J. Bot. 54: 1104-1119.
Hicklenton, P. R., and W. C. Oechel (1977). Physiological as-
    pects of the ecology of *Dicranum fuscescens* in the Sub-
    arctic. II. Seasonal patterns of organic nutrient con-
    tent. *Can. J. Bot. 55:* 2168-2177.
Hitchcock, C. L., and A. Cronquist (1973). "Flora of the
    Pacific Northwest." Univ. of Washington Press, Seattle.
Hopkins, D. M. (1967). The Cenozoic history of Beringia--a
    synthesis. *In* "The Bering Land Bridge" (D. M. Hopkins,
    ed.), pp. 451-484. Stanford Univ. Press, Stanford, Calif-
    ornia.
Horton, D. G., D. H. Vitt, and N. G. Slack, (1979). Habitats
    of circumboreal-subarctic sphagna: I. A quantitative analy-
    sis and review of species in the Caribou Mountains, north-
    ern Alberta. *Can. J. Bot. 57:* 2283-2317.

Horton, D. G. (1980). An evaluation of refugial theory relative to the western Canadian cordillera. *Bot. Soc. Am. Misc. Ser. Publ. 158:* 53.

Hult, R. (1885). Forsok till analytisk behandling af vaxtformationerna. *Meddel. Soc. Faun. Flor. Fenn. 8:* 1-156.

Hulten, E. (1968). "Flora of Alaska and Neighboring Territories: A Manual of the Vascular Plants." Stanford Univ. Press, Stanford, California.

Hustich, I. (1955). Forest-botanical notes from the Moose River area, Ontario, Canada. *Acta Geogr. 13:* 1-50.

Hutchinson, J. (1969). "Evolution and Phylogeny of Flowering Plants." Academic Press, New York.

Hygen, Georg. (1953). Studies in plant transpiration. *Physiol. Plant. 6:* 106-133.

Jackson, H. H. T. (1914). The land vertebrates of Ridgeway bog, Wisconsin. *Bull. Wisconsin Natural Hist. Soc. 12:* 4-54.

Jackson, H. H. T. (1961). "The Mammals of Wisconsin." Univ. of Wisconsin Press, Madison.

Janssen, C. R. (1967). A floristic study of forests and bog vegetation, northwestern Minnesota. *Ecology 48:* 751-765.

Jarvis, P. G., G. B. James, and J. J. Landsberg (1976). Coniferous forest. *In* "Vegetation and Atmosphere," Vol. II (J. L. Monteith, ed.), pp. 171-237. Academic Press, New York.

Jeglum, J. K. (1971). Plant indicators of pH and water level in peatlands at Candle Lake, Saskatchewan. *Can. J. Bot. 49:* 1661-1676.

Jeglum, J. K. (1972). Boreal forest wetlands near Candle Lake, central Saskatchewan. I. Vegetation. *Musk-Ox 11:* 41-58.

Jeglum, J. K. (1973). Boreal forest wetlands near Candle Lake, central Saskatchewan. II. Relationships of vegetation to major environmental gradients. *Musk-Ox 12:* 32-48.

Jeglum, J. K., A. N. Boissonneau, and V. F. Haavisto (1974). "Toward a Wetland Classification for Ontario." Dept. of Environment, Canada Forestry Service Inf. Rep. O-X-215, Sault Ste. Marie, Ontario.

Johnson, A. W., and J. G. Packer (1967). Distribution, ecology, and cytology of the Ogotoruk Creek flora and the history of Beringia. *In* "The Bering Land Bridge" (D. M. Hopkins, ed.), pp. 245-270. Stanford Univ. Press, Stanford, California.

Jones, H. E., and A. J. P. Gore (1978). A simulation of production and decay in blanket bog. *In* "Production Ecology of British Moors and Montane Grasslands" (O. W. Heal and D. F. Perkins, eds.). Springer-Verlag, New York.

Kartesz, J. T., and R. Kartesz (1980). "A Synonymized Checklist of the Vascular Flora of the United States, Canada, and Greenland." Univ. of North Carolina Press, Chapel Hill.

Kemp, G. A., and L. B. Keith (1970). Dynamics and regulation of the red squirrel *(Tamiasciurus hudsonicus)* populations. *Ecology 51:* 763-779.

Ketcheson, D. E., and J. K. Jeglum (1972). *Estimates of black spruce and peatland areas in Ontario.* Info. Rept. O-X-172, Canadian For. Serv., Dept. of the Environ., Great Lakes For. Res. Center, Sault Ste. Marie, Ontario.

King, William (1685). Of the bogs and loughs of Ireland. *Phil. Trans. Roy. Soc. London 15:* 948-960.

Kingsbury, J. M. (1964). "Poisonous Plants of the United States and Canada." Prentice-Hall, Englewood Cliffs, New Jersey.

√ Klopatek, J. M., and F. W. Stearns (1978). Primary productivity of emergent macrophytes in a Wisconsin freshwater marsh system. *Am. Midl. Nat. 100:* 320-332.

Kornas, J. (1972). Corresponding taxa and their ecological background in the forests of temperate Eurasia and North America. *In* "Taxonomy, Phytogeography, and Evolution" (D. H. Valentine, ed.), pp. 37-59. Academic Press, New York.

Koutler-Anderson, E. (1960). Geochemistry of a raised bog. Correlation between total nitrogen and ash alkalinity in bog-peats. *K. Lantbruksakad. Ann. 26:* 33-40.

Kozlowski, T. T. (ed.) (1968-1978). "Water Deficits and Plant Growth," Vols. 1-5. Academic Press, New York.

Kratz, T. K. (1981). "The Formation of a Northern Wisconsin Kettle-Hole Bog: A Spatial, Ecosystem Modeling Perspective." Ph. D. Thesis, Univ. of Wisconsin, Madison.

Lane, D. M. (1977). Extent of vegetative reproduction in elevan species of *Sphagnum* from northern Michigan. *Mich. Bot. 16:* 83-89.

Langille, W. M., and K. S. Maclean (1976). Some essential nutrient elements in forest plants as related to species, plant part, season, and location. *Plant Soil 45:* 17-26.

La Roi, G. H. (1967). Ecological studies in the boreal spruce-fir forests of the North American taiga. I. Analysis of the vascular flora. *Ecol. Monogr. 37:* 229-253.

La Roi, G. H., and M. H. L. Stringer (1976). Ecological studies in the boreal spruce-fir forests of the North American taiga. II. Analysis of the bryophyte flora. *Can. J. Bot. 54:* 619-643.

√ Larsen, J. A. (1965). The vegetation of the Ennadai Lake area, N. W. T.: Studies in subarctic and arctic bioclimatology. *Ecol. Monogr. 35:* 37-59.

√ Larsen, J. A. (1971a). Vegetational relationships with air mass frequencies: boreal forest and tundra. *Arctic 24:* 177-194.

Larsen, J. A. (1971b). Vegetation of Fort Reliance, Northwest Territories, Can. *Can. Field Nat.* *85:* 147-178.

Larsen, J. A. (1973). Plant communities north of the forest border, Keewatin, Northwest Territories. *Can. Field Nat.* *87:* 241-248.

Larsen, J. A. (1974). Ecology of the northern continental forest border. *In* "Arctic and Alpine Environments" (J.D. Ives and R. G. Barry, eds.). Methuen, London.

Larsen, J. A. (1980). "The Boreal Ecosystem." Academic Press, New York.

Lavkulich, L. M. (ed.) (1972). "Soils, Vegetation and Land-forms of the Fort Simpson Area, N. W. T." Dept. of Indian Affairs and Northern Development, Yellowknife, Northwest Territories, Canada.

Layne, J. N. (1954). The biology of the red squirrel, *Tamia-sciurus hudsonicus loquax* (Bangs), in central New York. *Ecol. Mongr.* *24:* 227-266.

Lazrus, A. L., E. Lorange, and J. P. Lodge, Jr. (1970). Lead and other metal ions in United States precipitation. *Environ. Sci. Technol.* *4:* 55-58.

Leach, D. G. (1972). The ancient curse of the Rhododendron. *Am. Hort.* *51:* 20-29.

Leisman, G. A. (1953). The rate of organic matter accumulation on the sedge mat zones of bogs in the Itasca State Park region of Minnesota. *Ecology 34:* 81-101.

Leisman, G. A. (1957). Further data on the rate of organic matter accumulation in bogs. *Ecology 38:* 361.

Leopold, E. B. (1967). Late-Cenozoic patterns of plant extinction. *In* "Pleistocene Extinctions" (P. S. Martin and H. E. Wright, eds.), pp. 203-246. Yale Univ. Press, New Haven, Connecticut.

Lewis, F. J., and E. S. Dowding (1926). The vegetation and retrogressive changes of peat areas ("muskegs") in central Alberta. *J. Ecol.* *14:* 317-341.

Lewis, F. J., E. S. Dowding, E. H. Moss (1928). The vegetation of Alberta. II. The swamp, moor, and bog forest vegetation of central Alberta. *J. Ecol.* *16:* 19-70.

Likens, G. E., and F. H. Bormann (1974). Acid rain: a serious regional environmental problem. *Science 184:* 1176-1179.

Likens, G. E., F. H. Bormann, R. S. Pierce, J. S. Eaton, and N. M. Johnson (1977). "Biogeochemistry of a Forested Ecosystem." Springer-Verlag, New York.

Loveless, A. R. (1961). A nutritional interpretation of sclerophylly based on differences in the chemical composition of sclerophyllous and mesophytic leaves. *Ann. Bot.* *25:* 179-184.

Loveless, A. R. (1962). Further evidence to support a nutritional interpretation of sclerophylly. *Ann. Bot. 26:* 551-561.

Loveless, A. R., and G. F. Asprey (1957). The dry evergreen
formations of Jamaica. I. The limestone hills of the
south coast. *J. Ecol. 45:* 799-822.

Lucas, R. E., and J. F. Davis (1961). Relationships between
pH values of organic soils and availability of 12 plant
nutrients. *Soil Sci. 92:* 177-182.

McIntosh, R. P. (1967a). The continuum concept of vegetation.
Bot. Rev. 33: 130-187.

McIntosh, R. P. (1967b). An index of diversity and the relation of certain concepts to diversity. *Ecology 48:* 392-
404.

McIntosh, R. P. (1975). H. A. Gleason--"individualistic ecologist" 1882-1975: his contributions to ecological theory.
Bull. Torrey Bot. Club 102: 253-273.

Malyuga, D. P. (1964). "Biogeochemical Methods of Prospecting."
Consultant Bureau Enterprises, New York.

Mankinen, G. W., and E. O. Korpijaako (1981). Peat is being
investigated as an energy fuel source. *Northern Miner,*
C7-C8, Jan. 15.

Marchand, P. J. (1975). Apparent ecotypic differences in the
water relations of some northern bog Ericaceae. *Rhodora
77:* 53-63.

Martell, A. M., and A. Radvanyi (1977). Changes in small
mammal populations after clearcutting in northern Ontario
black spruce forest. *Can. Field-Nat. 91:* 41-46.

Maycock, P. F. (1956). Composition of an upland conifer community in Ontario. *Ecology 37:* 846-848.

Maycock, P. F. (1961). The spruce-fir forests of the Keweenaw
peninsula, northern Michigan. *Ecology 42:* 357-365.

Maycock, P. F., and J. T. Curtis (1960). The phytosociology
of boreal conifer-hardwood forests of the Great Lakes
region. *Ecol. Monogr. 30:* 1-35.

Meyer, L. (1981). Basin plan fills gaps, not swamps. *Great
Lakes Communicator 11:* 3.

Mirick, S., and J. A. Quinn (1980). The reproductive biology
of six New Jersey and Pennsylvania populations of *Gaultheria procumbens* L. *Bot. Soc. Am. Misc. Ser. Publ. 158:*
76.

Moizuk, G. A., and R. B. Livingston (1966). Ecology of red
maple *(Acer rubrum L.)* in a Massachusetts upland bog.
Ecology 47: 942-950.

Monk, C. D. (1966). An ecological significance of evergreenness.
Ecology 47: 504-505.

Moore, P. (1980). The advantages of being evergreen. *Nature
285:* 535.

Moore, P. D., and D. J. Bellamy (1974). "Peatlands." Springer-
Verlang, New York.

Moore, T. R. (1974). Pedogenesis in a subarctic environment: Cambrian Lake, Quebec. *Arctic Alpine Res. 6:* 281-291.

✓Moss, E. H. (1953). Marsh and bog vegetation in northwestern Alberta. *Can. J. Bot. 31:* 448-470.

✓Moss, E. H. (1955). The vegetation of Alberta. *Bot. Rev. 21:* 493-567.

✓Nichols, G. E. (1915). The vegetation of Connecticut. *Bull. Torrey Bot. Club 42:* 169-217.

✓Nichols, G. E. (1918). The vegetation of northern Cape Breton Island, Nova Scotia. *Conn. Acad. Arts Sci. 22:* 249-467.

Noguchi, A. (1956). On some mosses of *Merceya,* with special reference to the variation and ecology. *Kumamoto J. Sci., Ser. B, Sec. 2, 2*(2): 239-257.

Page, G. (1971). Properties of some common Newfoundland forest soils and their relation to forest growth. *Can. J. Forest Res. 1:* 174-191.

Pakarinen, P. (1977). Element content of *Sphagna:* variation and its sources. *Bryophytorum Bibliotheca 13:* 751-762.

Pakarinen, P. (1978). Production and nutrient ecology of three *Sphagnum* species in southern Finnish raised bogs. *Ann. Bot. Fenn. 15:* 15-26.

Pakarinen, P., and K. Tolonen (1977). Nutrient content of *Sphagnum* mosses in relation to bog water chemistry in northern Finland. *Lindbergia 4:* 27-33.

Parker, G., and G. Schneider (1975). Biomass and productivity of an alder swamp in northern Michigan. *Can. J. Forest Res. 5:* 403-409.

Parker, J. (1961). Seasonal trends in carbon dioxide absorption, cold resistance, and transpiration of some evergreens. *Ecology 42:* 372-380.

Partch, M. L. (1949). *Habitat studies of soil moisture in relation to plants and plant communities.* Ph. D. thesis, University of Wisconsin, Madison.

Patrick, R., V. P. Binetti, and S. G. Halterman (1981). Acid lakes from natural and anthropogenic causes. *Science 211:* 446-448.

Patrick, W. H. Jr., and R. A. Khalid (1974). Phosphate release and sorption by soils and sediments: effect of aerobic and anaerobic conditions. *Science 196:* 53-55.

Pearsall, W. H., and E. M. Wray (1927). The physiology and ecology of the calcifuge habit in *Eriophorum angustifolium. J. Ecol. 15:* 1-32.

Persson, H. (1956). Studies in "copper mosses." *Hattori Bot. Lab. J. 17:* 1-18.

✓Persson, H. (1961). Mire and spring vegetation in an area north of Lake Tornetrask, Torne Lappmark, Sweden I. Description of the vegetation. *Opera Bot. 6*(1): 1-187.

Peterson, E. B. 1965. Inhibition of black spruce primary roots by a water-soluble substance in *Kalmia angustifolia. Forest Science 11:* 473-479.

Peterson, W. L., and J. M. Mayo (1975). Moisture stress and
    its effect on photosynthesis in *Dicranum polysetum*. *Can.
    J. Bot. 53*: 2897-2900.
Pielou, E. C. (1979). "Biogeography." Wiley, New York.
Pierce, R. S. (1953). Oxidation-reduction potential and speci-
    fic conductance of ground water: their influence on
    natural forest distribution. *Soil. Sci. Soc. Proc. 17:*
    61-65.
Polunin, N. (1959). "Circumpolar Arctic Flora." Oxford Univ.
    Press, London.
Porsild, A. E. (1943). Materials for a flora of the continental
    Northwest Territories of Canada. *Sargentia 4:* 1-79.
Porsalid, A. E. (1955). "The Vascular Plants of the Western
    Canadian Arctic Archipelago." National Museum of Canada
    Bull. 135, Ottawa.
Porsalid, A. E. (1957). "Illustrated Flora of the Canadian
    Arctic Archipelago." National Museum of Canada Bull. 146,
    Ottawa.
Porsalid, A. E. (1958). Geographical distribution of some
    elements in the flora of Canada. *Geogr. Bull. 11:* 57-77.
Potzger, J. E., and A. Courtemanche (1955). Permafrost and
    some characteristics of bogs and vegetation of northern
    Quebec. *Rev. Can. Geogr. 9:* 109-114.
P'yanchenko, N. I. (1967). Some results of station research
    on the interrelation of forest and bog in Western Siberia.
    In "Interrelation of Forest and Bog" (N. I. Pyanchenko,
    ed.). Amerind Publ. Co., New Delhi, India. [transl.
    from Russian, publ. for the National Science Foundation,
    1976].
Railton, J. B., and J. H. Sparling (1973). Preliminary stud-
    ies on the ecology of palsa mounds in northern Ontario.
    Can. J. Bot. 51: 1037-1044.
Raup, H. M. (1934). Phytogeographic studies in the Peace and
    Upper Laird River regions, Canada. *Contrib. Arnold Arb.
    6:* 1-230.
Raup, H. M. (1941). Botanical problems in boreal America. II.
    The development and distribution of plant communities.
    Bot. Rev. 7: 209-248.
Raup, H. J. (1947). The botany of southwestern Mackenzie.
    Sargentia 6: 1-275.
Reader, R. (1971). Impact of three leaf-feeding insects on
    three bog ericads. *Can. J. Bot. 49:* 2107-2112.
Reader, R. J. (1977). Bog ericad flowers: self-compatibility
    and relative attractiveness to bees. *Can. J. Bot. 55:*
    2279-2287.
Reader, R. J. (1978). Primary production in northern bog
    marshes. In *Freshwater Wetlands* (R. E. Good, Dennis
    Whigham, R. L. Simpson, and C. G. Jackson, Jr., eds.),
    Academic Press, New York.

Reader, R. J. (1978a). Contribution of overwintering leaves to the growth of three broad-leaved, evergreen shrubs belonging to the Ericaceae family. *Can. J. Bot. 56:* 1248-1261.

Reader, R. J. (1979). Flower cold hardiness: a potential determinant of the flowering sequence exhibited by bog ericads. *Can. J. Bot. 57:* 997-999.

Reader, R. J., and J. M. Stewart (1971). Net primary productivity of bog vegetation in southeastern Manitoba. *Can. J. Bot. 49:* 1471-1477.

Reader, R. J., and J. M. Stewart (1972). The relationship between net primary production and accumulation for a peatland in southeastern Manitoba. *Ecology 53:* 1024-1037.

Reiners, W. A. (1972). Structure and energetics of three Minnesota forests. *Ecol. Mongr. 42:* 71-94.

Rencz, A., and A. N. D. Auclair. (1978). Biomass distribution in a subarctic *Picea mariana-Cladonia alpestris* woodland. *Can. J. For. Res. 8:* 168-176.

Rhodes, J. W. (1933). An ecological comparison of two Wisconsin peat bogs. *Milwaukee Publ. Mus. Bull. 7:* 305-362.

Rice, E. L., and S. K. Pancholy (1973). Inhibition of nitrification by climax ecosystems. II. Additional evidence and possible role of tannins. *Am. J. Bot. 60:* 691-702.

Richardson, C. J., D. L. Tilton, J. A. Kadlec, J. P. M. Chamie, and W. A. Wentz (1978). Nutrient dynamics of northern wetland ecosystems. *In* "Freshwater Wetlands" (R. E. Good, D. F. Whigham, R. L. Simpson, and C. G. Jackson, eds.), pp. 217-241. Academic Press, New York.

Ridler, R. H., and W. W. Shilts (1974). Exploration for archean polymetallic sulphide deposits in permafrost terrains: an integrated geological geochemical technique; Kaminak Lake area, District of Keewatin. *Geol. Surv. Can. Paper 73-34,* Ottawa.

Rigg, G. B. (1913). The effect of some Puget Sound bog waters on the root hairs of Tradescantia. *Bot. Gaz. (Chicago) 55:* 314-326.

Rigg, G. B. (1916). Physical conditions in sphagnum bogs. *Bot. Gaz. (Chicago) 61:* 159-163.

Rigg, G. B. (1922a). The bog forest. *Ecology 3:* 207-213.

Rigg, G. B. (1922b). The sphagnum bogs of Mazama Dome. *Ecology 3:* 321-324.

Rigg, G. B. (1923). Birch succession in sphagnum bogs. *J. For. 20:* 1-3.

Rigg, G. B. (1925). Some sphagnum bogs of the north Pacific coast of America. *Ecology 6:* 260-278.

Rigg, G. B. (1940a). Comparison of the development of some Sphagnum bogs of the Atlantic coast, the interior, and the Pacific coast. *Am. J. Bot. 27:* 1-14.

Rigg, G. B. (1940b). The development of *Sphagnum* bogs in North America, Part 1. *Bot. Rev. 6:* 666-693.

Rigg, G. B. (1951). The development of *Sphagnum* bogs in North America, Part 2. *Bot. Rev. 17:* 109-131.

Ritchie, J. C. (1960). The vegetation of northern Manitoba. V. Establishing the major zonation. *Arctic 13:* 211-229.

Roberts, B. A. (1980). A forest site classification for larch, *Larix laricina* (Du Roi) K. Koch. *Bot. Soc. Am. Misc. Ser. Publ. 158:* 95.

Rønning, O. I. (1969). Features of the ecology of some arctic svalbard (Spitzbergen) plant communities. *Arctic Alpine Res. 1:* 29-44.

Rosatti, T. J. (1981). Ecological studies bearing on the systematics of the *Arctostaphylos uva-ursi* complex in North America. *Bot. Soc. Am. Misc. Ser. Publ. 160:* 77.

Rosendahl, C. O. (1955). "Trees and Shrubs of the Upper Midwest." Univ. of Minnesota Press, Minneapolis.

Rosswall, Th. (ed.). (1971). "Systems Analysis in Northern Coniferous Forests." IBP Workshop, Swedish Natural Science Research Council, Stockholm.

Rowe, J. S. (1956). Use of undergrowth plant species in forestry. *Ecology 37:* 461-473.

Running, S. W. (1976). Environmental control of leaf water conductance in conifers. *Can. J. Forest. Res. 6:* 104-114.

Rusch, D. H., and L. B. Keith (1971a). Ruffed grouse-vegetation relationships in central Alberta. *J. Wildl. Manage. 35:* 417-429.

Rusch, D. H., and L. B. Keith (1971b). Seasonal and annual trends in numbers of Alberta ruffed grouse. *J. Wildl. Manage. 35:* 803-822.

Rusch, D. H., E. C. Meslow, P. D. Doerr, and L. B. Keith (1972). Response of great horned owl populations to changing prey densities. *J. Wildl. Manage. 36:* 282-295.

Sakai, A., and K. Otsuka (1970). Freezing resistance of alpine plants. *Ecology 51:* 665-671.

Sakai, A., and C. J. Weisner (1973). Freezing resistance of trees in North America with reference to tree regions. *Ecology 54:* 118-126.

Savile, D. B. O. (1969). Interrelationships of *Ledum* species and their rust parasites in western Canada and Alaska. *Can. J. Bot. 47:* 1085-1100.

Savile, D. B. O. (1972). "Arctic Adaptations in Plants." Monogr. No. 6, Research Branch, Canada Dept. of Agriculture, Ottawa.

Scarpace, F. L., B. K. Quirk, R. W. Kiefer, and S. L. Wynn (1981). Wetland mapping from digitized aerial photography. *Photogramm. Eng. 47:* 829-838.

Schimper, A. F. W. (1903). *Plant Geography on a Physiological Basis.* (Translation of 1898 edition). Clarendon Press, Oxford.

Schlesinger, W. H., and B. F. Chabot (1977). The use of water and minerals by evergreen and deciduous shrubs in Oke-fenokee swamp. *Bot. Gaz. (Chicago) 138:* 490-497.

Schwintzer, C. R. (1978a). Nutrient and water levels in a small Michigan bog with high tree mortality. *Am. Midl. Nat. 100:* 441-451.

Schwintzer, C. R. (1978b). Vegetation and nutrient status of northern Michigan fens. *Can. J. Bot. 56:* 3044-3051.

Schwintzer, C. R. (1979a). Vegetation changes following a water level rise and tree mortality in a Michigan bog. *Mich. Bot. 18:* 91-98.

Schwintzer, C. R. (1979b). Nitrogen fixation by *Myrica gale* root nodules in a Massachusetts wetland. *Oecologia 43:* 283-294.

Schwintzer, C. R. (1981). Vegetation and nutrient status of northern Michigan bogs and conifer swamps with a compari-son to fens. *Can. J. Bot. 59:* 842-853.

Schwintzer, C. R., and G. Williams (1974). Vegetation changes in a small Michigan bog from 1917 to 1972. *Am. Midl. Nat. 92:* 447-459.

Scoggan, H. J. (1978). "The Flora of Canada," Vols. 1-4. National Museum of Canada, Ottawa.

Shacklette, H. T. (1967). "Copper Mosses as Indicators of Metal Concentrations." Geol. Survey Bull. 1198-G, U. S. Geol. Survey, Washington, D. C.

Shaw, C. H. (1909). The causes of timberline on mountains: the role of snow. *Plant World 12:* 3-15.

Shields, L. M. (1950). Leaf xeromorphy as related to physio-logical and structural influences. *Bot. Rev. 16:* 399-439.

Sifton, H. B. (1963). On the hairs and cuticle of Labrador tea leaves. A developmental study. *Can. J. Bot. 41:* 199-207.

Silvola, J., and I. Hanski (1979). Carbon accumulation in a raised bog. *Oecologia 37:* 285-295.

Silvola, J., and S. Heikkinen. (1979). CO_2 exchange in the *Empetrum nigrum-Sphagnum fuscum* community. *Oecologia 37:* 273-283.

Sims, R. A. (1980). Classification and characteristics of three treed peatland types, southern James Bay, Ontario. *Bot. Soc. Am. Misc. Ser. Publ. 158:* 105.

Sims, R. A. and J. M. Stewart (1981). Aerial biomass distrib-ution in an undisturbed and disturbed subarctic bog. *Can. J. Bot. 59:* 782-786.

Sjörs, H. (1948). Mire vegetation in Bergslagen, Sweden. *Acta Phytogeogr. Suec. 21:* 1-299.

Sjörs, H. (1950). On the relation between vegetation and electrolytes in north Swedish mire waters. *Oikos 2:* 241-258.

Sjörs, H. (1950). Regional studies in north Sweden mire vegetation. *Bot. Not. 103:* 173-222.

Sjörs, H. (1959). Bogs and fens in the Hudson Bay lowlands. *Arctic 12:* 3-19.

Sjörs, H. (1963). Bogs and fens on Attawapiskat river, northern Ontario. *Nat. Mus. Can. Bull. 186:* 45-133.

Sjörs, H. (1965). Northern mires. Regional ecology of mire sites and vegetation. *Acta Phytogeogr. Suec. 50:* 180-188.

Slack, N. G., D. H. Vitt, and D. G. Horton. (1979). Vegetation gradients of minerotrophically rich fens in western Alberta. *Can. J. Bot. 58:* 330-350.

Slatyer, R. O. (1963). Climatic control of plant water relations. *In* "Environmental Control of Plant Growth" (L. T. Evans, ed.), pp. 33-54. Academic Press, New York.

Small, E. (1972a). Ecological significance of four critical elements in plants of raised *Sphagnum* peat bogs. *Ecology 53:* 498-503.

Small, E. (1972b). Photosynthetic rates in relation to nitrogen recycling as an adaptation to nutrient deficiency in peat bog plants. *Can. J. Bot. 50:* 2227-2233.

Small, E. (1972c). Water relations of plants in raised *Sphagnum* peat bogs. *Ecology 53:* 726-728.

Smith, E. M., and E. B. Hadley (1974). Photosynthetic and respiratory acclimation to temperature in *Ledum groenlandicum* populations. *Arctic Alpine Res. 6:* 13-27.

Soper, J. H. (1963). Botanical observations along the Lake Superior route. *Proc. Roy. Can. Inst. 5:* 12-24.

Soper, J. H., and P. F. Maycock (1963). A community of arctic-alpine plants on the east shore of Lake Superior. *Can. J. Bot. 41:* 183-198.

Sparling, J. H. (1966). Studies on the relationship between water movement and water chemistry in mires. *Can. J. Bot. 44:* 747-758.

Spatt, P. D., and M. C. Miller (1981). Growth conditions and vitality of *Sphagnum* in a tundra community along the Alaskan pipeline haul road. *Arctic 34:* 48-54.

Sprent, J. I., R. Scott, and K. M. Perry (1978). The nitrogen ecology of *Myrica gale* in the field. *J. Ecol. 66:* 657-668.

Staats, D. (1981a). Wetland programs in the Great Lakes basin. *Great Lakes Communicator 11:* 5.

Staats, D. (ed.) (1981b). The destruction continues, but protection is growing. *Great Lakes Communicator 11:* 1-3.

Stanek, W., J. K. Jeglum, and L. Orloci (1977). Comparisons of peatland types using macro-nutrient content of peat. *Vegetatio 33:* 163-173.

Stearns, F. W. (1951). The composition of the sugar maple-hemlock-yellow birch association in northern Wisconsin. *Ecology 32:* 245-265.

Stebbins, G. L. (1974). "Flowering Plants: Evolution Above the Species Level." Harvard Univ. Press, Cambridge, Massachusetts.

Stout, A. B. (1914). A biological and statistical analysis of the vegetation of a typical wild hay meadow. *Trans. Wis. Acad. Sci., Arts and Lett. 17:* 405-469.

Swan, J. M. A., and A. M. Gill (1970). The origins, spread, and consolidation of a floating bog in Harvard Pond, Petersham, Massachusetts. *Ecology 51:* 829-840.

Swingle, D. B. (1946). "A Textbook of Systematic Botany." McGraw-Hill, New York.

Tamm, C. O. (1964). Growth of *Hylocomium splendens* in relation to tree canopy. *Bryologist 67:* 423-426.

Taylor, J., and R. Smith (1980). Power in the peatlands. *New Sci. 88:* 644-646.

Thompson, D. Q. (1952). Travel, range, and food habits of timber wolves in Wisconsin. *J. Mammal. 33:* 429-442.

Tranquillini, W. (1963). Climate and water relations of plants in the subalpine region. *In* "The Water Relations of Plants" (A. J. Rutter and F. W. Whitehead, eds.), pp. 153-167. Wiley, New York.

Tranquillini, W. (1979). "Physiological Ecology of the Alpine Timberline." Springer-Verlag, New York.

Transeau, E. N. (1903). On the geographic distribution and ecological relations of the bog plant socieites of northern North America. *Bot. Gaz. (Chicago) 36:* 401-420.

Transeau, E. N. (1905). The bogs and bog flora of the Huron River valley. *Bot. Gaz. (Chicago) 40:* 351-375.

Transeau, E. N. (1909). Present problems in plant ecology. *Am. Nat. 43:* 487-498.

Ugolini, F. C., and D. H. Mann (1979). Biopedological origin of peatlands in southeast Alaska. *Nature 281:* 366-369.

Usik, L. (1969). "Review of Geochemical and Geobotanical Prospecting Methods in Peatland." Geol. Survey of Canada Paper 68-66, Ottawa.

Van Cleve, K., and L. A. Viereck (1972). Distribution of selected chemical elements in even-aged alder *(Alnus)* ecosystems near Fairbanks, Alaska. *Arctic Alpine Res. 4:* 239-255.

Van Cleve, K., L. A. Viereck, and R. L. Schlentner (1971). Accumulation of nitrogen in alder *(Alnus)* ecosystems near Fairbanks, Alaska. *Arctic Alpine Res. 3:* 101-114.

Verme, L. J., and J. J. Ozoga (1981). Changes in small mammal populations following clear-cutting in Upper Michigan conifer swamps. *Can. Field-Nat. 95:* 253-256.

Vitt, D. H., and R. E. Andrus. (1977). The genus *Sphagnum* in
    Alberta. *Can. J. Bot. 55:* 331-357.
Vitt, D. H., and N. G. Slack (1975). An analysis of the vege-
    tation of Sphagnum-dominated kettle-hole bogs in relation
    to environmental gradients. *Can. J. Bot. 53:* 332-359.
√ Vitt, D. H., P. Achuff, and R. E. Andrus (1975a). The vegeta-
    tion and chemical properties of patterned fens in the
    Swan Hills, north central Alberta. *Can. J. Bot. 53:* 2776-
    2795.
Vitt, D. H., H. Crum, and J. Snider (1975b). The vertical
    zonation of *Sphagnum* species in hummock-hollow complexes
    in northern Michigan. *Mich. Bot. 14:* 190-200.
Voigt, G. K., and G. L. Steucek (1969). Nitrogen distribution
    and accretion in an alder ecosystem. *Soil Sci. Am. Proc.*
    33: 946-949.
Voss, E. B. (1978). "Botanical Beachcombers and Explorers."
    Contrib. Univ. of Michigan Herbarium, No. 13, Ann Arbor.
Vowinckle, T., W. C. Oechel, and W. G. Boll (1975). The effect
    of climate on the photosynthesis of *Picea mariana* at the
    subarctic tree line. I. Field measurements. *Can. J. Bot.*
    53: 604-620.
Walker, D. (1970). Direction and rate in some British post-
    glacial hydroseres. *In* "Studies in the Vegetational
    History of the British Isles" (D. Walker and R. G. West,
    eds.). Cambridge Univ. Press, Cambridge.
Warming, E. (1909). Oecology of Plants. (Translation of 1895
    edition). Clarendon Press, Oxford.
Watt, R. F., and M. L. Heinselman (1965). Foliar nitrogen and
    phosphorus level related to site quality in an northern
    Minnesota spruce bog. *Ecology 46:* 357-361.
Weaver, J. E., and F. E. Clements (1938). Coniferous forests
    of North America. *In* "Plant Ecology," 2nd ed., pp. 488-
    492, 496-504. McGraw-Hill, New York.
Weller, M. W. (1978). Management of freshwater marshes for
    wildlife. *In* "Freshwater Wetlands" (R. E. Good, D. F.
    Whigham, R. L. Simpson, and C. G. Jackson, Jr., eds.),
    pp. 267-284. Academic Press, New York.
Wells, K. (1980). A rolling spud gathers new moss. *Maclean's*
    Mag. p. 35. Nov. 10.
Wells, R. W. (1978). "Daylight in the Swamp." Doubleday,
    Garden City, New York.
Whitehead, N. W., and R. R. Brooks (1970). Aquatic bryophytes
    as indicators of uranium mineralization. *Bryologist 72:*
    501-507.
Whitford, H. N. (1901). The genetic development of the forests
    of northern Michigan. A study in physiographic ecology.
    Bot. Gaz. (Chicago) 31: 276-289.

Whittaker, R. H. (1962). Classification of natural communities. *Bot. Rev. 28:* 1-239.

Whittaker, R. H. (1975). "Communities and Ecosystems." Macmillan, New York.

Wickland, D. E. (1981). Lead, zinc, and copper concentrations in plants from derelict heavy metal mine sites in the Carolina slate belt. *Bot. Sci. Am. Misc. Ser. Publ. 160.*

Wilde, S. A., and A. L. Leaf (1955). The relationship between the degree of soil podzolization and the composition of ground cover vegetation. *Ecology 36:* 19-22.

Wilde, S. A., and G. W. Randall (1951). Chemical characteristics of ground water in forest and marsh soils of Wisconsin. *Trans. Wisconsin Acad. Sci. Arts Lett. 40:* 251-259.

Wilde, S. A., C. T. Youngberg, and J. H. Hovind (1950). Changes in composition of ground water, soil fertility, and forest growth produced by the construction and removal of beaver dams. *J. Wildl. Manage. 14:* 123-128.

Wildi, O. (1978). Simulating the development of peat bogs. *Vegetatio 37:* 1-17.

Wilson, L. R. (1939). A temperature study of a Wisconsin peat bog. *Ecology 20:* 432-433.

Wilton, W. C. (1964). "The Forests of Labrador." Canada Dept. of Forestry Publ. No. 1066, Ottawa.

Wisconsin Dept. of Natural Resources. (1979). "Wisconsin's Endangered and Threatened Species List." Madison, Wisconsin.

Wolfe, J. A. (1972). An interpretation of Alaskan Tertiary flora. *In* "Floristics and Paleofloristics of Asia and Eastern North America" (A. Graham, ed.), pp. 201-233. Elsevier, Amsterdam.

Wolfe, J. A. (1978). A paleobotanical interpretation of Tertiary climates in the northern hemisphere. *Am. Sci. 66:* 694-703.

Wolfe, J. A., and E. B. Leopold (1967). Neogene and early quaternary vegetation of northwestern North American and northeastern Asia. *In* "The Bering Land Bridge" (D. M. Hopkins, ed.), pp. 193-206. Stanford Univ. Press, Stanford, California.

Woodell, S. R. J. (1973). "Xerophytes." Oxford Univ. Press, London.

Wuenscher, J. F., and T. T. Kozlowksi (1971). The response of transpiration resistance to leaf temperature as a desiccation resistance mechanism in tree seedlings. *Physiol. Plant. 24:* 254-259.

Wynne, F. E. (1944). *Drosera* in eastern North America. *Bull. Torrey Bot. Club 71:* 166-174.

Younkin, W. E. (1973). Autecology studies of native species
    potentially useful for revegetation, Tuktoyaktuk region,
    N. W. T. *In* "Botanical Studies of Natural and Man-Modi-
    fied Habitats in the Mackenzie Valley, Eastern Mackenzie
    Delta Region, and the Arctic Islands" (L. C. Bliss, ed.).
    Dept. of Indian Affairs and Northern Development, Yellow-
    knife, Northwest Territories, Canada.
Zimmerman, J. H. (1959). Data published in Curtis, J. T., "The
    Vegetation of Wisconsin," Univ. of Wisconsin Press, Mad-
    ison, Wisconsin.
Zoltai, S. C. (1971). Southern limit of permafrost features in
    peat landforms, Manitoba and Saskatchewan. *Geol. Assoc.*
    Can. Spec. Paper No. 9, 305-310.
Zoltai, S. C. (1972). Palsas and peat plateaus in central
    Manitoba and Saskatchewan. *Can. J. Forest. Res. 2:* 291-302.

INDEX

A

Acidity, sclerophylly and, 113-123
Allelopathy, nutrient supplies and, 166-167
Alpine plants, bog plants compared to, 254-255
Andromeda glaucophylla, description and habitat of, 41, 84-85
Andromeda polifolia, description and habitat of, 41-42, 84
Arctic plants, bog plants compared to, 254-255
Arctostaphylos alpina, description and habitat of, 42
Arctostaphylos rubra, description and habitat of, 42
Arctostaphylos uva-ursi, description and habitat of, 43

B

Birds, in bogs, 270-272
Bog(s)
  alpine and arctic comparisons to, 254-255
  characteristics of, 26
  community composition and structure of, 22-35
  community relationships in, 61
    development of, 203-247
    ecological aspects, 216-247
    regional, 203-215
    structure, 208-212
    variations, 240-242
  ecology of, 1-10
  ericaceous shrubs of, 36-54, 75, 79-80, 83-92
  location and occurrence of, 67-74
  marshes and swamps compared to, 205
  microbiology of, soil conditions and, 173-177
  mosses in, 188-202
    list of, 302-303
  ombotrophic, 27-28
  organic production in, 213-215
  pioneer plants in, 219-224
  plant species of, 26, 28-30, 32, 36-57
    adaptive diversity, 252-254
    comparison of families, 35
    list of, 298-302

paleobotany, 90-92
physiological ecology, 248-257
transpiration in, 142-145
regional differences in, 229-231
species distribution in, 68, 70
structure variations in, 234-240
transpiration in, 255-257
tree importance in, 231-234
utilization of, 258-265
water-mineral-species interaction in, 242-247
waters of, 177-182
as wildlife habitats, 266-272

C

Chamaedaphne calyculata, description and habitat of, 44-45, 83-84
Chimaphila umbellata, description and habitat of, 54
Conifer forests, ecology of, 1-10
Copper, in bog plants, 170-171
Cranberry crops, bog temperatures and, 173-174

E

Ecology
  of conifer forests, 1-10
  of lowland bogs, 1-10
  principles of, 4-5
Elements, precipitation of, by bog plants, 162
Empetrum nigrum, description and habitat of, 55, 79
Environment, plants and, 7-10
Epigaea repens, description and habitat of, 45, 46
Ericaceae
  in bogs, 36-37
  conditions of life for, 104-106
  leaf characteristics of, 133-147
  North American habitats of, 38-40, 75, 79-80, 83-92
  origins of, 93-96
  sclerophylly of, 102-112
Evergreens, nutrient dynamics of, 148-163